Reflections on the Newgate Calendar

BY THE SAME AUTHOR

Novels

The Blaze of Noon
The Greater Infortune
The Lesser Infortune
The Connecting Door
The Woodshed
The Shearers

Literary Criticism

Léon Bloy
The Fourfold Tradition
Raymond Roussel

Memoirs

Four Absentees
The Intellectual Part
Portrait of the Artist as a Professional Man

Criminal History

A Little Pattern of French Crime
French Crime in the Romantic Age
Bluebeard and After
The Sex War and Others

Verse

Poems 1933–1945

Old Newgate Gateway, 1750
From an old print in the British Museum. The roof windmill was for ventilation

Reflections on the Newgate Calendar

by

Rayner Heppenstall

W. H. Allen · London
A division of Howard & Wyndham Ltd
1975

PRINTED AND BOUND BY
BUTLER & TANNER LTD, FROME AND LONDON
FOR THE PUBLISHERS W. H. ALLEN & CO. LTD,
44 HILL STREET, LONDON W1X 8LB

ISBN 0 491 01692 1

Contents

Preface

MOST OF my life, I have taken what I imagine to be rather less than the average masculine interest in crime. There may have been deeper, underlying causes, but it seems to me to have been almost by accident that, about six years ago, I found myself writing what would turn out to be only the first of no fewer than four volumes of French criminal history. I finished the last of these in March 1972. After a brief rest, I took it into my head that I ought to extend my knowledge of the criminal history of my own country.

The first step, I thought, would be to read *The Newgate Calendar*. I mentioned this thought in a letter to Basil Donne-Smith, a specialised dealer by post in secondhand books of criminological interest, with whom I had enjoyed dealing over the past few years. By return, he sent me, not as an article of sale but as a gift, a copy of an omnibus *Newgate Calendar* published by T. Werner Laurie Ltd, in 1932, thus becoming the first of those to whom in this preface I must acknowledge my indebtedness.

That omnibus volume, arranged by B. Laurie, dealt more or less briefly with two hundred cases between the years 1700 and 1790. Most of these cases had ended with a hanging. Among the names of those hanged, some had a familiar look. There were, for instance, Captain Kidd, John Sheppard, Jonathan Wild, Catherine Hayes, Captain Porteous, Richard Turpin, Lord Lovat, Eugene Aram, Elizabeth Brownrigg, William Wynne Ryland. For the most part, they were familiar in a literary connection, associated with Fielding, Thackeray, Scott, W. Harrison Ainsworth, Lord Lytton.

Presently, there reappeared on the bookstalls a *Newgate Calendar* in three paperback volumes with hideously sensational covers. These volumes dealt more or less briefly with ninety cases between the years 1701 and 1824, reverting also for one to fifteenth-century Scotland. Twenty-five of the eighteenth-century cases were also in the Laurie omnibus. Comparing the treatment of these in the two publications, I found it to be in part identical, in part different. Here were two abridged Newgate Calendars drawing on some of the same and some divergent sources. The paperback volumes advertised themselves as a special arrangement of *The Newgate Calendar Improved* by George Theodore Wilkinson, Esq. The omnibus called itself *The Newgate Calendar or Malefactors' Bloody Register*, without saying from what earlier compilation it had been taken.

I need not recount all the steps by which I was led to discard the supposition I had long and vaguely entertained, that there existed a single work to which we might all agree that we were referring when we spoke of *The Newgate Calendar*. Itself cannibalising single pamphlets and earlier compilations, one so entitled had first appeared two hundred years ago, its publisher J. Cooke, whom we may at least credit with devising a memorable title, and that was no doubt the one that William Godwin read. The Calendars most frequently quoted, however, have been those published forty or fifty years later. What Bulwer-Lytton and Harrison Ainsworth, Dickens and Thackeray had would be Wilkinson or, a little earlier, *The New and Complete Newgate Calendar or Malefactor's Universal Register* by William Jackson, Esq., of the Inner Temple, barrister-at-law, assisted by Other Gentlemen, issued in weekly parts to make up five volumes, to which a double Supplement and two further volumes were to be added, or, more probably and somewhat later, the four handy volumes compiled by Andrew Knapp and William Baldwin, attorneys at law, again simply called *The Newgate Calendar*. By the time they were out, the *Celebrated Trials* attributed to George Borrow had lodged another durable, if somewhat Frenchified, title in the public mind.

I am sorry to intrude so much bibliographical matter into a preface. It is, however, necessary, I feel, that the reader should understand at the outset what it is the present volume affects to reflect on and that it is something large, composite, various and even at moments a little shadowy. What I quote from is, unless otherwise stated, Knapp & Baldwin. The Werner Laurie omnibus, I may say, turned out, illustrations and all, to be an abstract of the first two and one third of their four volumes, its two hundred cases approximately a quarter of theirs for the eighteenth century alone.

For all Newgate Calendars begin in 1700, and most continue until a little before or after 1820, K. & B. to 1825. What we must therefore see as the Newgate Calendar period in criminal if not in literary history thus covers a century and a quarter. Of more than a thousand cases in any of the later Calendars, it is clear that a short book like this cannot touch on more than a small proportion. Apart from Kidd and two Scottish cases, and two which show the position of foreigners in London in the last years of William III and the reign of Queen Anne, there is nothing of unusual interest before the accession of George I. There is much to be said for treating the Newgate Calendar period rather as that of the Hanoverian monarchy than as the eighteenth century plus a quarter of the nineteenth. The legislator, who is much concerned, numbers his enactments, after all, not by century or by Christian year but by the reigns of monarchs and the years of these.

By way of further reducing my theme, I say little about the early years even of George I or about Scottish cases in the period, interesting as these are, so that one might very well write a separate book on Scottish cases in *The Newgate Calendar*. I toyed with the notion of further confining myself to the cases of persons who themselves had been confined in Newgate prison, which, after all, *The Newgate Calendar* might have been expected to do, had it taken its title seriously. But this would have deprived me of Thurtell and Corder, Dick Turpin, Abraham Thornton, Mary Blandy, the Hampshire smugglers, the Luddites and, above all, Eugene Aram.

It so happens that of Calendar cases one day to be made the subjects of Notable British Trials volumes, though five were tried in London (two of these in the House of Lords) only one was for a felony committed there. The defendant in this, moreover, was one of only three whose metropolitan careers were ever to give rise to much in the way of imaginative literature. Apart from Jack Sheppard's, the two stories most effectively to inspire those whom we know as the Newgate novelists both ended at York.

A sad London story was greatly to preoccupy Dr Johnson and to extract a sort of literature from him, as two others did from the author of *Jonathan Wild*. To the unfolding of their London stories, Fielding and Johnson were to contribute directly. The relevance of their literature should therefore be admitted by the kind of reader who likes his criminal history free of literature in general. The amateur criminologist may feel that I need to justify the attention I pay to the writings of later novelists and a poet.

The dyer's hand will show, of course. Devoted to criminal history for only a few years, I have been concerned with literary history for at least forty, and it was literature which led me to crime. Among French cases, I found those most interesting which had provided themes for novels and plays, from *Le Rouge et le Noir* to *Les Bonnes*. There is no less interest in treading the middle ground between English literary and criminal history, from, say, *Arden of Faversham* to *The Secret Agent*.

The Newgate Calendar itself is literature, for the most part of a rather poor kind, fit only to inspire literature in others. The best of it is evidence heard in court, which, once transcribed and published, is literature. Law itself is literature. In court, lawyers compose literature with great deliberation. The spontaneous cut-and-thrust of courtroom drama on stage, screen or radio is rarely heard in court. There, judges and counsel dictate their works slowly to the clerk of the court and to reporters, much as Henry James dictated his to a devoted secretary or as modern authors may dictate theirs to tape recorders, with all the more care because it will not be possible for them to make alterations in the transcript.

Among the literary compositions of lawyers in court, what we notably lack throughout our period are great speeches by defending counsel, who were not heard, except occasionally on legal points. What speeches for the defence we have were delivered by the accused themselves. There were other differences. Throughout the Newgate Calendar period, for instance, we shall find our magistrates acting more like French *juges d'instruction* than they do now. The system, as jurists say, was still inquisitorial rather than accusatory.

We may care to remind ourselves that it was not until late in the period that the French adopted from us trial by jury, which we have throughout. On the other hand, France has always had a ten years' prescriptive period, after which proceedings may not be started or renewed. This would have saved Eugene Aram, to say nothing for the moment about William Sheward. As Messrs Knapp & Baldwin were to point out towards the end of the period, our penal laws were also charged by foreign writers with being too sanguinary in lesser offences, and philanthropists of our own nation had accorded with their opinion.

They had only begun to do so. The later Calendars were among the first products of a reforming age which looked back fascinated at one during which too many were hanged for too little. The topper covered heads more merciful than those which had worn three-cornered hats. Nine years before the Reform Act, five statutes specifically exempted a hundred felonies from the death penalty. The pendulum had begun to swing towards our opposite extreme. The only people hanged now are those who hang themselves. There are some who doubt whether criminals should be punished at all or even confined in luxury prisons, where they are bothered by psychiatrists. Those on whom our society inflicts the death penalty are not the wicked but the young, the old, the silly, who won't keep their eyes on the traffic, and the unhappy, of whom it drives seven thousand a year to suicide. Luckily, I have no need in this book to consider the general arguments for and against all capital punishment. With the exception of Jeremy Bentham, nobody of great note gave them much thought at the time.

I offer, in fact, no general argument whatever. To a criminal historian, the changing spectacle of criminal activity and the attempts to cope with it must suffice. Human criminality is inexhaustible and, apparently, irreducible. A Christian theologian might find an explanation of it in Original Sin, a Buddhist in *karma*, a Marxist in capitalism, a psychiatrist in broken families. Our period ends at the point at which people were beginning to say that crime is caused by poverty and ignorance. There are still bemused or atavistic people who continue to say that in the Welfare State, in which the evidence suggests rather that it is caused by easy money and too much education. Cures are still proposed. But, if there is no general cause, there is no cure. I take the view that there is no general cause or cure. The next generation of murderers is at this moment growing up in our midst, and the Cambridge Institute of Criminology will not prevent a single one of their murders.

The Police College at Basingstoke may anticipate a few. Even if it doesn't, I shall still be grateful to P. J. Stead there, who from its library extracted for me information about Henry Fielding's writings on criminal matters which I had failed to discover at the London Library. Mr Stead is, of course, a leading criminal historian in his own right. So is Jonathan Goodman, whom here, however, I must thank in the lowlier capacity of a collector who doesn't mind lending his books and who, into the bargain, will pick up on the secondhand market things he is supplied with but knows his friends want. I must further acknowledge debts to the curator of the museum of the Royal College of Surgeons of England and the deputy keeper of Corporation of London records, Miss Elizabeth Allen and Miss Betty R. Masters, for arranging photocopies, the former of her predecessor's individual studies of the four college criminals, as well as general essays on the anatomising of criminals and cases of cardiac action after 'death' by hanging, the latter of the holograph transcript of evidence in the trial of the Cock Lane ghost. This, I understand, has never been published. I wish I had room for it.

I

Newgate and Tyburn

THE CITY OF London had seven gates. The other six were Ludgate, Moorgate, Cripplegate, Bishopsgate, Aldersgate and Aldgate. Temple Bar was also a gate, erected for ceremonial purposes at the extent of the city liberties. The gatehouses of Ludgate and Newgate were prisons, the former a prison for debt for freemen of the city only, the latter a prison for criminals, both for London and Middlesex, and for debtors also for Middlesex.

Understood in a larger sense, London contained more than twenty public gaols, of which those of the King's Bench and Marshalsea were in the borough of Southwark. There were also tolerated prisons, among which Defoe numbers Bethlehem or Bedlam, fifteen private mad-houses, three pest-houses and a hundred and nineteen spunging houses. Newgate spanned the roadway, facing east and west, both sides ornamented with pilasters and statues, one of these that of Liberty, with Dick Whittington's cat coiled at its feet, the original gatehouse having been replaced in the fifteenth century by one erected with money left by the most famous of lord mayors. This in turn had been demolished by the fire of London, when Daniel Foe or Defoe was six years old.

The south wing was at the corner of the street called Old Bailey, in which stood the sessions house. The street still exists and bears the same name, but there has been no Newgate prison since 1904, when what we now usually mean by the Old Bailey took over the site occupied for the past hundred and thirty years by prison buildings without an archway.

Despite contemporary prints and engravings, descriptions and even plans, I find it difficult either to visualise the Newgate of Defoe's time clearly or to understand how its various quarters were distributed and connected. Many of the facts we learn were, I suspect, facts only at one moment or another, though at any given moment there would be a master and a common side among both debtors and felons, with some but far from complete segregation not only between the sexes but also of debtors from felons and of common debtors or felons from master debtors and felons, those who could afford or whose friends could afford the extra space, garnish, bedding and firing, the provision of which was among the keeper's numerous perquisites. The keeper at that time was William Pitt, who was also conveniently a grocer.

The most famous and frequently illustrated rooms were the chapel and the condemned hold. The former was on the top floor, apparently of the gatehouse. It contained a pen for the prisoners under sentence of death, who sat about a table on which stood a coffin, and a gallery for visitors who enjoyed listening to condemned sermons on the Sunday morning before executions.

When those under sentence of death included women or privileged master felons or were very numerous, last nights would be spent elsewhere, but the condemned hold proper appears to have been at ground level on the south side of the gatehouse, its small, barred window looking into the archway but admitting light also through the semi-circular opening over a spiked gate from a part of the lodge used as a tap room, so that visitors and drinking prisoners were able to converse with those inside, who would be heavily fettered and perhaps also chained to staples set in the stonework. There was a fireplace in the condemned hold.

On the night before executions, the sexton of St Sepulchre's, the parish within which the prison lay, stationed himself beneath the archway, so as to be distinctly heard in the condemned hold. First, with a handbell, he gave twelve solemn tolls with double strokes. He then recited the following words, beginning with a perhaps unintentional rhymed couplet but quickly lapsing into prose.

> You prisoners that are within, who for wickedness and sin, after many mercies shown you, are now appointed to die tomorrow in the forenoon, give ear and understand that tomorrow morning the greatest bell of St Sepulchre's shall toll for you in form and manner of a passing bell, as used to be tolled for those at the point of death, to the end that all godly people, hearing that bell and knowing that it is for your going to your deaths, may be stirred up heartily to pray to God to bestow His grace and mercy upon you while you live. I beseech you for Jesus Christ's sake to keep this night in watching and prayer for the salvation of your own souls, while there is yet time and place for mercy, as knowing tomorrow you must appear before the judgment seat of your Creator, there to give an account of all things done in this life and to suffer eternal torments for your sins committed against Him, unless upon your hearty and unfeigned repentance you find mercy through the merits, death and passion of your only Mediator and Advocate, Jesus Christ, who now sits at the right hand of God to make intercession for as many of you as penitently return to Him.

This form of words had been written for and possibly by Robert Dow of the Merchant Taylors, who had thus, in the reign of James I, though his purpose may have been wholly benevolent, ensured himself an immortal place in criminal and even in literary history for the price of a handbell and £50 left to the parish.

It had been his original stipulation that a clergyman should speak the words, but the annual interest on £50 was not much. For this part of his parish duties the sexton was annually paid only £1. 6*s*. 8*d*., and its repetition a hundred times a year must have been burdensome, especially in winter. Nor was that the whole of it. There was a second instalment in the morning.

The carts bearing prisoners to the place of execution halted before the porch of St Sepulchre's church. The sexton then had to reappear and speak from the steps or other point of vantage, first exhorting everyone else within hearing and then addressing himself again, in much the same terms but more briefly, to the prisoners (there might be only one) in the cart or carts. The morning formula was:

> All good people, pray heartily unto God for these poor sinners who are now going to their death and for whom the great bell doth toll.
>
> You who are condemned to die, repent with lamentable tears. Ask mercy of the Lord, for the salvation of your souls through the merits of the death and passion of Jesus Christ, who now sits on the right hand of God, to make intercession for as many of you as penitently return unto Him.
>
> Lord have mercy upon you. Christ have mercy upon you.

A ringer in the square tower of the church, surmounted by four pinnacles, may at this point have started chiming the tenor bell or might have started earlier as the procession began to assemble. He was, at any rate, supposed to keep at it until the execution might be presumed to be over. This must have been calculated by the clock. More often than not, the moment at which an execution was in fact over must have been impossible to communicate to St Sepulchre's within half an hour or so.

The place of execution was not invariable. For treasonable noblemen, there were still Tower Hill and the block. They, however, would have been confined in the Tower, not in Newgate. For pirates, there was Execution Dock, a small inlet at Wapping, where, after hanging, their bodies were at low tide fastened to a post and there left until three tides had washed over them, a proceeding whose ritual significance escapes me. A judge might also order that a murderer should be hanged near the scene of his crime.

Thus, in the second year of the reign of George I, in consequence of Prince James Edward Stuart's ill-advised trip to Scotland, Lords Derwentwater and Kenmure were beheaded on Tower Hill. Three tides had washed over Captain Kidd and his principal accomplice and would wash over Captain Massey,

Philip Roche, John Gow and seven of his crew. The very first case in Jackson's *New and Complete Newgate Calendar* is of two Dutchmen and the wife of one of these hanged in East Smithfield. For shooting a watchman who caught him breaking into a house in Drury Lane, a burglar had shortly thereafter been executed at the end of Long Acre. The reign of Queen Anne had further seen gallows set up in St James's Street, Old Bailey and Clerkenwell, and the new reign would have a hanging of special piquancy in Bunhill Fields.

Such departures from custom were uncommon, however. In general, for seventy years more, the procession halted before St Sepulchre's church would move off either down Snow Hill or along Giltspur Street into Cock Lane. Either way, it presently crossed the Fleet river and climbed into Holborn, whence the way was level and straight and a little less than two miles long.

At the head of the procession rode the city marshal, followed by an under-sheriff. There were constables also on horseback and javelin men on foot. In the cart or carts, the prisoners sat with their halters bound about their breasts, perhaps holding with difficulty nosegays given them at St Sepulchre's. With them was expected to travel the Ordinary the prison chaplain of Newgate, or his deputy. The hangman sat with the driver of the first cart, if there were more than one.

Administratively, this was Middlesex, but the Oxford road had been built up and was Oxford Street almost as far as the Tyburn and the north-east corner of Hyde Park, which, not its south-east, was then known as Hyde Park Corner. The beam from which malefactors were to be left suspended by the neck had formerly been placed between the forks of two convenient elms, as was still the case at many places of execution in the provinces. At Tyburn, however, there had long stood, and would continue to stand until very near the end of the next reign, a permanent structure of three uprights joined at the top by three beams forming an equilateral triangle. This was known by analogy as the triple tree. Formerly here and still elsewhere, the last solid place beneath a hanged man's feet had been the rung of a ladder, the executioner's art consisting in giving this a sudden sharp twist, so that his patient might properly be said to have been 'turned off'. The expression (alternating with the more genteel 'launched into eternity') was still used in the metropolis, but at Tyburn the tails of as many as three carts might be simultaneously backed under beams and, when all the nooses were in place, simultaneously driven away, with remarkable effect.

After a period of not less than half an hour, the still figures were cut down. Their clothes became the hangman's perquisite. Their bodies might be claimed by family or friends and buried, but might equally go to the surgeons for public anatomising or be wrapped in tarred canvas and hung 'in chains' (in fact suits of metal bands) on gibbets at roadsides, alternatives later regularised by legislation. Those of traitors were subjected to special indignities, as were those of men who had 'cheated the gallows' by committing suicide in prison.

The hangman at the accession of George I was John Price, a former seaman. The following year, on his way back from an execution, he was arrested in Holborn for a debt of 7*s*. 6*d*. This he was able to discharge by selling three suits of clothes taken from the bodies of men hanged that day, but other writs were taken out against him, so that more than two years later we find him in the Marshalsea prison, without salary (it had been about £40 a year) or the perquisites of his trade. It was Price's immediate successor, William Marvell, who beheaded Lords Kenmure and Derwentwater and hanged the other rebels brought to London, subsequently decapitating them also, quartering their bodies and boiling, it seems, these quarters as well as the heads.

With seven fine suits of noblemen's and gentlemen's clothes, handsome tips from their former wearers and extra *per capita* payment, this was remunerative if arduous work. Marvell also, however, was soon imprisoned for debt (and later transported for stealing). When John Price escaped from the Marshalsea and murdered a woman resisting his attempt to ravish her, it was a third Georgian metropolitan hangman, Banks, whose Christian name we do not know, who turned him off in Bunhill Fields, eventual resting place of Daniel Foe or Defoe and many other dissenters. The first Georgian hangman was hanged on May

31st, 1718. He was afterwards hung in chains near Holloway. We hear little of Banks. He was presently succeeded by Richard Arnett.

At that time, we reasonably believe the population of the United Kingdom of Great Britain and Ireland to have been about twelve million, of whom a third were in Ireland and two thirds in Britain. The populations of Ireland, Scotland and Wales have not changed much, their surpluses making for England and especially London, which they, rather than the English, have gradually overpopulated and would now like to disown.

A little over fifty years before, it is supposed that the population of London was about half a million. Although as many as a fifth of these are calculated to have died of the plague, this population had since doubled. France, with a larger extent of fertile territory, had twice our total population, but Paris was smaller, perhaps because it was not also a seaport, the tides up the Seine reaching no further than Rouen, whereas only London Bridge kept tall ships from tying up in the Thames at Westminster. It was the only bridge. There was none at Westminster, only a ferry for horses and, downstream to the bridge, countless small craft.

As the bridge connected the city of London with the borough of Southwark, the Strand joined the former to Westminster. The rest was in Middlesex, but it was all known as London, of which Kensington and even Chelsea and, to the north, the town of Islington would soon form part. With a second bridge at Westminster, the Thames would flow through London.

This was the conurbation Defoe had seen grow out of something half its size. Born before the end of the Commonwealth, he had outlived Charles II, James II, William III and Queen Anne before, with the exception of one or two poems, he wrote any of those works of his we still read, *Robinson Crusoe* appearing in 1719 when he was in his sixtieth year and George I in the fifth of his reign.

He would remember the fire of London, the more so in that his parish, that of St Giles, Cripplegate, had remained comparatively little damaged. The old church (not his, since James Foe, butcher, was a dissenter) still stood. He had equally seen St Paul's cathedral and Wren's other churches and his fine municipal buildings and Newgate prison rebuilt. He had himself spent two years of his busy life in prisons, once, in the reign of Queen Anne, standing also three times in the stocks, for publishing, albeit anonymously ('a middle-sized, spare man about forty years old, of a brown complexion and dark brown-coloured hair, but wears a wig; a hooked nose, a sharp chin, grey eyes and a large mole near his mouth'), *The Shortest Way with Dissenters*, and once, more recently and briefly, for naming names in connection with plans for the Jacobite rising which almost at once occurred and justified him.

Among Londoners, Defoe was uncommon in the extent of his knowledge also of the provinces. When *Robinson Crusoe* had assured him of some leisure, he began to set out that knowledge systematically in the form of letters for publication. First, however, he wrote about the London of his childhood and pickpockets' London, about the inwardness of which he had doubtless learnt something from his prison companions.

Journal of the Plague Year and *Moll Flanders* both appeared in 1722. We search the Newgate Calendars vainly for clues to the identity of a possible original for the heroine of the first true English novel. The seven earlier female criminals there listed were all executed, not transported. A Moll King, a street robber in the city of London, transported, may be found however, in a curious document brought to light in the published proceedings of the Royal College of Surgeons of England for 1951 by Jessie Dobson, then recorder of their museum (which houses what remains of the Hunterian collection). This is a petition addressed, on New Year's Day, 1721, to the lord mayor and court of aldermen by Jonathan Wild. He states that he has been at great trouble and charge in apprehending and convicting felons for returning from transportation since the previous October, that he has never received any reward or gratuity for such his service and that he is very desirous to become a freeman of this honourable city. He lists ten names of men whom he has so apprehended and convicted and two more of persons taken by him and afterwards sent abroad, one of these Moll King.

Returning from transportation before the expiry of the allotted time (usually seven or fourteen years) was added that year to the growing list of capital offences, and a son of Huguenot parents was hanged for it that September. This was not the only way in which Jonathan Wild may be thought to have influenced legislation. The Calendars state that it was in the hope of suppressing his own iniquitous practices that an act had been passed between two and three years before, deeming every person guilty of a capital offence who should accept a reward for restoring stolen effects without prosecuting the thief. This act was in fact to hang Wild four years later.

One act older than that which had not yet produced its full effect was the Riot Act, passed in the first year of the reign. One passed more recently, in the year of the South Sea Bubble, making it capital to forge power of attorney, would not begin to reap its dreadful harvest for seventeen years more. An act passed before the downfall of Wild's criminal empire (or alternative society), lately shown to have its literary interest, was the Black Act of 1723. This was aimed at deer-stealing, conducted in the daytime by armed gangs with blackened faces.

The famous gang, at once caught by the act, were known as the Waltham Blacks. They, however, had killed a keeper while poaching on the bishop of Winchester's estate of Waltham Chase and so would no doubt have been hanged for murder without the new act. They feature in *The Newgate Calendar*. The Berkshire or Windsor Blacks do not. In the late summer of 1973, two distinguished scholars, Pat Rogers and E. F. Thompson, were engaged in the pages of the *Times Literary Supplement* at unusual length on the fact that the poet Alexander Pope's brother-in-law, Charles Rackett, and his son Michael were implicated in blacking in Windsor Forest shortly before the act was passed. It transpires from the research of the second of the two scholars that many Blacks were Roman Catholics and suspected of Jacobite conspiracy. There was, it is clear, in the country widespread resentment against the new Hanoverian game laws and the deer themselves, which were often shot and left lying. It was no doubt from fear of the failure of a county gaol to hold or a jury of local gentry and farmers to convict them that the seven Waltham Blacks, Hampshire men for the most part, were brought to London, imprisoned in Newgate, tried before a court of King's Bench and hanged at Tyburn.

II

Four Themes

JONATHAN WILD demands attention because he received it, in his lifetime or shortly after his death or twenty years later, from three great writers. We cannot, unfortunately, be sure just how much attention any of the three paid him. In the case of Fielding, we know, indeed, that he wrote a whole novel or anti-novel, his first, of which Wild is the eponymous hero or anti-hero, but we do not know how much of its remoteness from the known facts of Wild's life and death was due to conscious fantastication and how much to simple ignorance. In the case of Defoe and Swift, we cannot even be sure what they wrote, though it appears to be certain that the latter first designated Jonathan Wild 'the Great' and thus provided Fielding with his eventual theme for a satire on false greatness, aimed elsewhere.

In himself, Wild was not much of a criminal in any usual sense. *The Newgate Calendar* calls him 'the prince of thieves'. He was not even that, unless we think of a prince as one for whom his subjects toil. He was a murderer only if we restore the misused expression 'judicial murder' to the sense of the use of judicial process to ensure the death of someone whose death will gratify a personal wish or motive. He once directly caused grievous bodily harm, for which it seems no proceedings were taken against him and which it seems he regretted.

Wild did not lack courage. He never avoided the dangerous confrontations with which his line of business faced him. His gifts were those required of many a successful business man who benefits in a variety of ways from knowing how the law works. That it was criminal rather than civil law with which he played and that the play was so close may have been due in part to early circumstance.

Born in Wolverhampton in 1683, the eldest son of respectable parents, Jonathan Wild went to school till the age of fifteen, when he was apprenticed to a bucklemaker in Birmingham. At the end of seven years, he returned to Wolverhampton and married a young woman of good character, who bore him a son but whom, after two years, he deserted and went to London, where before long he was imprisoned for debt in Wood Street Compter.

There he spent four years. Also there for debt was Mary Milliner, a pickpocket and prostitute. The two formed an attachment, and it was from her he learned of the iniquitous practices of the city marshal, Charles Hitchin, on two of which his own career was to be based. Hitchin acted as a receiver of stolen goods but also blackmailed thieves, arresting only those who could not or who refused to pay him not to arrest them, no doubt also some who rejected his homosexual advances, for it appears that Hitchin also organised transvestite and sodomitical orgies.

After regaining his freedom in the last years of the reign of Queen Anne, Wild lived as man and wife with Mary, who conducted the business of a small public house in Cock Alley, facing Cripplegate church. For a while, he worked with Hitchin, who had been dismissed from his post as city marshal and against whom a law was passed, which we still have, making it a criminal offence to receive stolen goods, knowing them to have been stolen. Presently, the confederates quarrelled, publishing scurrilous pamphlets against each other.

The better organiser, Wild gradually supplanted his master, and presently we find him living in Old Bailey with an office in Newtoner's Lane at which stolen goods were restored to their owners, often for as much as half their value, which enabled him to pay the thieves a fair rate. Thieving itself became more lucrative.

> Articles which had been before considered as of no use but to the owners now became matters claiming a particular attention from the thieves by whom the metropolis and its environs were infested. Pocket-books, books of accounts, watches, rings, trinkets and a variety of articles of but small intrinsic worth were now esteemed very profitable booty. Books of accounts and other writings, being of great importance to the owners, produced very handsome rewards; and the same may be said of pocket-books, for they generally contained memorandums and sometimes bank-notes and other articles on which money could be readily procured.

While awaiting restoration to their owners, such goods were kept on premises elsewhere. Goods best disposed of otherwise were transported to Holland or Flanders by a sloop bought and manned for that purpose.

> Wild accumulated money so fast that he considered himself a man of consequence, and, to support his imaginary dignity, he dressed in laced clothes and wore a sword. He first exercised his martial instrument on the person of his accomplice and reputed wife, Mary Milliner, who having on some occasion provoked him, he, with an oath, declared he would 'mark her for a bitch' and, instantly drawing his sword, struck at her and cut off one of her ears. This event was the cause of a separation; but, in acknowledgement of the great service she had rendered him by introducing him to so lucrative a profession, he allowed her a weekly stipend till her decease.

The anecdotes abound, and we know the names of a fair number of those who worked for Wild, as well as of those whom he sent to the gallows. They were sometimes the same people, who had served their turn and could themselves be sold, at least for safety. This will seem, to most tastes, the truly execrable thing about Jonathan Wild. Our sympathy for his discarded minions may, however, in some cases be tempered by their readiness to inform on each other. One who displayed such readiness was the swarthy Joseph Blake, known as 'Blueskin' (under which name he appears in Fielding), who, by arrangement with Wild, swore away the lives of three of the gang in February 1723. It was not to do him much good.

· · ·

That year, a carpenter's apprentice, John Sheppard, commenced as a housebreaker. He was a small, wiry young man, with a good head for heights and a remarkable way with locks. The first exploit for which he was noted was the rescue, from St Giles roundhouse in Soho, of a large young woman, Elizabeth Lyon (known as 'Edgworth Bess'), a doxy he shared with a soldier. The first of his own four escapes was effected from the same place. His next evasion, in company with Bess, was from the New prison, in Clerkenwell. He then joined forces with Blueskin. Together, in July 1724, they burgled the house in the Strand of William Kneebone, a woollen draper, who had been very kind to Sheppard at the time of his father's death, and, a week later, with horses hired from an inn in Piccadilly, committed a highway robbery in Hampstead.

It was Jonathan Wild, who with one of his men, arrested them, on information abjectly supplied by Edgworth Bess. Brought to trial at the Old Bailey, Sheppard was, on August 14th, sentenced to death for the burglary in the Strand. Twice he escaped from Newgate, once from the condemned hold, once from the dungeon on an upper floor known as the Castle, a feat deemed impossible.

On October 14th, Blueskin, awaiting trial, stood in the bail dock outside the Old Bailey sessions house, when he was approached by Jonathan Wild, who offered him a dram of brandy. Blueskin begged Wild to speak for him at his trial. Wild said: 'I cannot do that. You're a dead man.' Whereupon Blueskin seized Wild by the hair and, with a little clasp knife he was provided with, cut his throat in a very dangerous manner. Had it not been for a muslin stock twisted in several plaits round Wild's neck, Blueskin would in all likelihood have finished him off. He triumphed afterwards in what he had done, swearing many bloody oaths that, if he had murdered Mr Wild, he should have died with satisfaction and that his intention was to have cut off his head and thrown it among the rabble in the sessions house yard.

In a ballad on this episode which was circulated at the time, it is pretended that Blueskin had succeeded in his barbarous design and that anyone might henceforward rob at his pleasure.

This ballad was for long attributed to Swift and may be found in older editions of his verse. It is a poem not up to Swift's standard, but otherwise it is not difficult to believe that he, then in Ireland, where he was engaged in a dangerous polemic against Wood's halfpence, imagined 'Jonathan Wild the Great' indeed dead already and thought this a bad thing, for ironists are not always ironic.

Of the two accounts of Jack Sheppard attributed to Defoe, one was published while he was still at large. The other, put into the mouth of Sheppard himself, could have been a transcript of what had been said by him to Defoe in the condemned hold, where he was much visited. He was painted there by Sir James Thornhill, who noted the strong hands, the handcuffs, the great, imploring eyes.

Blueskin was hanged on November 11th, Jack Sheppard on the 16th. He took a long time to die, being a lightweight. A soldier cut him down early, and there was an attempt to get him to a house where a surgeon waited to revive him. It is believed that this arrangement had been made by Defoe and his publisher. It is not beyond imagination that, at sixty-four, Defoe was still ready for such adventures. A superficial critical study of the internal evidence in the two published accounts does not disprove that Defoe wrote them both. If he did, he contributed a few phrases directly to *The Newgate Calendar*, whose account echoes, without acknowledgement, those attributed to him.

The balladry was extensive. There were also sermons. The Calendars amusingly quote one, Jackson at greater length than Knapp & Baldwin.

> Now, my beloved, what a melancholy consideration it is, that men should shew so much regard for the preservation of a poor perishing body, that can remain at most but a few years; and at the same time be so unaccountably negligent of a precious soul, which must continue to the age of eternity! Oh, what care! what pains! what diligence! and what contrivances are made use of for, and laid out upon, these frail and tottering tabernacles of clay: when, alas! the nobler part of us is allowed so very small a share of our concern that we scarce will give ourselves the trouble of bestowing a thought upon it.

> We have a remarkable instance of this in a notorious malefactor, well known by the name of Jack Sheppard! What amazing difficulties has he overcome, what astonishing things has he performed, for the sake of a stinking, miserable carcass, hardly worth hanging? how dexterously did he pick the padlock of his chain with a crooked nail? How manfully did he burst his fetters asunder, climb up the chimney, wrench out an iron bar, break his way through a stone wall and make the strong doors of a dark entry fly before him, till he got upon the leads of the prison? and then, fixing a blanket to the wall with a spike he stole out of the chapel, how intrepidly did he descend to the top of the turner's house, and how cautiously pass down the stairs and make his escape at the street door?
>
> Oh, that ye were all like Jack Sheppard!—Mistake me not, my brethren, I don't mean in a carnal but in a spiritual sense, for I purpose to spiritualise these things.—What a shame it would be if we should not think it worth our while to take as much pains and employ as many deep thoughts to save our souls, as he has done to preserve his body.
>
> Let me exhort ye, then, to open the *locks* of your *hearts* with the *nail of repentance;* burst asunder the *fetters* of your *beloved lusts;* mount the *chimney* of *hope*, take from hence the *bar* of *good resolution*, break through the *stone wall* of *despair* and all the *strong holds* in the *dark entry* of the *valley of the shadow of death;* raise yourselves to the *leads* of *divine meditation;* fix the *blanket of faith* with the *spike* of the *church;* let yourselves down to the *turner's house* of *resignation* and descend the *stairs* of *humility*. So shall you come to the *door of deliverance* from the *prison of iniquity* and *escape the clutches* of that old *executioner* the *devil*, who goeth about like a roaring lion, seeking whom he may devour.

There were also plays. The first of these, *Harlequin Sheppard* by John Thurmond, with a flash chant by the actor who played Blueskin and the lines attributed to Swift also sung, was put on at Drury Lane less than a fortnight after the execution. It was a failure.

On February 15th, 1725, three months after Sheppard's execution, Jonathan Wild was arrested on a charge of having assisted in the escape of the captain of his sloop, Roger Johnson, then in custody at an alehouse, pursued for theft by a former accomplice. On

March 2nd, Wild was still held in Newgate on a warrant of detainer, other charges having been brought against him.

That day, the exposure on a pole in St Margaret's churchyard of a head discovered in a pail on Thames mud near the Horse Ferry, Westminster, excited general speculation. The head had, as would presently transpire, till recently been on the shoulders of a Mr Hayes in the chandlery and coal trade. It had been held over the pail and detached, while he was paralytic on mountain wine from Malaga, by his wife Catherine and two friends of hers, Wood and Billings.

Wild made the false move which hanged him eight days later. On March 10th, he sent a message to a woman who had started proceedings against him and two others for a theft of lace from her shop, inviting her to call on him in prison. There he made an arrangement whereby the lace was returned to her on payment of a sum of ten guineas not to himself but to the messenger. On May 15th, the prosecution failed to convict him of theft but got a verdict under the act of 4 Geo. I for restoring stolen goods without prosecuting the thief.

Jonathan Wild was hanged by Richard Arnett on May 24th, 1725. Having lain briefly interred in St Pancras churchyard, his body was removed for dissection at the surgeons' hall in Old Bailey, where he had lived. In due course, his skeleton would be found in the possession of a Dr Thomas, a practitioner in Windsor.

Jack Sheppard rested his young head at St Martin's in the Fields. That year, his exploits were further celebrated in a play, *The Prison Breaker, or the Adventures of John Sheppard*, a farce, printed but never acted, as was intended, at the Theatre Royal in Lincoln's Inn Fields.

The year after, Wood, one of Catherine Hayes's accomplices in the murder and decapitation of her husband, having died of gaol fever, Arnett hanged Billings. The murder of a husband is petty treason, and the sentence passed on a woman convicted of it, as for coining and other high treasons, was then that she be burnt, though, as a customary measure of mercy, the hangman was expected to strangle her with a rope before the flames reached her.

Catherine Hayes was burnt alive. The flames reaching his hands before he had strangled her, Arnett let go the rope. The fire burned fiercely round her, and the spectators beheld her pushing away the faggots, while she rent the air with her cries and lamentations.

That was in May. In June, George I died. The following year, John Gay wrote *The Beggar's Opera* on a theme suggested by Swift and in consultation with Pope. That year, also in April, the former city marshal, Charles Hitchin, convicted of sodomitical practices, was sentenced to pay a fine of £20, to stand in the pillory and to suffer six months' imprisonment. In December, a minor but talented poet was convicted of murder.

Most students of English literature will have read the account of Richard Savage in Dr Johnson's *Lives of the English Poets*. They will therefore know for what version of his antecedents Savage gained widespread credence, including Johnson's. They may have noticed, on the other hand, that, in his *Life of Johnson*, Boswell is sceptical. We must take our choice. The matter has been carefully investigated, and it is quite uncertain whether Savage was a clever (or a demented) impostor or the illegitimate son of a cruel mother, Lady Macclesfield, and Lord Rivers, to whom it is certain, indeed, that she bore children.

The Calendars are credulous. Their accounts do not differ materially from Johnson, except in so far as Jackson speaks of Savage as playing the lead in his own *Sir Thomas Overbury* 'with considerable applause' whereas Savage, some ten years later, by Johnson's account, was so shamed that he tried to conceal the fact that the performance had ever taken place (in 1724, the year of Jack Sheppard's failure on the stage at Drury Lane). That he wrote a tragedy on that old but indubitably real murder case gives Richard Savage a place in a tradition with which we are concerned, but here we shall come rapidly to the night of November 21st, 1727.

> Mr Savage had at the time a lodging at Richmond and another at London; and having come to town to pay off the latter, and

> casually meeting with Gregory and Merchant, with whom he had been acquainted for some time past, they went to a coffee-house, where they drank till late in the evening. Savage would have engaged a bed at the place; but, there not being accommodations for him, he and his friends went into the street, proposing to spend the night as they could and in the morning to walk to Richmond. Strolling about, they saw a light in Robinson's coffee-house, into which they entered, . . . much disguised in liquor, . . . and went into a room where a Mr Sinclair and other company were drinking. Merchant, entering first, kicked down the table; and, Savage and Gregory drawing their swords, they were earnestly desired to put them up but refused to do so.
>
> A scuffle now ensued, in which Mr Sinclair received a mortal wound* and was heard to say, 'I am a dead man.' Soon after which the candles were extinguished. . . . The perpetrators of this rash action having left the house, some soldiers were sent for, by whom they were taken into custody. . . . The deceased had been attended by a clergyman, who declared that he said he was stabbed before he had time to draw his sword; and his testimony was confirmed by that of other witnesses.

There seems to have been no doubt that it was Savage who inflicted the fatal wound and that Sinclair at that moment either had not drawn or held his sword pointed to the ground. Savage and Gregory, who also had drawn, were sentenced to death. Merchant, who seems not to have been armed, was convicted of manslaughter, burnt in the hand and released.

Interest having been made on behalf of Savage (by Lady Hertford), he and Gregory were, on January 20th, 1728, bailed. On the 28th, *The Beggar's Opera* had its first night and was an immediate success. On March 5th, Savage and Gregory pleaded to a pardon and were discharged.

The decade had produced themes for novels by Fielding and, much later, Harrison Ainsworth and Thackeray, as well as for the first of Johnson's *Lives*. For us, it and the third year of the reign of George II shall end with a bill to make the forging of wills a capital offence and with a trial or pair of trials which do

* Jackson specifies that it was in the lower part of the belly. Robinson's, which Johnson declares to have been a house of ill fame, was at Charing Cross.

not figure in *The Newgate Calendar*. These were the trials of Bambridge and Huggins, wardens of the Fleet prison, for murder of and theft from prisoners in their charge. These took place at the Old Bailey in May and were to be followed in August by similar trials at Surrey assizes in respect of the Marshalsea prison.

I do not feel that I can properly devote space to these cases. For a proper treatment of them, I can only refer the reader to a volume by Lord Birkenhead (F. E. Smith) which, though published fifty years ago, comes up with some frequency on the secondhand market. They explain the painting by Hogarth which so oddly shows a committee of the House of Commons meeting at the Fleet prison. This was, of course, long before the agitation started by John Howard, then a child of three. The wardenship of a prison, like magistracy, remained an office of profit, with all the abuses that this fact might give rise to. It troubled men of good will, but none of them quite knew what to do about it. For some five years past, there had been fewer debtors in prison.

III

Hanged for Sheep-Stealing

In 1734, a new member of the Newgate Calendar family, a volume of *Select Trials* printed for J. Wilford, contained the account of Jack Sheppard which was to go on being reproduced in the Calendars proper. That year, a rioting mob in Edinburgh provided the future Sir Walter Scott with a theme by, as we might say (under American influence), lynching Captain John Porteous, who had ordered soldiers to fire on a previous rioting mob and who, at that moment, was under sentence of death but respited. That year also, we are justified in supposing, Samuel Johnson of Lichfield, in London, made the acquaintance of Richard Savage, reprieved murderer and plausible talker, though genuinely gifted, a man some twelve years older than himself but at the moment no less indigent.

The laws under which so many forgers were to be hanged were, basically, those of 6 Geo. I and 4 Geo. II, already noted, neither to produce much of a crop for eighteen years, after emendation. Forgery is, essentially, a literate man's crime, and some of the hanged forgers were to be of considerable note. The first noted in Calendars was hanged in 1738. He was a lawyer's clerk from Chichester, William Newington, who, from a coffee-house called Child's in St Paul's churchyard, sent a porter to Child's, bankers, in Fleet Street with an order signed Thomas Hill, whom he knew to be one of their clients, on behalf of Sir Rowland Hill, Bart. or order, for the sum of one hundred and twenty pounds. He omitted the date, and it was this omission, rather than the obscure joke, which cost him his life, at the hands not of Richard Arnett or of John Hooper, but of John Thrift, a bungling and unpopular hangman who was yet to see fourteen more years' service.

The names of provincial hangmen have not come down to us, and we do not know who, the following year, at York, finished Richard Turpin, most overrated of highwaymen, for horse-stealing. As the famous ride to York on Black Bess never took place, we can hardly say that Turpin provided the theme of Harrison Ainsworth's *Rookwood* and other future romances. He indeed got from London to York, doubtless on horseback, but by easy stages over a period of years.

The month after his execution at York, Thrift did have a horse-thief to launch into eternity at Tyburn. This was Abraham Wells, by trade a butcher, who had quarrelled with his wife.

That men were formerly hanged for stealing sheep has for long seemed more shocking than that they were formerly hanged for stealing horses or even deer. By people who would find it difficult to name any other offence for which men were formerly hanged, this fact is quoted with dark, ideological purpose. The notion seems to be that only a starving peasant would steal a sheep and that his rich oppressor would hardly miss it.

First let us note, however, that to roast a whole sheep is a conspicuous proceeding and that few starving peasants would possess the kind of vessel in which it could be boiled, while it would take a great many hungry mouths to eat all the meat while it was reasonably fresh. Sheep were the property rather of humble graziers than of lords of the manor. Their small flocks were the livelihood of such men. In Thomas Hardy's *Far from the Madding Crowd*, we may see what the loss of a man's sheep would mean to him. Gabriel Oak's sheep were not stolen.

When sheep were stolen, it was likely to be the work of gangs from the towns, tipped off perhaps by some member of the local peasantry.

Apparently, sheep-stealing on a great scale still goes on. In 1973, I read in one of the colour supplements that, over a period of twelve years, a Mrs Kirby in Wales had had over two thousand stolen and that, in the previous year alone, a Mr Evans had lost two hundred. A Mr Jones was quoted on the speed with which the thieves might operate. He recalled a theft of lambs from Denbigh, believed to have gone to a slaughterhouse in Liverpool. 'We went straight from Denbigh to Liverpool, but by the time we got there they'd all been killed. They were on the hook. Unidentifiable.' A Mr Lloyd of the National Farmers' Union believed that continued thefts could disrupt the entire hill economy. But, indeed, it was not only hill farmers who suffered. A Mr Ward who farmed near King's Lynn in Norfolk, after having two hundred and forty fat lambs stolen in three years, had given up sheep altogether.

It appears that the law still allows prison sentences of up to ten years for what is now known by another American term ('rustling') and that very stiff fines are sometimes imposed. A Caernarvonshire man had been fined £1,000 for the theft of a single sheep, a Pembrokeshire man £500 for stealing one elderly ewe (which was produced, struggling, in court), with a further, suspended prison sentence of eighteen months for attempting to sell her at market.

The measure which made sheep-stealing a capital offence was one of 14 Geo. II, for the security of farmers, whereby it was enacted that

> If any person or persons, after the first of May, 1741, shall feloniously drive away, or in any other manner feloniously steal, any sheep . . . or shall wilfully kill one or more sheep of any person or persons whatsoever, with an intent to steal the whole or part of any of the carcasses, the person or persons so offending shall suffer death without benefit of clergy.

The denial of benefit of clergy, which meant of course that literacy was no excuse, was becoming increasingly frequent. It appeared in the legislation concerning forgery, where perhaps it was necessary, only those who might have claimed that benefit being in a position to commit the offence. The literate might, on the other hand, be thought comparatively unlikely to steal sheep.

Added more than seventy years later, a note in Jackson says:

> In the course of a year it generally happens that several persons are convicted of sheep-stealing, who are usually thought proper objects of the lenity of the judges before whom they are tried; and it has rarely happened that a man has been hanged for the simple fact of sheep-stealing, though the offence be capital in the eyes of the law.

The one case of which he and Knapp & Baldwin offer identical accounts is, as he points out, of a very different complexion from that of a poor countryman, with a large family, who, if he were tempted to steal a sheep, might do it from mere want of the necessaries of life.

> Patrick Bourke and George Ellis were indicted at the Old Bailey, in December 1744, for killing fifteen ewe sheep, the property of John Messenger of Kensington, with intention to steal part of the carcasses, to wit, the fat near the kidneys.
>
> Mr Messenger deposed that he had lost fifteen ewes, that their throats were cut, their bellies ripped open and the fat taken out. He likewise said that he had lost twenty-seven lambs, which were taken out of those ewes, and he deposed that both the prisoners had confessed the crime before Sir Thomas Deveil on the Tuesday following; and that Bourke acknowledged they had sold the fat to a tallow-chandler for forty-one shillings and twopence halfpenny.
>
> Richard Twyford proved the finding the sheep ripped open and the fat taken out, and that the lambs were dragging by the sides of them; and swore that the prisoners had owned taking the gates from the farm to pen the sheep up.
>
> Joseph Agnew, a constable, swore that Ellis came to him and, after having told him of a quarrel between him and Bourke, who had given him two black eyes, he acknowledged that he had been concerned with him in the commission of the crime beforementioned. Hereupon, the constable took with him three watchmen and, going to Bourke's, seized him in bed; and found a clasp-knife lying on the ground near the feet of the bed, on which was some fat, which likewise remained when the knife was produced in court on the trial.

> Bourke, in his defence, said that he was kept drunk by the constable, in order to induce him to make a confession; but this not being credited by the jury, and there being other proofs of the fact having been acknowledged, they were capitally convicted and, receiving sentence of death, were executed at Tyburn on the 20th of February, 1745.

The offence was committed towards the end of the year during which Samuel Johnson had published *The Life of Richard Savage*, Savage having died the year before in prison for debt at Bristol, his circumstances then so reduced that, as Knapp & Baldwin note, he was buried in the churchyard of St Peter at the expense of the gaoler. Johnson himself had not yet prospered, as one of Malone's notes to Boswell tells us.

> The following striking proof of Johnson's extreme indigence, when he published the *Life of Savage*, was communicated to the author, by Mr Richard Stow, of Apsley in Bedfordshire, from the information of Mr Walter Harte, author of the *Life of Gustavus Adolphus*.
>
> Soon after Savage's *Life* was published, Mr Harte dined with Edward Cave and occasionally praised it. Soon after, meeting him, Cave said, 'You made a man very happy t'other day.' 'How could that be?' says Harte. 'Nobody was there but ourselves.' Cave answered by reminding him that a plate of victuals was sent behind a screen, which was to Johnson, dressed so shabbily that he did not choose to appear; but, on hearing the conversation, was highly delighted with the encomiums on his book.

In the northern part of the kingdom, there were to be stirring events in the year which may be said to have opened with the execution of Bourke and Ellis. We shall pay more attention, however, to a curious disappearance reported, during their last weeks of life, in a small town half-way between London and Edinburgh. Perhaps the best known of all tales from *The Newgate Calendar*, this is best reconsidered in two parts, widely separated by simple chronology.

IV

A Man of Forty

NOWADAYS, we see Knaresborough almost as a suburb of Harrogate, a little town three miles to the north-east, on the Nidd. Two hundred and fifty years ago, it was quite the reverse. In his *Tour through the Whole Island of Great Britain*, Defoe does not name the insignificant hamlets of High and Low Harrogate, to the south-west of Knaresborough. He knew of the mineral springs there, but thought of them as belonging to Knaresborough, known as the Yorkshire Spaw. The town returned two members to parliament, and the whole, vast area of unenclosed land, mainly to the west, on which Harrogate was to develop with the discovery of more and more mineral springs, had long been Knaresborough Forest.

The town stood on the steep north or left bank of the Nidd, here flowing through a wooded valley, hemmed in by limestone cliffs. Just across the river, the late Daniel Foe or Defoe had noted that, in a little cave, a petrifying water dropped from the roof of the cavity, which, as they said, turned wood to stone. He had not noted St Robert's cave on the bank, far less the one kept vacant for Mother Shipton, a reputed prophetess of the reign of Henry VIII, who was to have her vogue later. He does not mention the remains of a castle, demolished under the Commonwealth. He was unaware of a blind boy, John Metcalf, who, despite his disabilities, was to establish a reputation as a maker of roads and bridges, transport organiser and sportsman.

The bridges in the area had already struck Defoe as noteworthy. The Nidd he had found furiously rapid and very dangerous to pass in many places, especially upon sudden rains, notwithstanding such lofty, high-built bridges as were not to be seen over small rivers in any other place. For no part of England could show such noble, large, lofty and long stone bridges, nor so many of them. On Knaresborough Forest, he had noted the posts set up for fear of bogs and holes.

Linen and leather were manufactured, and there were limestone quarries. At the beginning of 1745, a heckler or flax-dresser, Richard Houseman, a heavily built man, bald and wearing a brown wig, lived in a yard behind the White Horse inn. A thin young friend of his, a shoemaker, Daniel Clark, tall but pock-broke and a stutterer, had just married a wife with a fortune of £200 or more, daughter of an exciseman, her sister the wife of no less a worthy than Philip Coates, an attorney or so described.

We know the names of a good many other citizens of Knaresborough at the time. Among the publicans, for instance, was Henry Terry, ale-draper at the Barrel inn. A builder was William Tutin. Almost a gentleman was Francis Iles, who lived east of the town, where the York road began, a man of great influence but doubtful avocation. The vicar was Mr Collins. The justice of the peace, William Thornton, Esq., lived further along the York road. John Yeats was a barber, Stephen Latham another shoemaker. Bryan Hardcastle kept a livery stable. Barbara Leatham, a widow, lived south of the town, at the foot of Thistle Hill.

Daniel Clark's credit was good. He was seized of two freeholds and kept a horse at bait in Hardcastle's stable. At the time of his marriage, he had taken up a great quantity of goods, undertaking to pay for these as soon as he came into possession of his wife's fortune. From Mr Beckwith, the draper, he had velvets and cambrics, and Beckwith had further lent him fifteen guineas. From Ward, a saddler, he had whips and leather, from Iles and others blankets and other linen and woollen goods, wanting not only clothes to appear in on the occasion but also table and bed linen. From the landlords of the White Horse and the Crown, for the use of company he was to have at supper, he had borrowed three tankards, four silver pints and a milkpot, ordering ale and other sorts of liquors. His own servant, Peter Moor, had lent him £38. He had further procured a ring set with an emerald and two brilliant diamonds, another with three rose diamonds, a third with an amethyst in the shape of a heart, six plain rings, eight watches and two snuff-boxes. There were even books from a bookseller in York and another without Temple Bar, London. These included Ephraim Chamber's *Universal Dictionary of Arts and Sciences* in two volumes, folio, and Pope's Homer in six volumes, bound.

Having some urgent business with him, Philip Coates, seeing his new brother-in-law in the High Street, about nine o'clock in the evening on February 7th, asked him to call next morning. Clark promised to do so, but did not call. Mr Coates therefore went to his house. That was at nine o'clock in the morning. Clark's maid told him that her master had gone to see his wife who was visiting her parents. On Sunday, the 10th, Mr Coates went out to the village where his own parents-in-law lived, but Clark had not been there. In Knaresborough, the maid and Peter Moor looked around in Clark's house but found neither plate nor money.

The conclusion seemed obvious. Daniel Clark had absconded with his wife's fortune, the plate and jewellery. On Tuesday, he was advertised for in the York *Courant*, with a list of the missing goods and the offer of a reward for information, no questions asked. The horse, still at Bryan Hardcastle's stable, was turned over to a common friend, John Holliday, who paid for its keep.

His brother-in-law had not been the last person to see Clark on the night of his disappearance. Between eleven o'clock and midnight, he had called on William Tutin, his neighbour, to leave some leather. At about two of the clock, Tutin had again been visited by Clark, who called him out of bed. Looking out of the window to speak to Clark, Tutin had, he said, seen two men standing in the moonlight near Clark's cellar door. On perceiving that they were observed, they had withdrawn to the end of the street, towards Castle Yard. One, said Tutin, had been Richard Houseman, the heckler. The other had been the schoolmaster, Eugene Aram.

In the evening, Clark had been seen with Richard Houseman at the Crown inn. Earlier that day, Peter Moor, with his master, had visited the schoolhouse, bearing a parcel. It looked as though Clark had had accomplices. There had been rumours about these three before, in connection with a Jew who had been briefly in the town.

With or without authority, premises were searched. In Houseman's garden, Tutin found a mason's pick or hammer he had missed. Concealed beneath drying flax in Houseman's shed lay skins from Clark's stock of leather. The Arams lived meanly in one of a pair of cottages up a ginnel off Vicarage Lane, but the schoolhouse was in White Horse Yard. Its bit of garden adjoined Houseman's. It, too, was searched, and in it were found buried several kinds of goods bound together in a coarse wrapper, among them velvets and a piece of cambric, which Beckwith claimed. No plate was found, nor any jewellery. Clark himself had no doubt gone off with those.

There is no record of any proceedings being taken against Houseman. A process was served on Aram in respect of a debt to a gentleman, William Norton, whom he had served as steward when he first came to Knaresborough ten years before. This was done with a view to detain him until a warrant could be had from Justice Thornton, then absent in York. On Mr Thornton's return, Aram appeared before him, but no charge was pressed. Though reputed very poor, Aram discharged the debt without difficulty.

The birthplace of Eugene or Eugenius Aram was Ramsgill in upper Nidderdale, some twenty miles north-west of Knaresborough, though most of his childhood had been spent in the neighbourhood of Ripon, nearer and to the north, his father having been gardener to Sir Edward Blackett of Newby Hall.

It may be assumed that he was called Eugene after Prince Eugene of Savoy, Marlborough's friend and co-victor at the Battle of Blenheim, the month before his birth in September 1704. It is true that in later documents he is commonly shown as Eugenius (spelt variously, in his marriage entry at Lofthouse as 'Ujenius'). This may have been due to affectation on his part. There was no hint of popery in the family. His father, on the other hand, might well have known the name in its Latin form. A gardener may not be quite a gentleman, but Peter Aram had been fully literate and had studied botany, which inclines to Latinisation, more especially of continental names. He had also published verse, though his only known surviving work is a celebration in heroic couplets of the beauties of Studley Park, which contains the ruins of Fountains Abbey and lies some four miles west of Newby Hall. It is not as good as *Windsor Forest*, but at least suggests that Sir Edward Blackett's gardener had read Pope.

His other sons, Stephen and Henry, lived now in Hull. It is likely enough that the latter had been christened after Henry Compton, bishop of London, by whom Peter Aram had been recommended to the Blacketts. The present Newby Hall is owned by Comptons. They acquired the old house and the estate very shortly after the demise of Sir Edward Blackett, whose own posterity thrives grandly in Northumberland. Newby Hall is known as one of the great Adam houses, abounding in Gobelin tapestries and classical statuary. The old house had no doubt had its own splendour. Eugene Aram later wrote:

> It was here my propension to literature first appeared, for, being always of a solitary disposition and uncommonly fond of retirement and books, I enjoyed here all the repose and opportunity I could wish. My study at that time was engaged in the mathematics. . . . I was even then equal to the management of quadratic equations and their geometrical constructions.

Though he does not tell us so (was not, that is to say, to tell the Rev. Mr Collins, in the letter from which this comes), it seems likely that he had looked after the books at Newby, with some prospect of being appointed steward. When Sir Edward had died shortly thereafter, the heir, clearly, did not wish to continue his father's arrangements, perhaps from the outset meaning to sell the place. The Blacketts had not turned the Arams loose, however. The gardener had been found a post with Sir John Ingilby at Ripley Hall, six miles south-west of Newby and still occupied by Ingilbys.

> Being about the age of sixteen, I was sent for to London, being thought upon examination by Mr Christopher Blackett, qualified to serve him as book-keeper in his counting house. Here, after a year or two's continuance, I took the small pox and suffered severely under that distemper. My mother was so impatient to see me that she was very near upon a journey to London, which I by an invitation from my father prevented, by going to her.
>
> At home, with leisure upon my hands and a new addition of authors to those brought me from Newby, I renewed not only my mathematical studies but began and prosecuted others of a different turn, with much avidity and diligence. These were poetry, history and antiquities, the charms of which quite destroyed all the heavier beauties of numbers and lines, whose applications and properties I now pursued no longer, except occasionally in teaching.
>
> I was, after some time employed in this manner, invited into Nidderdale, my native air, where I first engaged in a school and where I married. . . .

His bride had been Anna Spence, of Lofthouse, and the marriage had taken place on May 4th, 1731, he being then twenty-seven, she twenty-three. From their prompt embraces had resulted a daughter, christened Anna the following January, buried in June. Their quiver, however, had not long remained empty.

> . . . unfortunately . . . During my marriage here, perceiving the deficiencies of my education, sensible of my want of the learned languages and prompted by an irresistible covetousness of knowledge, I commenced . . . the labour of grammar. I selected Lilly from the rest, all of which I got and repeated by heart. The task of repeating it all every day was impossible while I attended the school, so I divided it into portions, by which method it was pronounced thrice every week. This I performed for years.
>
> Next I became acquainted with Camden's *Greek Grammar*, which I also repeated in the same manner, *memoriter*. Thus instructed, I entered upon the Latin classics, whose allurements

> repaid my assiduities and my labours. I remember to have at first hung over five lines for a whole day. . . . After I had accurately perused every one of the Latin classics, historians and poets, I went through the Greek Testament, first parsing every word as I proceeded. Next, I ventured upon Hesiod, Homer, Theocritus, Herodotus, Thucydides and all the Greek tragedians. A tedious labour was this, but my former acquaintance with history lessened it extremely, because it threw a light upon many passages which, without that assistance, must have appeared obscure.
>
> In the midst of these literary pursuits, a man and horse, from my good friend William Norton, Esq., came for me from Knaresborough, along with that gentleman's letter inviting me thither. . . .

That stewardship cannot have gone well. There, at any rate, ten years later, was Eugenius Aram, reputed very poor, pursued for a debt by Norton, teaching in a schoolroom without a fireplace, up White Horse Yard. He had in the meantime wrestled with Hebrew, reading the *Pentateuch* but no further in the original, begetting with certainty three and with a fair likelihood seven children. He was a man with a very small head, wearing his own hair, strong-jawed, the profile aquiline.

After discharging the debt, he continued in Knaresborough for a month without further molestation. He then left that place and went, it is supposed, at first to Nottingham, there to stay with kinsfolk of his late father.

> In April, I think the 18th, . . . I went again to London. Here I agreed to teach the Latin and writing for the Rev. Mr Painblanc, in Piccadilly, which he, along with a salary, returned by teaching me French, wherein I observed the pronunciation the most formidable part. . . . But this my continual application every night or other opportunity overcame, and I soon became a tolerable master of French.

Later that year, Prince Charles Edward Stuart, whose French was perfect, brought a skirl of sheep's guts and a gabble of Irish first into Edinburgh and then to Manchester. Wisely, he kept to the west side of the Pennines, seeing that Justice Thornton (greatly aided by Blind Jack Metcalf) had raised a regiment of Yorkshire Blues. On Micklegate Bar in York, the heads of two rebels, James Mayne and William Connolly, were posted. In Knaresborough, at least a part of the cottage up a ginnel off Vicarage Lane was taken as a weaving shed by Richard Houseman. To weave, he employed John Barber and, to spin, Polly Powell, who lived in the other of the pair. Daniel Clark, as he had failed to appear when advertised for, was outlawed by a promulgation dated October 20th, 1746. His brother-in-law, Philip Coates, heard of a Daniel Clark, a shoemaker, in Limerick, but, going into Ireland, found it was not the same man or, returning, said so.

Eugene Aram stayed, he was to write, with the Rev. Mr Painblanc, presumably a Huguenot pastor, in Piccadilly for two years and above.

> Some time after this, I went to Hayes, in the capacity of writing master, and served a gentlewoman there, since dead, and stayed after that with a worthy and reverend gentleman. I succeeded to several other places in the south of England and all that while used every occasion of improvement. I then transcribed the acts of parliament to be registered in Chancery; and after went down to the free school at Lynn.

This is all we know, with anything resembling certainty, of the course of that man's life during a period over twelve years, except that on a number of occasions he visited the embankment at Chelsea and that he lost some back teeth.

There is, indeed, one story of him in London, which we may credit or not, as we please. It appears that, while he was taking tea with a lady, a gentleman of Leeds, her keeper, surprised them. The strong jaw and hooked nose of the unwelcomed guest seemed familiar to the gentleman. He behaved with civility, but next day desired his fair one to question Aram whether he were not from Knaresborough in Yorkshire and acquainted with one Daniel Clark, whether Clark was with him in London and so forth, to all of which questions the visitor replied evasively and took tea no more at that house.

The authority for this story was presumably the gentleman from Leeds, whose name the anonymous scribe of York would choose to omit, so that we do not know it. It is not an improbable story. A greater improbability would be that no such encounter should take place in twelve years, for it is given no date. If we believe that it took place as recounted, we still do not know whether it was while Aram taught at Mr Painblanc's or, later (perhaps ten years later), when he was reduced to copying, in Gothic script, those acts of parliament, generally both old and of minor importance, to be exemplified under the Great Seal, at intervals removed by *certiorari* and deposited in the Rolls Chapel.

Of his intellectual preoccupations during that period, he tells us (was to tell Mr Collins) a fair amount.

> From my leaving Knaresborough . . . is a long interval, which I . . . filled up with the further study of history and antiquities, heraldry and botany, in the last of which I was very agreeably entertained, there being so extensive a display of Nature. I well knew . . . Linnaeus. . . . I made frequent visits to the Botanic Garden at Chelsea and traced pleasure through a thousand fields. At last, few plants, domestic or exotic, were unknown to me.
>
> Amidst all this, I ventured upon the Chaldee and Arabic. . . . I had not time to obtain any great knowledge of the Arabic. The Chaldee I found easy enough, because of its connection with the Hebrew. I then investigated the Celtic, as far as possible in all its dialects, began collections and made comparisons between that, the English, the Latin, the Greek and even the Hebrew. I made notes and compared above three thousand [words] of these together and found such a surprising affinity, . . . beyond any expectation or conception, that I was determined to proceed through the whole of all these languages and form a comparative Lexicon, which I hoped would account for numberless vocables in use with us, the Latins and the Greeks, before concealed and unobserved. . . . Most of my books and papers are now scattered and lost.

Two later papers were to be recovered. It is generally admitted that they constitute a step forward in the understanding of relations between the historical languages, which is still by no means complete and may never be so.

In the terms he uses, the Yorkshire scholiast betrays a dependence on notions of his time which have been or must presently be discarded. The term 'Chaldee' has long been given up, for instance, and it may amuse us to note that the term by which it has been replaced is 'Aramaic'. This term comes from the name of a territory now regarded as part of Syria, although indeed there was once a King Aram of Urartu (known as Armenia till the Russians overran it). The language forms one of a group to which the term 'Semitic' was to be given by a German historian, August Ludwig von Schlözer, twenty-two years after Aram's death.

The term 'Celtic' began its history in our language when he was two years old. No word cognate with it had ever existed in any of what are nevertheless still known as the Celtic languages, namely, on the one hand, Welsh, Old Cornish and Breton and, on the other, Irish, Manx and the Gaelic of some parts of highland Scotland and its offshore islands.

The misunderstanding had first arisen in the mind of a Breton Frenchman, Brother Paul-Yves Pezron, a Cistercian monk, who, the year before Mrs Peter Aram of Ramsgill in the West Riding of Yorkshire bore a son christened Eugenius or Eugene, published a volume called *L'Antiquité de la Nation et de la Langue des Celtes.* In Caesar's *De Bello Gallico*, Book I, it is said that the Gauls of the greater part of what is now France were, in their own tongue, called *Celtae*. They were the only people ever, in their own tongue, on record as being called anything like that, though Strabo and other Greek geographers designated *Keltoi* all the fair-haired tribes north of the Alps, including those whom Caesar distinguished as Germans. A thousand years before Pezron, the languages theretofore spoken throughout south-western Europe, including that of the Gauls or *Celtae*, had, except along the Pyrenees, been replaced by varieties of decayed Latin, remarkably consistent in their grammar and syntax, differing in the extent and source of alien admissions to their vocabulary, most of those in French being of German words, a mere fifty or so of Gaulish (or Celtic) surviving, except, thought Pezron, in his native Brittany. That was where he made his mistake. Breton had been introduced from south-west Britain, which was why the Armorican peninsula was called Bretagne or Brittany, as it might have been Little Britain. The Breton of the peasants of Brittany was still recognisably the Cornish not yet quite dead in south-west Great Britain. It was not in the least a survival of ancient Gaulish or Celtic.

Three years after its publication in France, when Eugene Aram was two years old, there had appeared in English a modified translation of Pezron's book by one D. Jones, who called it *The Antiquities of Nations, more particularly of the* Celtae *or* Gauls, *taken to be originally the same people as our ancient* Britains. To the glossaries with which Pezron's book concludes D. Jones had added from some evident knowledge of Welsh, and his volume contains an advertisement for a forthcoming book, the *Archeologia Britannica* of Edward Lhuyd, keeper of the Ashmolean museum, who proposed 'a British etymologicon or the British collated with the Greek, Latin, Celtic, Teutonic, etc.' and also 'a Latin-Celtic dictionary or vocabulary of the original languages of Britain and Ireland and of the Armoric British.' The false revelation to these Welshmen had been that Breton was a survival of Gaulish or Celtic. Since affinities between Welsh and Breton had long since been noted, Welsh also, they concluded, must be a form of Celtic, and Irish must be yet another form, since affinities between Welsh and Irish had also been noted. The remarkable Celtomania of the eighteenth and early nineteenth centuries had been born.

It is not yet extinct. The uneducated still firmly believe that, while the English are Anglo-Saxons with a dash of Norman-French in the upper class, the Welsh, the Cornish and Manx, the Irish and even the lowland Scots are Celts, like the Bretons. Similar fantasies obtain abroad, and even respectable academic circles cling to the notion of 'the Celtic languages'. The academics have, of course, contrived to persuade themselves that a few Gallo-Roman inscriptions and some French place-names prove affinity between Welsh, Irish *et cetera* and the Gaulish so irrecoverably lost. Even if they are right, to call Welsh and Irish the Celtic languages is as though we were to call Latin and Greek the Illyrian languages.

The Pezron-Jones confusion having shown itself so durable, we ought not to be surprised that, in his time, so discerning a philologist as Eugene Aram, when he meant Welsh or Irish, spoke of 'the Celtic, in some dialect of it or other'. The term 'Chaldee' was not so misleading, and 'Phoenician' is perhaps not misleading at all. Two notions adopted by the Yorkshire schoolmaster were that the *Cymry*, as the Welsh call themselves, were the same as the *Cimbri* or Cimmerians from Jutland who had once so frightened the Romans and that it meant that the Welsh at least were children of Gomer, eldest son of Japhet, second or third son of Noah. These notions he may have picked up from Theophilus Evans, Moses Williams or some other Welshman, but the importance of Gomer goes back to Josephus, as do most eighteenth-century ideas about the migrations of peoples and how nations came to receive their names, all of course originally Jewish.

In those of his papers which have survived, we may see Eugenius Aram indulging in flights of historical fancy about the *Celtae* (who were, for instance, he says, both Scythians and Tatars) as wild as those of the Rev. William Stukeley, M.D., F.R.S., in his famous *Stonehenge, a Temple Restored to the British Druids*, which, although it had appeared in 1740, he may have read during his lost years. We know that he read or at least that he read about or heard of the same author's *Paleographia Britannica*, published three years later.

This we know by deduction. By the same process, we know the titles of some other books he read or at least heard about and remembered things from, not always with perfect accuracy. They include Sir William Dugdale's *Antiquities of Warwickshire*, Nathan Drake's *Eboracum*, William Howell's *Medulla Historiae Anglicanae* and John Gerard Voss's *De Origine ac Progressu Idolatriae*. None of these was at all recent. Of two works of translation he can only have become aware late in his lost years. One was of the poems of Callimachus by the Rev. William Dodd, a brilliant young curate in West Ham who also held a lectureship at St Olave's, had published a volume of *Beauties of Shakespeare* and a saucy, satirical novel, *The Sisters*, and who was to attain a notoriety which will concern us. Marsilius Ficinus's Plato in Latin we know Aram to have annoted in Latin.

In London in 1746, it is impossible that he should not have heard of the executions on Tower Hill of the Jacobite Lords Kilmarnock, Balmerino and, later, Lovat, of the awkwardness of Thrift, a stranger to the axe, with the first two and of the collapse of a spectators' scaffolding just before the unpleasant Lovat's old head fell. Two criminal cases we know him to have learnt of, in both a miscarriage of justice, one in Surrey and one at Winchester, those of Coleman and Fainloth, the one adequately treated in *The Newgate Calendar*, the other not there at all. Richard Coleman was a brewer's clerk in Southwark, hanged for a murder in the course of rape which, two years later, was brought home to three other men.

V

Smugglers, Forgers and Two Workhouse Children

AMONG the miscellaneous horrors of those years, it is impossible, if one's Calendar is Knapp & Baldwin (Jackson doesn't include it), not to be struck by the case of William York.

> This unhappy child was but just turned of ten years of age when he committed the dreadful crime of which he was convicted. He was a pauper in the poorhouse belonging to the parish of Eye, in Suffolk, and was committed, on the coroner's inquest, to Ipswich gaol, for the murder of Susan Mayhew, another child, of five years of age, who had been his bedfellow. The following is his confession, taken and attested by a justice of the peace and which was, in part, proved on the trial, with many corroborating circumstances of his guilt.
>
> He said that, a trifling quarrel happening between them on the 13th of May, 1748, about ten in the morning, he struck her with his open hand and made her cry: that, she going out of the house to the dunghill opposite to the door, he followed her, with a hook in his hand, with an intent to kill her, but before he came up to her he set down the hook and went into the house for a knife. He then came out again, took hold of the girl's left hand and cut her wrist all round to the bone, and then threw her down and cut her to the bone just above the elbow of the same arm. That, after this, he set his foot upon her stomach and cut her right arm round about and to the bone, both on the wrist and above the elbow. That he still thought she would not die,

> and therefore took the hook and cut her left thigh to the bone; and, observing she was not dead yet, his next care was to conceal the murder, for which purpose he filled a pail with water at a ditch and, washing the blood off the child's body, buried it in the dunghill, together with the blood that was spilled upon the ground, and made the dunghill as smooth as he could. Afterwards he washed the knife and hook and carried them into the house, cleaned the blood off his own clothes, hid the child's clothes in an old chamber and then came down and got his breakfast. When he was examined, he showed very little concern and appeared easy and cheerful. All he alleged was that the child fouled the bed in which they lay together, that she was sulky and that he did not like her.

There are cases on record of boys of William York's age being hanged, one in the previous century for burning a child in its cradle. The present 'boy murderer' (Knapp & Baldwin put the expression in inverted commas) was found guilty, and sentence of death pronounced against him. But he was respited from time to time and, on account of his tender years, was at length pardoned.

Along with pirates and highwaymen, smugglers are commonly viewed with indulgence even by respectable people. One of the less unattractive highwaymen, Henry Simms, known as Gentleman Harry, had recently met his end with fortitude. The Thames below London Bridge was infested with river pirates, usually dignified by the title of seamen (today they are registered dockers). Ports have always nurtured a criminal population not so much highly organised as tacitly united against people inland, some of whom will nevertheless be their agents, those for smugglers often being innkeepers. East Suffolk was smugglers' country. So were West Sussex, Hampshire and the hinterland of Poole, the geographical explanation no doubt being sufficiently obvious.

The indulgence we extend to smugglers we withhold from excisemen, none of us paying our taxes with enthusiasm (a fact which also accounted for the New England pirates and, ultimately, American independence). Yet to be an exciseman in the eighteenth century required at least courage. Smugglers assembled in such numbers that they were on occasion capable of routing the soldiery, while an exciseman who fell into their hands could expect to be tortured and murdered.

Knapp & Baldwin, in footnotes, quote East Anglian cases. Their principal cases, one a pendant to the other, come from the southern counties in a version largely identical with Jackson's. The two cases constitute a sequel to yet another, a robbery of the custom house at Poole, of which we are told little.

Seventeen smugglers, three innkeepers and some of their associates are named. The smugglers (the sweet symphony of their English names reduced to alphabetical order) were William Carter, John Cobby, John Diamond, Samuel Downer (known as Little Sam), John Hammond, William Jackson, John Mills, his father, Richard Mills, and his elder brother, also Richard Mills, William Pring, Edmund Richards, John Royce, Henry Sheerman (known as Little Harry), William Steele, Thomas Stringer and Thomas Winter, a Curtis and a Rowland being unprovided with Christian names. Of the innkeepers, a widow, Elizabeth Payne, who had two sons, was the most heavily committed, Scardefield and John Reynolds seeming a little nervous, while the positions of George Harris and his brother Peascod, William Comleah, a gardener and two Kemps, occasional highwaymen, remain a little uncertain. The Millses were Sussex men, as were Cobby, Hammond and Tapner. Carter and Jackson were Hampshire men, the latter a Roman Catholic. The setting is, for the most part, on the Hampshire side of the boundary between the two counties.

It is a famous smugglers' area, as any guidebook will inform us with pride. The wide and complicated sheet of water, more advantageous even than those before Poole or Southampton or than London pool, is that of Chichester harbour, branching round Hayling Island and cut off from Portsmouth.

The first victims were William Galley and Daniel Chater. The former was a custom-house officer of Southampton, the latter a shoemaker of Fordingbridge. Neither was a young man. For the most part, the smugglers were not very young. As one of his sons was in his late thirties, the elder Richard Mills must have been a man in advanced middle age.

On Sunday, February 14th, 1748, Galley and Chater set off

from Southampton with a letter from the collector of the customs there, Mr Shearer, to Major Battine, a justice of the peace at Stansted in Sussex,* requesting him to take a statement from Chater, a shoemaker, who had unwisely recalled seeing Diamond, described as a shepherd, then in custody at Chichester, among others, coming from Poole, loaded with, of all things (in view of what I have suggested about American independence), tea, of which Diamond had thrown him a packet. The two passed Havant and came to Leigh, where, at the New inn, they inquired their way of George Austin, his brother and brother-in-law. These said they were going the same road and would accompany the two to Rowlands Castle, where they might get better directions, it being close to the major's residence.

It was at the White Hart inn at Rowlands Castle that the trouble started, and it was the landlady, Elizabeth Payne, who started it. She said to Austin that she was afraid the two strangers meant harm to the smugglers. 'No, sure,' said he, 'they are only carrying a letter to Major Battine.' But she sent one of her sons for Jackson and Carter, who came as Galley and Chater were asking for their horses (but were told that Major Battine was not then at home). Elizabeth Payne advised Austin to go away, which he did, leaving his brother and brother-in-law. Her other son rounded up Steele, Downer, Richards and Sheerman.

> After they had drunk a little, Carter, who had some knowledge of Chater, called him into the yard and asked him where Diamond was. Chater said he believed he was in custody and that he was going to appear against him, which he was sorry for, but could not help it. Galley came into the yard to them, and, asking Chater why he would stay there, Jackson, who followed him, said, with a horrid imprecation, 'What is that to you?' and immediately struck him a blow in the face, which knocked him down and set his nose and mouth bleeding. Soon after, they all came into the house, when Jackson, reviling Galley, offered to strike him again, but one of the Paynes interposed. Galley and

* Place-names in this part of England show a disconcerting tendency to echo some better known in Essex. This was already the case with the Waltham Blacks, the Waltham in question being now called Bishop's Waltham. There is no proper village of Stansted in West Sussex, but maps still show a Stansted Forest and a Stansted House, in which latter Major Battine no doubt lived.

> Chater now began to be very uneasy and wanted to be going; but, Jackson, Carter and the rest of them persuading them to stay and drink more rum and make it up (for they were sorry for what had happened), they sat down again. . . . Jackson and Carter desired to see the letter, but they refused to show it. The smugglers then drank about plentifully, and made Galley and Chater fuddled, afterwards persuading them to lie down on a bed, which they did, and fell asleep. The letter was then taken away, read, and, the substance of it greatly exasperating them, it was destroyed.

They were joined by another of the gang, Royce, told him the contents of the letter and explained the two sleeping men. It was Steele who first proposed that they should be taken to a well about two hundred yards from the house, murdered and thrown in. This proposal was rejected, because the two men had been seen in the smugglers' company by the younger Austin and his brother-in-law, while also a Mr Garnett and a Mr Jenks were newly come into the house to drink.

> It was next proposed to send them to France; but that was objected against, as there was a possibility of their coming over again. Jackson's and Carter's wives, being present, cried out, 'Hang the dogs, for they come here to hang you!' It was then proposed and agreed to keep them confined till they could know Diamond's fate and, whatever it was, to treat these in the same manner; and each to allow threepence a week towards keeping them.
>
> Galley and Chater continuing asleep, Jackson went in and began the first scene of cruelty. For, having put on his spurs, he got upon the bed and spurred their foreheads, to wake them, and afterwards whipped them with a horsewhip, so that when they came out they were both bleeding. The abovesaid smugglers then took them out of the house; but Richards returned with a pistol and swore he would shoot any person who should mention what had passed.
>
> Meanwhile, the rest put Galley and Chater on one horse, tied their legs under the horse's belly and then tied the legs of both together. They now set forward, all but Royce, who had no horse. They had not gone above two hundred yards before Jackson called out, 'Whip 'em, cut 'em, slash 'em, damn 'em! upon which all began to whip, except Steele who led the horse, the roads being very bad. They whipped them for half a mile'

till they came to Woodash, where they fell off, with their heads under the horse's belly; and their legs, which were tied, appeared over the horse's back. Their tormentors soon set them upright again and continued whipping them over the head, face, shoulders &c. till they came to Dean, upwards of half a mile farther. Here they both fell again as before, with their heads under the horse's belly, which were struck at every step by the horse's hoofs.

Upon placing them again in the saddle, they found them so weak that they could not sit, upon which they separated them and put Galley before Steele and Chater before Little Sam; and then whipped Galley so severely that, the lashes coming upon Steele, at his desire they desisted. They then went to Harris's well, near Ladyholt Park, where they took Galley off the horse and threw him into the well: upon which he desired them to dispatch him at once and put an end to his misery. 'No,' says Jackson, cursing, 'if that's the case, we have more to say to you!' then put him on a horse again and whipped him over the downs, till he was so weak that he fell off, when they laid him across the saddle with his breast downwards, and Little Sam got up behind him, and as they went on he squeezed Galley's testicles so that he groaned with agony and tumbled off. Being then put on astride, Richards got up behind him, but soon the poor man cried out, 'I fall, I fall, I fall!' and Richards, pushing him, said, 'Fall, and be damned!' Upon which he fell down and expired; and the villains, taking up the body, laid it again on the horse, and proposed to go to some proper place, where Chater might be concealed till they heard the fate of Diamond.

Jackson and Carter called at one Peascod's house, desiring admittance for two sick men. But he absolutely refused it.

Being now one o'clock in the morning, they agreed to go to one Scardefield's, at the Red Lion, at Rake, which was not far. Here, Carter and Jackson got admittance, after many refusals. While Scardefield went to draw liquor, he heard more company come in; but, though they refused to admit him into the room, he saw one man stand up very bloody and another lie as dead. They said they had engaged some officers, lost their tea, and several of them were wounded if not killed.

Jackson and Little Harry now carried Chater down to Old Mills's, which was not far off, and chained him in a turf-house; and, Little Harry staying to watch him, Jackson returned again to the company. After they had drunk gin and rum, they all went out, taking the body of Galley with them. Carter compelled Scardefield to show them a place before used to bury smuggled tea, and to lend them spades and a candle and lantern. There they began to dig, and, it being very cold, he helped to make a hole where they buried 'something that lay across a horse like a dead man'.

They continued at Scardefield's, drinking, all that day, and in the night went to their own homes in order to be seen on Tuesday, agreeing to meet again on Thursday at the same house and bring more of their associates. They met accordingly, and brought old Richard Mills and his sons, . . . Stringer, . . . Cobby, . . . Tapner and . . . Hammond, who, with the former, made fourteen. They consulted now what was to be done with Chater. It was unanimously agreed that he must be destroyed. Richard Mills junior proposed to load a gun, clap the muzzle to his head, tie a long string to the trigger, then all to pull it, that all might be guilty of his murder. This was rejected, because it would put him out of his pain too soon; and at length they came to resolution to carry him up to Harris's well . . . and to throw him in.

All this while, Chater was in the utmost horror and misery, being visited by one or other of them, who abused him both with words and blows. At last, they all came, and, Tapner and Cobby going into the turf-house, the former pulled out a clasp-knife and said, with a great oath, 'Down on your knees, and go to prayers, for with this knife I'll be your butcher!' The poor man knelt down; and, as he was at prayers, Cobby kicked him, calling him 'informing villain'. Chater asking what they had done with Mr Galley, Tapner, slashing the knife across his eyes, almost cut them out and the gristle of his nose quite through. He bore it patiently, believing they were putting an end to his misery. Accordingly, Tapner struck at him again and made a deep cut in his forehead. Upon this, Old Mills said, 'Do not murder him here, but somewhere else.' Accordingly, they placed him upon a horse, and all set out together for Harris's well, except Mills and his sons, they having no horses ready and saying in excuse that there were enough without them to murder one man. All the way, Tapner whipped him till the blood came; and then swore that, if he blooded the saddle, he would torture him the more, which, as he could not stop his wounds from bleeding, was an incredible instance of barbarity.

When they were come within two hundred yards of the well, Jackson and Carter stopped, saying to Tapner, Cobby, Stringer, Steele and Hammond, 'Go on and do your duty on Chater, as we have ours upon Galley.' In the dead of the night of the 18th, they brought him to the well, which was nearly thirty feet deep, but dry, and paled close round. Tapner having fastened a noose round Chater's neck, they bade him get over the pales to the well. He was going through a broken place; but, though he was covered with blood and fainting with the anguish of his wounds, they forced him to climb up, having the rope about his neck, one end of which being tied to the pales they pushed him into the well. The rope being short, he hung no farther within it than his thighs, and, leaning against the edge, he hung above a quarter of an hour and was not strangled. They then untied him and threw him head foremost into the well. They tarried some time and, hearing him groan, they concluded to go to one William Comleah's, a gardener, to borrow a rope and ladder, saying they wanted to relieve one of their companions who had fallen into Harris's well. He said they might take them; but they could not manage the ladder in their confusion, it being a long one.

They then returned to the well; and, still hearing him groan and fearful that the sound thereof might lead to a discovery, the place being near the road, they threw upon him some of the rails and gateposts fixed about the wall, also great stones, when, finding him silent, they left him.

Their next consultation was how to dispose of their horses. . . . They killed Galley's, which was grey, and, taking his hide off, cut it into small pieces and hid them so as to prevent any discovery. But a bay horse that Chater had rode on got from them. . .

The two unfortunate sufferers . . . not returning to their respective homes, . . . a search for them was . . . instituted.

Those employed for this purpose, after every inquiry, could hear no certain tidings of them, fear of the smugglers' resentment silencing such inhabitants on the road over which they had carried the unfortunate men as were not in connection with them. At length, a Mr Stone, following his hounds, came to a spot which appeared to have been dug not long before, and, from the publicity of the circumstance of the men . . . being missed, he conjectured that there they might have been buried and thereof gave immediate information. Upon digging there, nearly seven feet in the earth, the remains of Galley were found, but in so putrid a state as not to be known except by the clothes. The search after Chater was now pursued with redoubled vigilance, and his body was found in [the] well, with a quantity of stones, wooden rails and earth upon it. . . .

After a long and diligent search for the perpetrators of these crimes, some of the smugglers were taken up on suspicion, and . . . admitted evidences for the crown, on discovering all they knew of the horrid transaction. . . . At a special commission held

> at Chichester on the 16th of January, 1749, Benjamin Tapner, John Cobby, John Hammond, William Carter, Richard Mills the elder and Richard Mills the younger were indicted for the murder of Daniel Chater, the three first as principals and the others as accessories before the fact; and William Jackson and William Carter were indicted for the murder of William Galley. . . . Sir Michael Foster presided in court. . . . The jury, after being out of court about a quarter of an hour, brought in a verdict of guilty against all the prisoners. . . .
>
> The heinousness of the crime . . . rendering it necessary that their punishment should be exemplary, the judge ordered that they should be executed on the following day; and the sentence was accordingly carried [out] against all but Jackson, who . . . on the evening that he was condemned . . . was so struck with horror at being measured for his irons that he . . . expired. . . . Tapner and Carter gave good advice to the spectators and desired diligence might be used to apprehend Richards, whom they charged as the cause of their being brought to this wretched end. Young Mills smiled several times at the executioner, who was a discharged marine and, having ropes too short for some of them, was puzzled to fit them. Old Mills, being forced to stand tip-toe to reach the halter, desired that he might not be hanged by inches. The Millses were so rejoiced at being told that they were not to be hung in chains after execution that death seemed to excite in them no terror. . . .
>
> Carter was hung in chains near Rake, in Sussex; Tapner on Rook's Hill, near Chichester; and Cobby and Hammond [on Selsey Bill, near] the beach where they sometimes landed their smuggled goods and where they could be seen at a great distance east and west. . . . The body of . . . Jackson was thrown into a hole near the place of execution, as were those of Mills, the father and son, who had no friends to take them away. . . .

As we presently discover, John Mills (also concerned in the murder of the custom-house officer and the shoemaker and likewise one of the gang who most daringly broke open the custom house at Poole) had been travelling over Hind Heath with some associates when he saw the judges on their road to Chichester to try his father, his brother and the rest. He had proposed to rob the party, but his associates would not.

They planned to go to Bristol, with a view to embarking for France.

Stopping at a house on the road, they met with one Richard Hawkins, who they asked to go with them; but, the poor fellow hesitating, they put him on horseback behind Mills and carried him to the Dog and Partridge on Slindon Common, which was kept by John Reynolds.

They had not been long in the house when complaint was made that two bags of tea had been stolen, and Hawkins was charged with the robbery. He steadily denied any knowledge of the affair, but, this not satisfying the villains, they obliged him to pull off his clothes; and, having likewise stripped themselves, they began to whip him with the most unrelenting barbarity. Curtis, one of the gang, said he did know of the robbery, and, if he would not confess, he would whip him till he died, for he had whipped many a rogue and washed his hands in his blood.

These bloodthirsty villains continued whipping the poor wretch till their breath was almost exhausted: while he begged them to spare his life, on account of his wife and child. Hawkins drawing up his legs, to defend himself in some measure from their blows, they kicked him in the groin in a manner too shocking to be described: continually asking him what was become of the tea. At length the unfortunate man mentioned something of his father and brother, on which Mills and Curtis said they would go and fetch them; but Hawkins expired soon after they had left the house.

Rowland, one of the accomplices, now locked the door; and, putting the key in his pocket, he and Thomas Winter (who was afterwards admitted evidence) went out to meet Curtis and Mills, whom they saw riding up a lane leading from an adjacent village, having each a man behind him. Winter desiring to speak with his companions, the other men stood at a distance, while he asked Curtis what he meant to do with them, who replied, to confront them with Hawkins.

Winter now said that Hawkins was dead, and begged that no more mischief might be done; but Curtis replied, 'By God, we will go through it now!' But at length they permitted them to go home, saying that when they were wanted they should be sent for.

The murderers now coming back to the public house, Reynolds said, 'You have ruined me.' But Curtis replied that he would make him amends. Having consulted how they should dispose of the body, it was proposed to throw it into a well in an adjacent park; but, this being objected to, they carried it twelve miles and, having tied stones to it in order to sink it, they threw it into a pond in Parham Park, belonging to Sir Cecil Bishop; and in this place it lay more than two months before it was discovered.

This horrid and unprovoked murder gave rise to a royal proclamation, in which a pardon was offered to any persons, even outlawed smugglers, except those who had been guilty of murder or concerned in breaking open the custom house at Poole, on condition of discovering the persons who had murdered Hawkins, particularly Mills, who was charged with having had a concern in the horrid transaction.

Hereupon William Pring, an outlawed smuggler, who had not had any share in either of the crimes excepted in the proclamation, went to the Secretary of State and informed him that he would find Mills if he could be ascertained of his own pardon, adding that he believed he was either at Bath or Bristol.

Being assured that he need not doubt of his pardon, he set out for Bristol, where he found Mills, and with him Thomas and Lawrence Kemp, brothers, the former of whom had broken out of Newgate, and the other was outlawed by proclamation. Having consulted on their desperate circumstances, Pring offered them a retreat at his house near Beckenham in Kent, whence they might make excursions and commit robberies on the highway.

Pleased with this proposal, they set out with Pring and arrived in safety at his house, where they had not been long before he pretended that, his horse being an indifferent one and theirs remarkably good, he would go and procure another, and then they would proceed on the intended expedition. Thus saying, he set out, and they agreed to wait for his return; but, instead of going to procure a horse, he went to the house of . . . an officer of the excise at Horsham, who, taking with him seven or eight armed men, went to Beckenham at night, where they found Mills and the two brothers Kemp just going to supper on a breast of veal. They immediately secured the brothers by tying their arms; but Mills, making resistance, was cut with a hanger before he would submit.

The offenders, being taken, were conducted to the county gaol for Sussex; and, being secured till the assizes, were removed to East Grinstead, where the brothers Kemp were tried for highway robberies, convicted, sentenced and executed.

Mills, being tried for the murder of Hawkins, was capitally convicted and received sentence of death. . . . The country being at the time filled with smugglers, a rescue was feared, wherefore he was conducted to the place of execution by a guard of soldiers. . . . He was executed on Slindon Common on the 12th of August, 1749, and afterwards hung in chains near the same spot.

Those whom tax phobia inclines to regard smugglers as champions of freedom may care to reflect that only excise duty provided them with a trade. Without it, they would have been as deprived as militant shop stewards in the Russia of their dreams or I.R.A. gunmen in an Ireland without British soldiers. But, since the early middle ages, Ireland has never had any history which was not also British and, as a rule, specifically English history.

To British criminal history Ireland has made a notable contribution. Around the exact middle of the eighteenth century, Irishmen suddenly became prominent as forgers, perhaps a measure of their unusual literacy.

The outbreak was, it is true, initiated by a Londoner and a Welshman, and the first of the Irish was a Protestant operating in Scotland. Of the next three Irish forgers, indeed, only one was with certainty a Roman Catholic, another certainly a Protestant, the third doubtful.

From November 16th, 1747, to March 23rd, 1752, the Calendars record eight forgers hanged. The instruments forged were in several cases the wills of seamen actually at sea, whose tickets had been stolen.

Thereafter, the catalogue shows only twenty forgers in thirty-seven years, with a massive resurgence in the last decade of the century, during which there were to be thirty cases. It is among the twenty that we find the forgers of best social position.

Before we come to the first of these, there is a great deal that seems worth considering. The case of Mary Blandy, to which we turn next, was seven years ago made the subject of a novel. It is surprising that it had to wait so long, since its romantic interest is not small. Everything is provided by the documents, and sixty years ago the best of these were conveniently put together in a Notable British Trials volume.

VI

The Fair Parricide

IN THE *Tour*, Defoe had contrasted the Yorkshire bridges with those in the Thames valley.

> No part can show such noble, large, lofty and long stone bridges as this part of England, nor so many of them; nor do I remember any such thing as a timber bridge in all the northern part of England, no, not from the Trent to the Tweed, whereas in the south parts of England there are an abundance, as particularly over the great river of Thames at Kingston, Chertsey, Staines, Windsor, Maidenhead, Reading, Henley, Marlow and other places.

The order of these is upstream as far as Maidenhead, but then downstream from Reading. There, after collecting the Kennet, the Thames turns left and flows north-east past Sonning and Shiplake to Wargrave, where it again turns left, as though wishing to return to Oxford. This disposition is corrected in part at Henley.

It is supposed that Defoe took part in the Monmouth rebellion. By his own account, he was in Henley three years later, when the Prince of Orange entered it in pursuit of James II and his big-mouthed Irish rabble. Thirty-six years after that, he would pair Henley with Maidenhead as two towns which had little or nothing remarkable in them but that they had great business by the trade for malt and meal and timber, which they loaded on their great barges for London. At Henley, they also loaded glass.

Near the wooden bridge, on the London road, stood the White Hart inn. In the old-fashioned house which faced it lived Francis Blandy, attorney-at-law, town clerk and steward to most of the gentry in that most southerly part of Oxfordshire, himself a gentleman of old family and solid means, though not quite so much so as he gave out. Married to a woman also of good legal family, he had an only child, a daughter, Mary after her mother (but known at home as Molly), born in 1720 and baptised on July 15th of that year.

At twenty-six, she was unmarried, despite (but also because of) a settlement of £10,000 which was supposed to go with her to the most suitable bidder. An ambitious apothecary, a worthier Mr H. and a Mr T. had in turn been dismissed by her father with more or less civility. In person, she appears to have been sufficiently pleasing, perhaps a little angular but with splendid dark hair, only very little pockmarked, proper in her behaviour but animated, well read and witty.

In the spring of 1746, a Captain D. walked delightfully with Miss Blandy in the meadows about Henley, but then went with his regiment abroad, there to await the peace of Aix-la-Chapelle. In August, the Blandys were invited to dine with the bachelor General Lord Mark Kerr at Paradise, a house which the attorney had obtained for him. Miss Blandy was placed beside a nephew of Lord Mark's and younger brother of Lord Cranstoun, the Honourable William Henry Cranstoun, a lieutenant in Sir Andrew Agnew's regiment of marines, stationed at Southampton.

In appearance, Lieut. the Hon. W. H. Cranstoun, known as Captain Cranstoun, was unimpressive. His stature was low, his face both freckled and badly pockmarked, his eyes small and weak, his eyebrows sandy and his legs clumsy. With these, he nevertheless took his turn in the already less verdant meadows, a proceeding Lord Mark viewed with disfavour for reasons unguessed by the young lady or her parents. On leave in England, Captain D. failed to renew his advances. The following summer, Captain C. was again at Henley-on-Thames. He did not fail.

His connections appealed to Mr Blandy. He flattered Mrs Blandy, and she was besotted with him. We must, I think, do Mary Blandy the credit of supposing that she fell quite simply in love with him. Whatever tender feelings he may on occasion have experienced, there seems no doubt that he was in the first place a fortune-hunter. Lord Mark's sister had borne the late Lord Cranstoun twelve children, and the provision for them was not large. Captain Cranstoun believed in the £10,000 and meant to have it. He had debts and a mistress in London.

He also had a wife and a daughter in Scotland. Lord Mark Kerr told Blandy this. Cranstoun denied it. There was, he said, a woman in Scotland, a Miss Murray, who claimed to be his wife, but a process was pending whereby this claim would soon be disproved. When he proposed to Mary, Cranstoun had told her that such a difficulty existed. And so she believed him, and so did her mother. Her father believed him at first. Cranstoun stayed six months with the Blandys.

In March 1748, his marriage was upheld by the Scottish courts. He again stayed six months with the Blandys. The marines were disbanded, and he was on half-pay. In September 1749, Mrs Blandy died. Not for two years more did Blandy decisively forbid Cranstoun the house.

On a penultimate visit, he had, with Mary's approval, put into her father's tea what he said was a love philtre, designed to sweeten tempers. This cannot have been poisonous, for its immediate sequel had been that for the moment tempers were sweetened. It may be argued from this that to the very end Mary Blandy contrived to believe that the powder Cranstoun sent her from Scotland after his final departure from Henley could not be fatal poison. The Calendar account, which is identical in Knapp & Baldwin and Jackson allows her the benefit of this doubt.

The powder was sent marked 'powders to clean the Scotch pebbles'. Scotch pebbles also were sent. Scotch pebbles were, it appears, agates and other semi-precious stones. They cannot have been highly polished, or they would not have needed a powder to clean them. I have never seen any, but they were fashionable at the time as 'ornaments' (presumably rather of furniture and ledges than of the person). Mr Blandy was first taken ill after drinking tea in June 1751. A letter from Cranstoun suggested gruel. In August, Mr Blandy was twice taken ill after eating gruel. A servant, for whom it was warmed up, almost died. Fully informed, after forgiving his daughter, Francis Blandy, a man in his early sixties, died on the 14th. On the 15th, Mary, aged thirty-one, ran from the house half-dressed and crossed the wooden bridge. Beset by a mob, she was saved by the landlady not of the White Hart but of the Angel on the Berkshire side. She ordered a pint of wine and a toast.

Very early on Saturday morning, the 17th, she was taken to Oxford Castle. For the first two months unfettered, she was allowed her maid, free access to the keeper's garden and frequent visitors, from one of whom she learned that the £10,000 were fewer than half that, from another perhaps that Cranstoun had fled the country. He was in Boulogne, at the house of a Mrs Ross, a kinswoman, whose maiden name of Dunbar he adopted. He had been got out to oblige Lords Cranstoun and Home, who failed to reimburse their agent.

Not until Tuesday, March 3rd, 1752, did Mary Blandy, spinster, late of the parish of Henley-upon-Thames, who by then had worn fetters five months, appear at the assizes held in the Divinity school, Oxford, for the county of Oxford, before the Honourable Heneage Legge, Esq., a baron of His Majesty's Court of Exchequer. Counsel for the Crown were the Honourable Mr Bathurst, Mr Serjeant Hayward, the Honourable Mr Barrington and three others. Miss Blandy had three counsel, who of course would not speak unless it were to raise points of procedure.

Instructed by the clerk of arraigns to hold up her hand (which she did), the prisoner was indicted for that she, not having the fear of God before her eyes but being moved and seduced by the instigation of the Devil, contriving and intending Francis Blandy, her late father, in his lifetime to deprive of his life and him feloniously to kill and murder on the 10th day of November in the twenty-third year of the reign of our sovereign lord

George the Second, then King of Great Britain, and on divers days and times between the said 10th day of November and the 5th day of August in the twenty-fifth year of the reign of His said Majesty, did knowingly, wilfully and feloniously and of her malice aforethought mix and mingle certain deadly poison (to wit, white arsenic) in certain tea which had been prepared for the use of the said Francis Blandy to be drank by him, then and there well knowing that the said tea was then and there prepared for the use of the said Francis Blandy, with intent to be then and there administered to him for his drinking the same, and furthermore, that she might more speedily kill and murder the said Francis Blandy, on the said 5th day of August and at divers other days and times between that day and the 14th of August, with force of arms and at the parish of Henley-upon-Thames aforesaid in the county aforesaid, did mix and mingle certain deadly poison (to wit, white arsenic) in water gruel and, in short, that the said Francis Blandy, of the poison aforesaid and by the operation thereof, became sick and greatly distempered in his body and, not to put too fine a point on it, died, whereof it might reasonably be said that she him in manner and form aforesaid did poison, kill and murder against the peace of our said lord the King, his crown and dignity. To the reading of this formal piece of literature, which the clerk of the arraigns had suitably adapted to the occasion, Mary Blandy formally pleaded not guilty and, asked how she would be tried, said by God and her country, whereupon twelve good and lawful men were sworn as a jury, which country to be.

Mr Bathurst then first proceeded to create original literature, with the assistance of the clerk of the arraigns, and literature went on being created, some of it by unlettered persons (but always with the assistance of the clerk), for thirteen hours. Without retiring, the jury found the prisoner guilty, and Mr Baron Legge pronounced the sentence of the law upon her, which was that she be carried to the place of execution and there hanged by the neck until she was dead.

The prisoner then said:

'My lord, as your lordship has been so good as to show so

much candour and impartiality in the course of my trial, have one more favour to beg, which is that your lordship would please to allow me a little time till I can settle my affairs and make my peace with God.'

Mr Baron Legge replied:

'To be sure, you shall have a proper time allowed you.'

On leaving the hall to be taken back to prison, Mary Blandy stepped into the coach with as little concern as if she had been going to a ball. At the castle, the verdict being already known to them, she found the keeper's family in some disorder, the children all in tears.

'Don't mind it,' she said. 'What does it signify? I am very hungry. Pray let me have something for supper as speedily as possible.'

She sat down to mutton chops and an apple pie.

Five weeks were allowed her. During that time, partly in her own hand and partly by dictation to the castle ordinary, the Rev. J. Swinton, the indomitable spinster herself added to the literature upon which she had already made a beginning with a spirited and pathetic defence. Her principal work was to be *Miss Mary Blandy's Own Account of the Affair between Her and Mr Cranstoun*. This is described by Bleackley and in his turn Roughead as 'the most famous apologia in criminal literature'. No doubt they meant English criminal literature, for I suppose that Lacenaire's is more famous. The *Own Account* is indeed rather splendid. I don't think it quotes well, but, if this were a much longer book, I would print it in full.

There was also her correspondence. In one letter, she begs her godmother, Mrs Mounteney, to use influence (for a reprieve) with the bishop of Winchester, on the ground that she, Mary, had once had the honour of dancing with the late Prince of Wales, 'Fred, who was alive and is dead.' She asked to have the letter back, for she meant to print it.

In the public mind and in that of some of her betters, her case was linked with the one which immediately precedes it in

Jackson (occurring some thirty pages later in Knapp & Baldwin). This was the case of Elizabeth Jeffries, tried at Chelmsford, the week after her own trial at Oxford, for abetting her lover, John Swan, in the violent murder of her uncle, a murder committed six weeks before her own. An exchange of letters between the two murderesses was clearly an idea which might suggest itself to the mind of a publisher, and the *Genuine Letters between Miss Blandy and Miss Jeffries* cannot now be authenticated. It is certain, however, that Mary Blandy took an interest in the other's case.

'It was barbarous,' she said of the murder, 'but I am sorry for her and hope she will have a good divine to attend her in her last moments, if possible a second Swinton, for, poor unhappy girl, I pity her.'

A visitor having reproved these excessively Christian sentiments and withdrawn, she added:

'I can't bear with these over-virtuous women. I believe, if ever the Devil picks a bone, it is one of theirs.'

There is a possibility that the two exchanged letters. Together, they occasioned literature in others.

On Monday, March 23rd, Horace Walpole wrote to Horace Mann, his old friend in Venice:

> There are two wretched women that just now are . . . much talked of, a Miss Jeffries and a Miss Blandy, the one condemned for murdering her uncle, the other her father. Both their stories have horrid circumstances, the first having been debauched by her uncle; the other had so tender a parent that his whole concern, while he was expiring and knew her for his murderess, was to save her life. It is shocking to think what shambles this country is grown! Seventeen were executed this morning, after having murdered the turnkey on Friday night and almost forced open Newgate. One is forced to travel, even at noon, as if one was going to battle.

Of that morning's seventeen, the Calendars name only three. These were Samuel Hill, who had been one of the Kentish smugglers but who was hanged for strangling his landlady after he had gone straight; John Andrews, for forgery, who, having been to sea himself, had done a brisk trade in seamen's tickets thereafter and in whose lodgings, when they were searched after his arrest, sixty-four forged wills and powers of attorney were found; and Anthony De Rosa, of Portuguese extraction, who also had been to sea and forged seamen's wills and powers, but who was hanged for a murder in Hoxton. There is no mention of the turnkey's murder.

To finish and strip seventeen in a morning is not light work even for a young hangman, and two days later John Thrift further had to see to the complicated business of launching a pirate into eternity at Execution Dock, where he would get his feet wet. During the course of the month, he also had a defrauder to whip publicly six times in different streets of Westminster, an exertion which doubtless hastened his end. For after eighteen years' service, Thrift had only five more weeks to live.

Elizabeth Jeffries and John Swan had only three more days. They were hanged, apparently not between trees, in Epping Forest, near the six-mile stone, on Saturday, March 28th, her body being delivered to friends for interment, his wrapped in tarred canvas and iron bands and suspended again from the gibbet, which had meanwhile been moved.

The following Saturday, Mary Blandy signed her *Own Account* in the Castle at Oxford, 'in presence of two clergymen, members of the University of Oxford'. Her execution had been appointed for that day. It was the University authorities who argued that this would not be proper, as it was still Holy Week. On Sunday, therefore, she was able to look out of an upper window of the Castle and see, on the Green, the pole laid across the arms of two trees. She said it was set very high.

At nine o'clock on Monday morning, the Rev. Mr Swinton led her out. She was dressed in black bombasine, her arms and hands tied with black ribbons, which did not prevent her holding and glancing at a book of devotions. She walked to the foot of the ladder with the utmost solemnity of deportment and, when there, acknowledged her fault in administering the powders to her father, but insisted that she had had no idea of doing injury, nor any suspicion that the powders were of a poisonous nature.

Having ascended some steps of the ladder, she said:

'Gentlemen, don't hang me high, for the sake of decency.'

Being desired to go something higher, she turned about and expressed her apprehension that she should fall. The rope being put about her neck, she pulled her handkerchief over her face and was turned off on holding out the book of devotions, the agreed signal. When she had hung the usual time, she was cut down and, the body being put into a hearse, conveyed to Henley, where she was interred with her parents at one o'clock the following morning, Tuesday.

On Wednesday, the principal magistrate for Westminster and Middlesex, Henry Fielding, author of *Jonathan Wild*, *Joseph Andrews*, *Tom Jones*, *Amelia* and numerous works for the stage, completed his notes on her case and that of Elizabeth Jeffries and, having added these to what would otherwise be a mere reprint of the work of a merchant of Exeter in the previous century, sent off to the printer a pamphlet entitled *Examples of the Interposition of Providence in the Detection and Punishment of Murder*. On Saturday, April 18th, the revised version of Mary Blandy's *Own Account* appeared.

To Horace Mann, on May 13th, Horace Walpole wrote:

> Miss Blandy died with a coolness of courage that is astonishing and denying the fact, which has made a kind of party in her favour. As if a woman who would not stick at parricide would scruple a lie! We have made a law for immediate execution on conviction for murder: it will appear extraordinary to me if it has any effect, for I can't help feeling that the terrible part of death must be the preparation for it.

By the law in question, 25 Geo. II, it was enacted that executions of murderers should take place on the second day after conviction, unless this were a Sunday. A backlog having been cleared, the first execution under the new dispensation took place on Wednesday, July 1st. It was carried out by Thomas Turlis, who would find the general pattern of his work different from that of his predecessors in London, a morning's labours generally less arduous but the trips to Tyburn more frequent. It was hard on the sexton at St Sepulchre's.

From accounts of the unspeakable Cranstoun which were published the following year, it appears that Scottish officers in the French service, related to his wife, discovered his whereabouts and that, after a fortnight in Paris in August, he took refuge at Furnes in Flanders, again with the Rosses, though another version is that the Rosses themselves, by reason of a financial awkwardness, absconded from France and sought the jurisdiction of, as it happened, the Queen of Hungary. He seems to have died a suitably unpleasant death, his body so swollen that it was expected to burst, but with the consolations of the Romish faith, and that, in view of this conversion, he was given a pompous funeral. His papers were sent to Scotland, to his brother, Lord Cranstoun, and a collection of his fancy waistcoats was sold for the discharge of his debts. His wife continued to draw the interest on his patrimony, which saved her from acute distress.

The date of Cranstoun's death is variously given as November 30th and December 2nd, 1752. The day on which he died was therefore either a Thursday or a Saturday, as it would have been in any other year. In England or Scotland, however, though not in Flanders, its date would have been the 19th or 21st of November had eleven days not been removed from the calendar in September.

VII

A House in Bow Street

MOST STUDENTS of English literature may be expected to know that the author of *Joseph Andrews* and *Tom Jones* was also a magistrate, and that he had something to do with the Bow Street runners. I suspect that, with a fine disregard for mere chronology, some may even have assumed that *The History of the Life of the Late Mr Jonathan Wild the Great* reflected his experience on the bench, though in fact this remarkable one-man Mafia was disbanded while the future novelist was in his last year at Eton.

There followed a year or two of idleness, including a dangerous attempt at the abduction of an heiress, and about the same of studies at Leyden University. Like so many others, the life of Henry Fielding thereafter may be said to have fallen into three parts. There was first the theatrical part, which was not unsuccessful. By 1736, a man not yet thirty, recently married, an original comic dramatist and translator of Molière, he was also manager of the Haymarket theatre. A year later, the Licensing Act severely curtailed the number of theatres in London, and Fielding's first career came to an end. We may think this a pity, but otherwise might never have had the novels.

With the exception of *Amelia*, these, together with a great deal of journalism, belong to the period of a second career as barrister. Called to the bar in June 1740, he joined the Western circuit. With what regularity we do not know, this took him, perhaps as often as three times a year into territory familiar to him from childhood and clearly not unloved. Diligent research in town and county archives may yet turn up a list of cases with which Fielding as a barrister was concerned. For the moment, all we can learn from one or another Newgate Calendar are some particulars of two murder cases that were heard at assizes on the Western circuit during the first of the eight years he travelled it, together with an absurdity at Taunton quarter sessions later.

We may further care to fancy that he would hear of Elizabeth and Mary Branch, mother and daughter, who, for beating an orphanage girl to death at Norton St Philip, north of his birthplace, had been hanged at Ilchester, south of it, the month before he was called. Eleven months later, in Dorchester, Henry Smythee, Esq., suffered for the murder of a girl pregnant by him and, in Bristol, Captain Samuel Goodere, with two Irishmen, Mahony and White, for that of Sir John Goodere. The outcome of this feud between brothers remains something of a *cause célèbre*, having found its way not only into the Calendars and Howell's *State Trials* but into a pamphlet by their kinsman, Samuel Foote, the topical playwright and mimic, and a hundred and fifty years later, into one of H. B. Irving's best essays on an English case. The absurdity at Taunton in 1746 involved a Mary Hamilton who had succeeded in going through a form of marriage, according to the rites of the established Church, with no fewer than fourteen other women, for which he or she, whichever he or she might be, was sentenced to be imprisoned six months and, during that time, to be whipped in the towns of Taunton, Glastonbury, Wells and Shepton Mallet.

Tom Jones appeared in 1748. By then, Henry Fielding, already troubled with gout, had buried his wife and married her maid. He became a principal justice of the peace for Middlesex and Westminster at the end of the year and, the following May, was further appointed chairman of Westminster quarter sessions. This gave him the house in Bow Street, Covent Garden, at which he was to administer justice for some five years, being at first assisted and eventually succeeded in these appointments by his blind half-brother, John.

It is sometimes said that Henry Fielding was our first stipendiary magistrate. This does not appear to have been the case. In the last year of his life, he would describe the original proceeds of his office of profit as five hundred pounds a year of the dirtiest money upon earth, but he seems to have done without many of the perquisites and even paid a clerk out of his legitimate court charges. Before him, the London magistracy had been extortionate if not corrupt. In his time, it ceased to be either, though he remained, in his official capacity, one of the 'trading justices'. The Bow Street runners were his creation. If Fielding had never written an unofficial word, he would have enjoyed, in not the least important domain of history, a position of which he himself seems hardly to have been aware.

As a magistrate, he published a number of short works, listed in our bibliography, of which only two will much concern us. These are *A True State of the Case of Bosavern Penlez*, 1749, and *A Clear State of the Case of Elizabeth Canning*, 1753. To the mere criminal historian, the *Clear State* is of more interest than the *True State*. The case of Elizabeth Canning is one of those unsolved mysteries about which every amateur criminologist knows something and which has produced a literature of its own, even in our own time. We must nevertheless also look at the *True State*.

On a Sunday evening, July 2nd, 1749, three normally respectable lads were picked up for being concerned in a riot at the Star tavern near Temple Bar. The place had been half wrecked the previous evening by sailors, three of whom complained of having been robbed either there or at another house of ill fame in the Strand. The names of the three youths were John Wilson, Benjamin Launder and Bosavern Penlez. Born and brought up in Devonshire, this last was the son of a parson, a Jerseyman, to whom no doubt he owed his unusul name and who died while his unfortunate son was still a boy, thereafter apprenticed to a barber and peruke-maker in Exeter and in due course proceeding to London.

The three were brought to trial at the next sessions at the Old Bailey. I quote the Calendars, here perfectly uniform.

> Several persons of reputation appeared to the character of the prisoners; but the positive evidence against them induced the jury to convict Penlez and Wilson; but Launder was acquitted. The inhabitants of the parish of St Clement Danes, and many individuals, made great interest to save these unfortunate youths, in consequence of which Wilson was reprieved, but Penlez was ordered for execution.
>
> It is said that the king was disposed to have pardoned them both; but that Lord Chief Justice Willes, before whom they were tried, declared in council that no regard would be paid to the laws except one of them was made an example of. Our account informs us that the king still inclined to pardon them both, and that the chief justice was three times sent for and consulted on this occasion; but that he still persisted in his former opinion.
>
> After conviction Penlez behaved in such a manner as evidently testified the goodness of his disposition. . . . It is not in language to describe how much he was pitied by the public. . . . When the day of execution arrived he prepared to meet his fate with the . . . courage of a Christian. . . . Sir Stephen Theodore Janssen . . . was at that time sheriff; and a number of soldiers being placed at Holborn Bars, to conduct Penlez to Tyburn (as a rescue was apprehended), the sheriff politely dismissed them, asserting that the civil power was sufficient to carry the edicts of the law into effectual execution.
>
> This unhappy youth was executed at Tyburn on the 18th of October, 1749. The worthy inhabitants of St Clement Danes . . . did all possible honour to his memory, by burying him in a distinguished manner in a churchyard of their parish, on the evening after his unfortunate exit, which happened in the twenty-third year of his age.

That a gross miscarriage of justice had occurred was clearly the view not only of many in the neighbourhood at the time but of the author of the pamphlet on which the Calendars severally rely. In their account of the trial proceedings, for instance, they quote only the manager of the Star and a Mr John Mixon, the collector of the scavenger's rate, who, to discredit their testimony, 'deposed that he did not think the oath of Mr or Mrs Wood was to be taken and that he would not hang a cat or a dog on their evidence', adding 'that the house they kept was of the most notorious ill fame; . . . and that the neighbours were afraid to appear against them'. The impression we receive is that Penlez had been picked out by the Woods and that theirs was the only evidence against him. This was not so.

Fielding's *True State* begins with a substantial exposition of the Riot Act of George I and its precedents. We live in an age of organised rioting, which we view with what might be thought a strange complacency, extending our permissiveness to the young beyond precocious sex to something like a belief that it will be good for their personal development to indulge in a certain amount of criminal activity, still by tradition tolerated also in a 'working' class no longer poor and oppressed. To date, outside Ireland and Italy, recent rioting in Western Europe and North America has not been accompanied by a great deal of murder, but this always threatens. In those riots in the Strand two and a quarter centuries ago, nobody was killed. There was only destruction of property, theft, arson, intimidation and uproar, but they were bad riots, with a very large number of people involved, and the authorities were understandably frightened. It was a puritanical hatred of brothels which made respectable citizens later appear to condone what at the time had certainly worried them.

Bosavern Penlez was arrested not, as the Calendars imply, on the Star's premises at the instigation of Wood, but in Carey Street, between the Law Courts and Lincoln's Inn, towards Holborn, at one o'clock on the Monday morning, running as fast as he could go from a watchman of St Dunstan's in the West until he was pinned against railings by another of the Liberty of the Rolls. In his possession were ten laced caps, four laced handkerchiefs, three pair of laced ruffles, two laced clouts, five plain handkerchiefs, five plain aprons and one laced apron, the property indeed of Mrs Wood. The depositions of the two watchmen, Samuel Marsh and Edward Fritter, were sworn before H. Fielding, Esq., together with those of a beadle and a constable, Robert Oliver and John Hoare, all four illiterate men who appended their mark. The author of *Joseph Andrews* and *Tom Jones*, not yet of *Amelia*, prints the depositions of these four, as well as those, relative to the rioting but not specifically to Penlez, of Nathanael Munns, beadle, John Carter and James Cecil, constables, and Saunders Welch, gentleman, high constable of Holborn division, this last dealing with Launder, who, it may be remembered, was acquitted at the Old Bailey.

The year was the twenty-third of the reign of George II. The government was Pelham's. In his prefactory remarks to the *True State*, Fielding describes himself as reluctantly called forth to do an act of justice to his king and the administration by disabusing the public, which hath been in the grossest and wickedest manner imposed upon with relation to the case of Bosavern Penlez, executed for the late riot in the Strand. His reluctance, he says, is due in part to the fact that he has already been barbarously aspersed for defending the present government and in part to a character not devoid of the milk of human kindness.

> I was desirous that a man who had suffered the extremity of the law should be permitted to rest quietly in his grave. I was willing that his punishment should end there; nay, that he should be generally esteemed the object of compassion. . . . But when this malefactor is made an object of sedition, when he is transformed into a hero, and the most merciful prince who ever sat on any throne is arraigned of blamable severity, if not of downright cruelty, . . . I should then think myself worthy of much censure if, having a full justification in my hands, I permitted it to sleep there. . . .

Follow, first, the potted history of legislation against riots from the time of Richard II to the Riot Act of George I, then the depositions listed above and a series of conclusions about the rioters, notably that 'the clamour against bawdy-houses was in them a bare pretence only'. As to the sufferer:

> Whatever was the man's guilt, he hath made all the atonement which the law requires, or could be exacted of him. . . . If . . . there should remain any private compassion in the breast of the reader, far be it from me to endeavour to remove it. I hope I have said enough to prove that this was such a riot as called for

> some example and that the man who was made that example deserved his fate. . . . I doubt very much whether even he would have suffered had it not appeared that a capital indictment for burglary was likewise found by the grand jury against him. . . .

And to this is appended a note which, to a later understanding of what constitutes good law, may seem to contain the whole gist of the matter.

> Upon this indictment he was arraigned, but the judge said, as he was already capitally convicted for the same fact, though of a different offence, there was no occasion of trying him again: by which means the evidence which I have above produced, and which the prosecutor reserved to give on this indictment, was never heard at the Old Bailey, nor in the least known to the public.

It is difficult, as we are constantly reminded, for courts of law to deal with the mob. Doctrines of collective responsibility are constantly proclaimed and as quickly abandoned, a matter recently more agitated in France than in the English-speaking world. It is an unsound idea. However many people act together to commit a crime, each bears his own particular guilt, which may vary from person to person even within a close conspiracy. To apportion guilt among the members of a mob (the 1749 rioters in the Strand were estimated at seven hundred, with four thousand more sailors preparing to march from Tower Hill) is practically impossible. Yet most of us are, I fancy, repelled by the putting to death of anyone 'as an example'. It reminds us too much of the shooting of hostages in war-time. It reminds me of the hanging of Bentley in 1953 *because* the man with the gun was too young to be hanged, whereas, years before, Smith had been reprieved because Ley had to be, because he was mad.) In the case two hundred years before, we know too little about the related culpability of Launder and Wilson. If Penlez was to be hanged, it should have been purely for theft. It was not claimed that he instigated or caused the riots. As far as he was concerned, they merely provided circumstances of which he took advantage to commit a felony punishable at that time by death, as were already more than a hundred others.

. . .

There are cases during the next three years of which we may assume that Fielding took official cognisance, since the arrests were made in Westminster or Middlesex. In 1750, among those hanged in consequence at Tyburn were a highwayman, James Maclaine, son of a dissenting minister in Ulster, picked up at his lodgings in Pall Mall, and a thief, John Everett, caught between Kentish Town and Hampstead. The following year, William Parsons, Esq., arrested in Hounslow, was hanged for returning from transportation (he had been transported for non-capital forgery) and three men, of whom two were Irish, for street robbery in Long Acre. For murder, there were Hill and De Rosa, for fraud Stroud.

Two *causes célèbres* of which the novelist took unofficial cognisance that spring were, as we have noted, those of Mary Blandy and Elizabeth Jeffries. (It is difficult to see how in either was exemplified the interposition of Providence in the detection and punishment of murder.) One would have liked to read him on the pathetic case of Thomas Wilford, whose appearance before Justice Fielding is the only one specified in the Calendars to that time. As the case also has some juridical importance. I quote the account as it occurs in Jackson, including a footnote and the concluding reflections. Basically, Jackson's does not diverge from the version retained by Knapp & Baldwin, but he omits a peculiarly unfortunate first paragraph on Wilford's antecedents and the evils of jealousy and concludes in a vein less alien to our taste now (and we may think Fielding's) than are some of his reflections elsewhere.

> Thomas Wilford was the son of a poor man, who belonged to the parish of Fulham, and the boy, being born with one arm, was placed in the workhouse, where he was employed in going on errands for the paupers, and occasionally for the inhabitants of the town; and he was distinguished by his inoffensive behaviour.
>
> A girl of ill-fame, named Sarah Williams, being passed from the parish of St Giles in the Fields to the same workhouse, had art enough to persuade Wilford to marry her, though he was then only seventeen years of age; and, their inclinations being made known to the churchwardens, they gave the intended bride forty shillings, to enable her to begin the world.

The young couple now went to the Fleet and were married, after which they took lodgings in St Giles's; and it was only on the Sunday succeeding the marriage that the murder was perpetrated. On that day, the wife, having been out with an old acquaintance, stayed till midnight; and on her return Wilford, who was jealous of her conduct, asked her where she had been. She said to the Park, and would give him no other answer: a circumstance that enflamed him to such a degree that a violent quarrel ensued, the consequence of which was fatal to the wife, for Wilford's passions were so irritated that he seized a knife, and, she advancing towards him, he threw her down and, kneeling on her, cut her throat, so that her head was almost severed from her body.

He had no sooner committed the horrid deed than he threw down the knife, opened the chamber door and was going downstairs when a woman who lodged in an adjacent room asked who was there. To which Wilford replied, 'It is me, I have murdered my poor wife, whom I loved as dearly as my own life.'

On this, the woman went down to the landlord of the house and was immediately followed by Wilford, who said he had killed the woman that he loved beyond all the world and was willing to die for the crime he had committed; and he did not make the slightest effort to escape.

On this, the landlord called the watch, who, taking Wilford into custody, confined him for that night, and on the following day he was committed to Newgate by Justice Fielding.

Being arraigned on the first day of the following sessions at the Old Bailey, he pleaded guilty; but, the court refusing to record his plea, he was put by till the last day, when he again pleaded guilty, but was prevailed on to put himself on his trial.*

Accordingly, the trial came on, during which the prisoner did not seek to extenuate the crime of which he had been guilty: on the contrary, his penitent behaviour and flowing tears seemed to testify the sense he entertained of his offence. Every person present seemed penetrated with grief for his misfortunes.

The case of this malefactor has been the rather inserted because he was the first that suffered in consequence of an act that passed in the year 1751, for the more effectual prevention of murder, which decrees that the convict shall be executed on the second day after conviction: for which reason it has been customary to

* Much praise is due to the humanity of the judges, who frequently prevail on a prisoner to retract his first plea of guilty: which very prisoner has been acquitted on his second arraignment.

try persons charged with murder on a Friday, by which indulgence, in case of conviction, the execution of the sentence is necessarily postponed till Monday. And by the same act it is ordained that the convicted murderer shall be either hung in chains or anatomised.

The jury having found Wilford guilty, sentence against him was pronounced in the following terms: 'Thomas Wilford, you stand convicted of the horrid and unnatural crime of murdering Sarah your wife. This court doth adjudge that you be taken back to the place from whence you came, and there to be fed on bread and water till Wednesday next, when you are to be taken to the common place of execution and there hanged by the neck until you are dead; after which your body is to be publicly dissected and anatomised, agreeable to an act of parliament in that case made and provided. And may God Almighty have mercy on your soul!'

Both before and after conviction, Wilford behaved as a real penitent, and at the place of execution he exhibited the most genuine signs of contrition for the crime of which he had been guilty.

He was executed at Tyburn on the 23rd of June, 1752, and died more lamented than almost any murderer has ever done at the fatal tree.

REFLECTIONS

It is almost impossible to dismiss this article without remarking on that narrowness of conduct in parish officers which tempts them to get rid of the poor on any terms which they deem least burdensome to the parish.

If the officers of Fulham had not been so ready to give the paltry gratification as a marriage portion, it is probable that murder would never have happened. The richer people in a parish should consider themselves as guardians of the poor, whom it is their duty to protect, if it were only for their own sake: for 'he that giveth to the poor lendeth to the Lord.'

We are to suppose, I fancy, that Mrs Wilford had been in the Park raising money by the means to which she was accustomed.

What is not stated in the account here of 25 Geo. II, c. 37, is that, by a later resolution of the judges, it had been agreed that only dissecting and anatomising should be part of the sentence passed, but that, if it were thought advisable, the judge might afterwards, by special order to the sheriff, direct hanging 'in chains' (*i.e.*, in a suit of metal strips over tarred calico). It seems unlikely that Wilford would be so gibbeted at Fulham, and whether his one-armed body went to Surgeons' Hall we do not know.

By an act passed two years previously, that year was, as we have seen, shortened by eleven days. This was done by removing the dates September 3rd to 13th inclusive from the calendar. Eleven is, as it happens, the number of days by which the lunar is shorter than the solar year, but in that respect no more than a momentary coincidence was obtained. The date in Great Britain and its colonies would, however, thenceforward be the same as it was elsewhere in Europe. It would, of course, have been more convenient if other countries had adopted our calendar, the Julian for their own Gregorian. That the concession was ours could be seen as a triumph for Roman Catholicism. That we made it shows that the Jacobite threat was felt to be done with.

Those whose birthdays fell on the dates removed may have wondered whether they were a year older or not. For most people, the awkwardness would not be felt until Christmas. This, which should that year have fallen on a Friday, fell instead on a Monday, eleven days earlier, very shortly after the true or astronomical winter solstice. New Year's Day in 1753 would also fall on a Monday, eleven days early. The weather there should have been on Christmas Day would not occur until January 5th. Thenceforward, it would be as regularly true as it had always been that, as daylight lengthened, cold strengthened, but January would be a colder month than December. There would be fewer white Christmases than white second weeks in January. Meanwhile, the harvest was late.

We know to what unease summer time, double summer time, summer time in winter and decimal coinage have given rise within living memory. If there are newspapers, those who expect to be alive then may count on seeing, in twenty-five years' time, the correspondence columns dotted with letters debating whether a new century has begun or will not begin for another year, while even as little as five years from now someone will be insisting that we must wait a year more for a new decade, the 'eighties, to begin, 1980 being properly a 'seventy. We ought not, therefore, to be surprised that, in late 1752, both nature and religion seemed to many to have suffered an outrage, that people worried about the proper moment at which to celebrate Christ's nativity and doubted for the best part of a fortnight what year they were in.

Certainly, the Glastonbury thorn, *Crataegus oxyacantha praecox*, did not recognise the new dispensation. The original tree, called into miraculous existence sixteen hundred and ninety years previously on behalf of the widely travelled St Joseph of Arimathea, had, it was true, been felled by a zealous soldier in Cromwell's time (the axe glancing off to slice his leg and a stray thorn flying to blind him in one eye), but shoots had been acclimatised both at Glastonbury itself (in St John's churchyard) and elsewhere, for instance at Quainton near Aylesbury. Neither of these trees budded on Christmas Eve, new style, to the great mortification of families in Glastonbury who had tapped their ale eleven days too soon, while at Quainton upwards of two thousand people, who had gathered to watch the offshoot there, refused, in spite of the vicar's sound cursing, to go to church. In villages elsewhere, on the other hand, advantages were discovered in the Popish plot. In the less refined parts of Oxfordshire, for instance, the clergy keeping New Christmas and the villagers Old, they rang the bells and got drunk every night for three weeks.

Henry Fielding was born near Glastonbury, in a house once occupied by the last abbots. In later life, he had found its peaty water beneficial both to his gout and pocket, since it was marketed in London by the Universal Registry, in which he had an interest and whose business was conducted by John Fielding. As the spring from which it flowed had a legendary connection with Joseph of Arimathea, no doubt he would have preferred the holy thorn to bud earlier that year. It also happened that, on returning to Bow Street from a farm he had taken at Ealing, he found himself, in early February, reluctantly involved with the case of Elizabeth Canning, in which it was to be material whether Mary

Squires, an old gipsy, had been seen in Dorset at Old or New Christmas.

On Thursday, January 4th, new style (it was Christmas Eve, old style), the *Daily Advertiser* carried the following announcement:

> Lost, a girl about eighteen years of age dressed in a purple masquerade stuff gown, a white handkerchief and apron, a black quilted petticoat, a green undercoat, black shoes, blue stockings, a white shaving hat with green ribbons, and had a very fresh colour. She was left on Monday last near Houndsditch and has not been heard of since. Whoever informs Mrs Canning, a sawyer at Aldermanbury Postern, concerning her shall be handsomely rewarded for their trouble.

On Saturday, the advertisement was repeated with some variation.

> Elizabeth Canning went from her friends between nine and ten on Monday night, between Houndsditch and Bishopsgate, fresh-coloured, pitted with the small pox, high forehead, light eyebrows, about five feet high, well-set, had on a purple masquerade stuff gown, black stuff petticoat, a white chip hat bound round with green, white apron and handkerchief, blue stockings and leather shoes. Note, it is supposed she was forcibly taken away by some evil-disposed person, as she was heard to screek out in a hackney coach in Bishopsgate Street. If the coachman remembers anything of the affair, he shall have two guineas reward, to be paid by Mrs Canning, in Aldermanbury Postern, sawyer.

The girl was away for four weeks. On Monday evening, January 29th, she arrived home in a pitiable state, black and blue, wearing only her shift and an old bedgown, one ear bloody from an unwashed cut.

The story she told was that, on the way home from a visit to an uncle and aunt on New Year's Day, she had been abducted by two men and taken to a brothel on the Hertford road at Enfield Wash, where, preserving her virtue, she had been locked up and starved, finally making her escape with great difficulty and some danger. A week before Fielding was apprised of the affair, she had gone before the sitting alderman, Thomas Chitty, at the Guildhall, in consequence of which the house had been visited and, with warrants issued by a local justice, the proprietress, Mother Wells, and an aged gipsy of remarkable ugliness, Mary Squires, were in custody, respectively at Bridewell and the New prison. The magistrate novelist took a statement from Elizabeth Canning on February 7th and issued further warrants. On the 14th, he examined a young woman called Virtue Hall, from the same establishment, who at first denied but, after six hours' questioning, finally confirmed Elizabeth's story. Later, she was again to deny it.

The legal proceedings in this case dragged on for over a year. At a first trial on March 21st, Mary Squires was sentenced to death. That April, she was first respited and then pardoned. In late April of the following year, Elizabeth Canning was brought to trial for perjury and in early May sentenced to seven years' transportation. She was to marry and die in Connecticut, where her descendants would be found prospering in the present century.

Before she sailed, Henry Fielding, a very sick man, had set off for Lisbon. What he there died believing, we do not know. While the original case against Squires and Wells was still *sub judice*, he, a senior magistrate, had committed what we should regard as the grossest contempt of court by publishing a pamphlet affirming his belief in Canning's truthfulness and Squires's guilt. He had been prepared to see the girl swear the gipsy's life away.

The case against Elizabeth Canning rests on the inaccuracies in her story and on the strength of the gipsy's alibi, many witnesses being found to swear that Mary Squires was up and down the country west of London at the time when Elizabeth said she had been at Enfield. There is no doubt at all that the old gipsy was in Enfield and at Mother Wells's house, but the question is when. It may also be doubted whether Elizabeth was ever at Enfield before the official visit as a consequence of which arrests were first made. And all this was at a time when town and country, the literate and the illiterate, held opposed views on how the days should be dated.

Such a case, we may feel, had to arise at that time. We might even believe in a conspiracy to ensure that such a case did arise at that time. It would not tell us what had really happened to Elizabeth Canning during the month she was away from home or whether Mary Squires was in any way to blame for the condition in which she returned. A pamphlet by Alan Ramsay persuaded Voltaire, who was in London at the time, that the girl had been away to have a baby. There is no evidence to support this view, and she bore a good character locally.

She may have been abducted and illegally restrained, but not where or how she said. It may have been at a brothel, but not that one. This is the territory within which the more recent speculators have elaborated their thoughts. The villains for Arthur Machen and Lillian de la Torre were well-to-do neighbours who both appeared in evidence, the one a publican for whom Elizabeth had worked.

The gifted woman writer whom we knew as 'Josephine Tey' and 'Gordon Daviot' (under the latter name as a playwright, author of *Richard of Bordeaux*) is no longer here to be asked, but I hazard the guess that, in her most successful novel, *The Franchise Affair*, she was consciously inspired by the case of Elizabeth Canning. I think that her purpose was to put that story into a modern setting. *The Franchise Affair* is an excellent novel. Its weakness, to my mind, is that the two women suspected of abduction and illegal restraint could never, in modern England, have been so easily suspected even by the most idiotic and class-conscious rural populace. That the girl who vanished is, in this novel, so very unpleasant suggests to me that Josephine Tey read Arthur Machen (this also was a pseudonym) rather than Lillian de la Torre, for the latter is kinder to Elizabeth and more inclined to morbid psychology, not perhaps without reason. To both of them, Elizabeth was a liar, to the latter unwittingly so, being an acute hysteric under great pressure.

At least before the first trial, Fielding simply believed her. The Newgate Calendars mention his part in the proceedings. Though Jackson doesn't, Knapp & Baldwin quote from *A Clear State of the Case of Elizabeth Canning*. They also quote a pamphlet written from the anti-Canning side. Their own view adds nothing to the common source. It was all enveloped in mystery, they agree, and we must learn to adore the inscrutable decrees of Providence.

VIII

The Wrong Bones

AT A congregation held in the guildhall of King's Lynn, Norfolk, on Tuesday, February 14th, 1758, St Valentine's and a market day, it was resolved that, John Knox, the schoolmaster, having informed the mayor and corporation by letter that he had dismissed John Birkes, his usher, and in his stead, subject to their approbation, engaged Eugenius Aram, they approved the said Eugenius during the pleasure and under the control of Mr Knox, to whom it was ordered that the usher's salary of thirty pounds a year should be paid during their pleasure. Having taken up his duties a fortnight before the Christmas vacation, the new usher was already a familiar figure in the streets of Lynn, a man of fifty-four muffled up in a horseman's great coat and a flapped hat.

The mayor that year was Benjamin Nuthall, and among the aldermen present that day was Sir John Turner, baronet, J.P. and M.P., for the town returned two members to Westminster. The other, briefly seen last year, was a son of the late earl of Orford, a younger brother of the second earl, by name Horatio Walpole, Horace for short.

Also proclaimed that day, the Mart assembly was held that month in the town hall by Mrs Eastland, who kept a young ladies' seminary. Among the youngest of her young ladies might be found the Misses Esther and Susanna Burney (hardly yet, at the age of six, Miss Fanny), daughters of the organist at St Margaret's. Her proudest exhibit was still Dr Lidderdale's daughter. She, already eighteen, was to be instructed out of school hours by Mr Aram, as were the little daughters of Justice Bulwer at Heydon. Among boys at the Free School were Dr Burney's elder son, James, two sons of the Rev. Mr Weatherhead, vicar of Heacham, one or more of Mr Davy, squire of Mileham, and perhaps an older brother of Stephen Allen, the wine-merchant's infant son.

There is no record of the social intercourse between the scholiast and the future historian of music. The schoolroom adjoined the church and had been its charnel chapel. Meeting at their respective entrances, the two men would have found more in common than that the older taught the younger's son Latin. We may certainly imagine Dr Burney at St George's Hall in April for the Latin play, just as we may suppose that in happier circumstances Aram would have attended Burney's subscription concert in August. A new book one might very well lend the other would be the translation of the Swiss poet Salomon Gessner's *Death of Abel*, currently much read, while a local work then current, published by Chace of Norwich, was *A Warning Piece against the Crime of Murder, with an Account of many Extraordinary and Providential Discoveries of Secret Murders*. If the usher did not talk about murder to his pupils, he may well have done so with the father of one of them, who perhaps reported the conversation at home.

The immediate suggestion was strong. The smell of blood must have been strong in the morning. The schoolroom was on a first floor over the town slaughterhouse. It was animal blood, but it must sometimes have been seen on human hands and even faces, certainly clothing.

Livestock were much in evidence. While on a visit to Mr Weatherhead at Heacham, the usher was recognised by a person from Yorkshire with a stallion. The man, Mr Davy would say, knew Aram and spoke to him, but Aram ignored him *in toto*. The man's dignity was offended.

That, we may think, was in late June or in July. At some point thereafter, we assume that, upon news of her father's whereabouts, Sally Aram, his daughter, nine years older than Miss Lidderdale, left Knaresborough and made her way to King's Lynn, where she was accommodated at a baker's and introduced as the usher's niece, since he had never admitted to being married. This journey she may have made at her leisure in July or with some haste in August.

On Tuesday, the first of that month, employed in digging for stone to supply a lime-kiln, a labourer by the name of Thompson, on Thistle Hill to the south of Knaresborough, having at the edge of the cliff dug about half a yard and half a quarter deep, found an arm bone and the small bone of the leg of a human skeleton. In digging forward on Thursday, he discovered all the rest of the bones belonging to the body, which, by the position of it, seemed to have been put in double, as the bones were all entire.

Next day, these bones were examined by two surgeons of the town, William Higgins and Aaron Locock. The suspicion formed and was soon near certainty in Knaresborough that the bones were those of Daniel Clark, who had vanished so unaccountably thirteen years before.

The coroner for the West Riding was John Theakston. He was unavailable before Saturday week, the 12th. On that day, an inquest was held at the house of Henry Mellor, a jury of thirteen having been nominated by John Barker, parish clerk and constable, acting as coroner's officer. Among those volunteering or required to give evidence were John Yeats, Barbara Leatham, Bryan Hardcastle, Stephen Latham and William Tutin. To Polly Powell and others, Mrs Aram had at various times murmured darkly about the murder of Daniel Clark, and it was hoped that at last she might consent to tell all.

She, a soft sort of woman, had been put to a variety of shifts since her husband's departure, but at present sold bread, black puddings and pies at a small shop in the High Street. Two daughters, Betty and Jane, were in service. The elder of two surviving sons, Henry, aged twenty-two, was an idiot and subject to fits, while Michael was studious like his father, but of the Bible and religious pamphlets only.

Thompson, who had found the bones, deposed first concerning his discovery. Yeats stated that, thirteen or fourteen years previously, nigh Candlemas, at the same spot he had observed a place fresh dug up. Mrs Leatham, a widow, passing that spot one morning at about the same time, had seen a place dug up which had not been so dug when she passed late the day before. The earth had been put back in a careless manner. Hardcastle spoke of Clark's horse, left at bait with him. The town's verdict first appeared in the testimony of Stephen Latham. After the report of Clark's departure, this examinant had been appointed by the honour of Knaresborough to serve a process on Eugenius Aram and to arrest him for a debt to his former patron, Mr Norton. Here I take the liberty of putting reported into direct speech.

> LATHAM: He, the said Eugenius, asked what the debt and charges were, and he would pay them. He drew out of his breeches' pocket a large quantity of gold in guineas and other large coin. I thought it amounted to above one hundred pounds. I knew Aram at the time to be very poor. That was his general character. He had great quantities of goods of different sorts of Clark's in his custody. So had Richard Houseman, of many different sorts, which were appraised to forty-five pounds. He pretended he had received them for a debt due to him from Clark.

Tutin told his story of being roused by Clark at three o'clock in the morning, of the two men he had seen with Clark, who were, he said, Houseman and the schoolmaster, and of finding a hammer he had missed at Houseman's.

> MRS ARAM, *much prompted:* Daniel Clark was an intimate acquaintance of my husband's. They had frequent transactions together, and Richard Houseman was often with them. On the 7th of February, in 1745 or the previous year, about six o'clock in the evening, my husband came home when I was washing in the kitchen. He directed me to put out the fire and make one above stairs. This I did.

My husband then went out. He returned at about two o'clock in the morning, with Clark and Houseman. They went upstairs to the room where I was. There they stayed about an hour. My husband asked me for a handkerchief, for Dicky (I mean Richard Houseman) to tie about his head. I accordingly lent him one. Then Clark said, 'It will soon be morning. We must get off.' Thereupon, Houseman, Clark and my husband all went out together.

Upon Clark's going out, I observed him take a sack or wallet upon his back, which he carried along with him. Whither they went I could not tell.

About five o'clock the same morning, my husband and Houseman returned. Clark did not come with them. My husband came upstairs and desired to have a candle, that he might make a fire below. To which I objected, and said there was no occasion for two fires, as there was a good one in the room above, where I then was. My husband answered, 'Dicky is below and does not choose to come upstairs.' Upon which I asked, Clark not returning with them, what they had done with Daniel. To this my husband gave no answer, but desired me to go to bed, which I refused. I told him they had been doing something bad.

Then my husband went down with the candle. Being desirous to know what he and Houseman were doing and being about to go downstairs, I heard Houseman say to my husband, 'She is coming.' My husband replied, 'We'll not let her.' Houseman then said, 'If she does, she'll tell.' 'What can she tell?' replied my husband. 'Poor, simple thing, she knows nothing.' To which Houseman said, 'If she tells that I am here, 'twill be enough.' My husband then said, 'I will hold the door, to prevent her coming.' Whereupon Houseman said something must be done to prevent me telling and pressed my husband to it very much and said, 'If she does not tell now, she may at some other time.' 'No,' said my husband, 'we will coax her a little, until her passion be off, and then take an opportunity to shoot her.' Upon which Houseman seemed satisfied and said, 'What must be done with her clothes?' Whereupon they both agreed that they should let me lie where I was shot, in my clothes.

I, hearing this discourse, was much terrified.

THEAKSTON: That may well be imagined, mistress. It may also be assumed that these threats against the examinant went unexecuted. Be so good as to tell us what in fact ensued.

MRS ARAM: I remained quiet until near seven o'clock, at which time Houseman and my husband went out of the house. Upon which coming down and seeing that, where a fire had been, all

> the ashes had been taken out from the grate, I examined the dunghill. Perceiving ashes of a different kind to lie upon it, I searched among them and found several pieces of linen and woollen cloth, very near burnt, which had the appearance of belonging to wearing apparel. When I returned into the house from the dunghill, I found the handkerchief I had lent Houseman the night before, and, looking at it, I found some blood upon it, about the size of a shilling. I immediately went to Houseman and showed him the pieces of cloth I had found. I said I was afraid they had done something bad to Clark. But Houseman then pretended he was a stranger to this accusation, and said he knew nothing of what I meant.

Upon being asked what her conclusion was, Mrs Aram stated that she believed him (Clark) to have been murdered by her husband and Richard Houseman.

Philip Coates spoke briefly on this occasion. He concluded that, as no other person in Knaresborough or the neighbourhood had ever been missing in his time, what lay on Mellor's table before them were the remains of Daniel Clark, his brother-in-law.

Mr Theakston expressing a desire to see both Aram and Houseman, he was informed that the former had long been absent from Knaresborough and that his whereabouts were uncertain, though latterly rumoured. Houseman, a widower living with his stepdaughter, Nancy Johnson, was sent for by a constable, Francis Moor. The two surgeons were meanwhile questioned.

Assuming the bones to be Clark's, they fitted their findings with great precision to what they knew about Clark. The body, they agreed, was that of a young man of about twenty-three, and it had lain in the ground for some thirteen or fourteen years, a fact they had discovered by breaking a thigh bone and finding it, as they said, fresh.

Dicky Houseman not yet having appeared, the jury deliberated briefly and brought in their verdict, which was that from all apparent circumstances the skeleton was that of Daniel Clark and that he had been murdered by some person or persons to them unknown. Francis Moor returned with Houseman.

Jack Shepherd in the Stone Room in Newgate.

Catherine Hayes assisting Wood & Billings in cutting of the head of John Hayes.

John Hayes's head exposed in St. Margarets church yard

The Bloody and Inhuman SMUGGLERS *throwing down Stones &c. on the expiring Body of* DANIEL CHATER *whom they had flung into Lady Holt-Well*

Mills & Rowland whipping Rich^d. Hawkins to death.

ELIZABETH CANNING,
Drawn from the Life, as she stood at the Bar to receive her Sentence, in th
Session's-House, in the *Old-Bailey*.

Theodore Gardelle having murder'd Mrs King, burns some of her Body & hides the rest.

Ryland Cutting his throat on Sight of the Officers of Justice

Informed of the jury's verdict, he was brought before the bones and invited to pick one up, it being well known that a murdered body would find some means to confound its murderer, perhaps by sweating blood. Nothing of the kind happened when Richard Houseman took up one of the bones which lay before him.

'This,' he said, 'is no more Dan Clark's bone than it is mine.'

The hush which had awaited his reaction would be prolonged.

The verdict being in, the inquest was over. Theakston, then already *functus officio*, had exceeded his duties in questioning Houseman at all. All that had properly remained for him to do was sign Barker's report of the proceedings. Houseman was under no obligation to speak. Further asked how he knew the bones were not Clark's, he nevertheless replied that he could produce a witness who had seen Clark on the road a few days after he was reported missing. Mr Theakston said that he would see this witness, whose name was Parkinson. He would see him that afternoon. He would see him, moreover, on Thistle Hill itself. That jury could hardly be expected to reverse its findings, and so Theakston discharged it, but at once ordered Barker to empanel another. They would all meet on Thistle Hill and there hold a further inquest after due attention had been paid to Mr Mellor's ale and his lady's meat.

In the afternoon, a concourse of people therefore crossed the Nidd, climbed Thistle Hill and poked about the spot where the wrong bones had been found. A jury this time of sixteen was sworn. All it heard Parkinson say was that he had heard someone else aver that, subsequently to Clark's disappearance, he had seen a man like him muffled up on a snowy day. No other evidence was taken that afternoon, and Barker did not even write this down. The sixteen men returned a verdict of murder of a person unknown by a person or persons unknown and were in their turn discharged.

These proceedings were void, as Theakston ought to have known. Only the court of King's Bench in London could authorise a second inquest on the same body. As to whose the wrong bones were, *vox populi* made up its mind on the *dies non* which followed. They were those of a Jew, murdered by Houseman, Aram and Clark, this last killed later in a quarrel over the booty.

On that Lord's Day, the Lord, we must suppose, was as mindful of His own as on any other, but to Him we may be sure that even the Rev. Mr Collins and his curate, Mr Broderick, devoted less than their customary attention. Polly Powell's and other tongues would be busy, some more guileful or malicious than hers. It is more than likely that Francis Iles spent a part of the day suborning possible witnesses. If Sally Aram was still in Knaresborough, we may imagine a distressful confrontation, long or short, between her and her mother, whose tongue had placed the father of the one, still the other's husband, in peril of his life. We must suppose that, had it not already done so, his whereabouts, as reported by the stallion-leader, became a matter of common knowledge in the town. If this is what she did, we cannot know just when Sally Aram set off to warn him, whether she waited to hear what more was said or in simple irresolution.

Of what Mr Theakston communicated to him in writing cognizance was certainly taken by William Thornton, Esq., J.P., of Thornville on the York road. Next day, he examined Philip Coates, Anna Aram, William Tutin and Richard Houseman.

To what they had already deposed Coates and Anna added something. The former:

> This informant further saith that talking sometimes with Mrs Aram about the missing of Daniel Clark, she, Mrs Aram, said that she believed Houseman deserved to be hanged about him, and her daughter said that in case her mother hanged Houseman she would hang her father, at which the girl seemed much concerned.

For her own part, the latter that, before the conversation she overheard she had refused to go to bed either with or without her husband and that after it she had tried to get out of the window but could not. Both she and Coates signed with a fair hand.

Houseman was circumstantial.

Who saith that he was in company with Daniel Clark the night before he went off, . . . and the reason of his being then with him was upon account of some money (*viz.* £20) that he had lent Clark, which he wanted to get again of him, and for which Clark then gave him some goods, which took up some time in carrying from Daniel Clark's house to his, and might take him from about eleven o'clock at night . . . till some time the next morning, the goods which he . . . took was leather and some linen cloth, which, as soon as he had possessed himself of and also a note of the prices he was to sell them at, he left Clark at Aram's house with Aram and another man not known to this examinant, who further saith that Aram and Clark immediately after followed him out of the house and went into the market place with the other unknown person, which he could very well observe and discover by the light of the moon, and does not know what became of them after and utterly disowns coming back with Aram again that morning to Aram's house, as charged by Mrs Aram, and without Clark, nor was ever with Aram at his house that night, but with Clark where he went to find him to obtain the note from Clark, . . . which he now says was obtained at Aram's house and not at Clark's, for that he only got all the goods at Clark's house, and when he secured the goods at his own house he went to seek Clark to obtain the note and found him at Aram's with the unknown person, and after he obtained the note he came away directly as before related.

Now Houseman saith that the unknown person was in the street the first time he saw him, and does not know whether he was in the house at all with Aram.

This examinant saith that he did not see Clark take any watch, plate or things of value along with him when they came out of the house the last time late in the morning.

The examinant admits that some time after Clark was a-missing, Anna Aram came to him in a passion and demanded money of him, and said he had money of her husband's in his hands, and pretended to show some shreds of cloth and demanded of him if he knew what they were, and he answered that he did not know what they were, and entirely disowns that he has ever been charged with the murder of Daniel Clark till now by Anna Aram.

Upon asking the examinant if he chose to sign this examination, he said he chose to waive it till further, for he might have something to add to it; therefore desired to have time to consider of it.

Houseman was then allowed to go home. In the morning, however, Mr Thornton thought proper to commit him to York castle, whither he was despatched in the company of John Barker and Francis Moor. Mr Thornton at the same time appointed his own carriage to be made ready. At Green Hammerton on the road to York, Houseman behaved to his conductors in such a manner as to show that he was concerned in the murder or knew of it and that he was desirous of making more ample confession on their arrival at York. Being come into Micklegate, he was taken to a house by the Minster. Being presently acquainted that Mr Thornton was passing by, Houseman desired he might be called into the house and in his presence made a further statement.

> This examinant [now saith] that true it is that Daniel Clark was murdered by Eugene Aram, late of Knaresborough, schoolmaster, as he believes, . . . for that he and Eugene Aram and Daniel Clark were together at Aram's house early on that morning, and there was snow upon the ground and moonlight, and went up the street a little before them, and they called him to go a little way with them to a place called St Robert's cave, near Grimble Bridge, where Aram and Clark stopped a little and there he saw Aram strike him several times over the breast and head and saw him fall as if he was dead and . . . came away and left them together, but whether Aram used any weapon or not to kill him with he can't tell, nor does he know what he did with the body afterwards, but believes Aram left it at the cave's mouth, for this examinant seeing Aram do this, to which he declares he was no way abetting or privy to, nor knew of his design to kill him at all, did . . . make the best of his way from him lest he might share the same fate and got to the Bridge end and then looked back and saw him coming from the cave side, which is in a private rock adjoining the river, and he could discern some bundle in his hand, but does not know what it was. On which this informant made the best of his way to the town without joining Aram again or seeing him again till next day, and from that time till this he never had any private discourse with him.

Houseman also appended a fair signature and was taken from that house to the castle.

Visited there next day by Barker, he described in careful

detail where the body lay in the cave, in the turn just within, its head to the right. The parish clerk and constable reported the same to Mr Thornton, who sent messages to Mr Theakston and appointed Thompson to join the gravediggers.

The position of these second bones was found to be exactly as Houseman said. This was strange, if the heckler had only seen Clark fall and had never thereafter consulted with the schoolmaster. We do not know whether Mr Thornton noticed the inconsistency. When Mr Theakston was known to be in the town on Thursday, an old woman called upon him to say that, a few days after the body was found on Thistle Hill, she had seen Houseman go into the cave. First peeping out as though fearful of being observed, he had, on emerging, gone and washed his hands in the Nidd. This old woman was not heard at the inquest next day, unless she was Mary Bransby, a widow, in which case the fact was not brought out in evidence.

Also then examined for the first time were Dorothy Clark, widow, the mother of Daniel Clark, and Thomas Barnett, a builder. Neither added much to what we know. This first part of the inquest was again held at Henry Mellor's house, before a jury of sixteen, who then adjourned to St Robert's cave. Those who gave evidence there were witnesses we have heard before. They added little that was new. The learned surgeons were again in perfect agreement. They had that day viewed the skeleton. They observed upon the back part of the skull a large fracture, supposed to have been done by a mason's pick or some suchlike tool and did verily believe the same to have been the cause of the death of Daniel Clark.

These were certainly the right bones. The jury (whose names we know, as we know so many others) signed a parchment engrossed in due form, whereby they collectively and individually upon their oath did say that Richard Houseman, of Knaresborough in the county of York, flaxdresser, and Eugenius Aram, late of the same place, yeoman, not having the fear of God before their eyes but moved and seduced by the instigation of the Devil and so forth, in and upon the said Daniel Clark and so forth made an assault and then and there, upon the back part of the head of the said Daniel Clark, struck and pierced, giving to the said Daniel Clark one mortal wound of which he then and there instantly died.

Of the two gentlemen who represented King's Lynn at Westminster, Horatio Walpole, Horace for short, rarely seen by the Ouse or on the Wash, was at Ragley, in Warwickshire, with Lady Hertford. He was in acquisitive mood and also enjoyed romps and jumping with the two boys, which greatly surprised a clergyman also present. Lynn's other parliamentary representative, Sir John Turner, rarely outside his borough, was at home, and the surprise was all his when, late that Saturday afternoon, a servant announced two Yorkshiremen, not, it appeared, cattle-dealers but constables who had posted all night from a town called Knaresborough, Barker and Moor, bearing a warrant from a magistrate there, one William Thornton, Esq., for the arrest of none other than Mr Knox's usher, the very Aram whose appointment Sir John had confirmed in February. He must have listened with consternation to the tale of caverns and skeletons these slow voices told. He trusted, nevertheless, to his ear not having misheard or his brain misunderstood the words these tired men so unemphatically mispronounced and the unfamiliar syntax which at times bound these together, and, having sent out for a constable of his own, one Ernest Day, he endorsed Mr Thornton's warrant for the county of Norfolk.

The arrest was made in the little room, formerly the vestry, off the schoolroom, overlooking the litter of the Saturday market. While the constable waited at the door, the gentlemen entering, Sir John asked Aram whether he knew Knaresborough, to which the usher answered that he did not. Being asked further whether he were acquainted with one Daniel Clark, he denied ever knowing such a man.

John Barker here entered and said:

'How do you do, Mr Aram?'

To which Aram replied:

'How do you do, sir? I don't know you.'

'What, don't you know me?' said Barker. 'Don't you remember that Daniel Clark and you had always a spite against me when you lived at Knaresborough?'

Here it may be noted that a young man will have changed much in thirteen years, while an older one won't, and that Aram presently recognised Barker, who said to him:

'And do you know St Robert's cave?'

Upon which Aram acknowledging that he did, Barker said:

'Aye, to your sorrow.'

Crossing the one Ouse (from *Isca*, as the scholiast had noted, like Isis, Usk and whisky) and heading for Spalding, they would come to the other at Selby by way of Lincoln, Gainsborough and Doncaster. On Monday morning, the chaise pulled up neither at the White Horse nor the Crown nor yet the Barrel or Windmill but at the Bell inn, where the notables assembled. Mrs Aram was admitted to see her husband, who barely acknowledged her presence. Then he was taken to Thornville, where a different clerk transcribed the statement on oath of Eugene Aram.

> Who saith that he was well acquainted with Daniel Clark, . . . but utterly disowns having any criminal connections with him, such as Clark stood charged with at or before the time of his disappearance, . . . when he, this examinant, was arrested by a process for a debt, during the time of which, being in custody, he first heard that Clark was a-missing. . . .
>
> This examinant . . . does not recollect being at Mr Carter's, a public house in Knaresborough, with a Jew and Richard Houseman . . . and Daniel Clark, . . . nor . . . ever being in company with Clark and Houseman . . . at Grimble bridge, nor at nor near a place called St Robert's cave . . . at that unseasonable time in the morning. . . .

In fact, at that first examination, Eugene Aram chose to remember almost nothing. Like Houseman, he also chose to waive signing for the present, that he might have time to recollect himself better and more fully, lest anything might be omitted or slip his memory that was material which might thereafter occur to him.

Like Houseman, he was committed to York Castle, but that very day, whither Barker and Moor were conducting him when he begged to be taken back to Thornville, for that he had something of importance to impart. After mature deliberation and at his own instance, Eugene Aram there stated that he desired to make further discoveries relating to the affair of Clark.

> And saith that true it was that he was at his own house on the 7th of February, year 1745, at night, when Richard Houseman and Daniel Clark came to him with some plate and went out for more several times both of them, sometimes one of them and sometimes the other, and came back with several pieces of plate, which Clark was endeavouring to defraud his neighbours of; and could not but observe that Houseman was all that night very diligent to abet him and assist him and did it to the utmost of his power; and this examinant insists this was Houseman's business that night and not the signing of any note or instrument or agreement as mentioned by Houseman, and . . . saith that Henry Terry, then of Knaresborough, alehouse keeper, was as instrumental in abetting the said frauds as either Houseman or Clark, but was not there because it was market day and his absence from his guests might have occasioned some suspicion, but that Terry notwithstanding brought two silver tankards that night upon Clark's account, which had been fraudulently obtained.
>
> This examinant further saith that Houseman at that time, so far from having lent Clark £20, as he hath insisted on, very well knows that he never owed him but £9, which he had paid him again before that night; and further saith that all the leather Clark had, which was of considerable value, he very well knows that Houseman had then concealed under flax in his own house and intended to dispose of little by little in order to prevent suspicion of his being concerned in Clark's fraudulent practices at all.
>
> And this examinant further saith that Mr Iles of Knaresborough by divers undue means and threatenings possessed himself of considerable effects belonging to Clark.
>
> And this examinant further saith that, as to the plate and other things that Clark had so fraudulently possessed himself of, after that Abraham Spence* had taken off the goods (which Mr Iles afterwards possessed himself of) into the Dales, then Richard Houseman took the watches, rings and several small things of value, and Clark took the plate in a bag, and, the above said Henry Terry having taken the great plate, Clark

* A brother of Anna Aram.

carried them into Long Flat, where they and this examinant all went together to St Robert's cave, which Richard Houseman and Terry only went into with Clark, without examinant, who stayed without. Where they beat most of the plate flat, and it was then too late at that time in the morning, being about four o'clock, for Clark to go off so as to get any distance, wherefore it was agreed that he should stay there till the night following, and Clark accordingly stayed there, as this examinant believes, all that day, they having agreed to send him victuals, which was carried to him by Henry Terry, he being the properest person and could do it with the least suspicion, being a shooter and could do it under pretence of sporting. And next night very early Henry Terry, Richard Houseman and himself went down to the cave to Clark, in order that he might have more time to get off, but this examinant did not go into the cave or see Clark at all, but Richard Houseman and Henry Terry alone went into the cave, and he stayed to watch at a little distance on the outside, lest anybody should come and discover them, and he believed they were beating some of the plate, for they told him so, for he heard them make a great noise, and they stayed there about an hour and then came out of the cave and returned and told him Clark was gone, but upon observing a bag they had along with them he took it into his hand and saw it was plate and asked, 'What, has not Daniel taken the plate along with him?' And Richard Houseman replied, as well as Terry, that they had bought it of Daniel, as well as the watches, and given him money for it, which was more convenient for him to go off with, as he found it cumbersome and dangerous, and both Houseman and Terry told this examinant that as they had bought these things of Clark he had nothing to do with them. After which, they all three went into Houseman's warehouse and concealed the watches and small plate there, save what Terry carried away with him, which was the great plate. And afterwards Terry told him he carried it to How Hill and concealed it there and afterwards carried it to Scotland and disposed of it there. But as to the murdering of Clark, he couldn't tell anything of it, nor couldn't tell what to say, whether he was murdered or not, only they told him he was gone off.

The following Saturday, August 26th, there appeared in *Lloyd's Evening Post*, *Owen's Weekly Chronicle*, the *Cambridge Journal* and the *London Evening Post* some account of Eugene Airham's committal to York Castle on suspicion for being an accomplice to the murder of Daniel Clark. On Tuesday, the *Leeds Intelligencer* and on Saturday following the *Ipswich Journal* noted that Terry also was in custody. The Saturday after that, in what we should consider flagrant contempt of court, the *Whitehall Post*, *Payne's* and *Lloyd's* printed a letter from a correspondent in Yorkshire in which it was stated that a woman of the town of Knaresborough had often been heard to say that she had it in her power to hang her husband (who had been from her several years) and others in that neighbourhood. Upon examining her, they discovered the murder of three men as follows. Several men in the town agreed together that one of them, under specious pretences, should borrow plate, jewels, etc. of all substantial people in the town and then make off with the booty. It fell to the lot of one Clark to borrow, and he met with the wished-for success. At that time, a Jew and his man were in the town. They sent for him, offered him the goods and sold them to him and received the money. When done, they murdered the Jew and his man and buried them. While they were throwing the earth upon them, one of the company, whose name is Arom and who is now in York Castle with another confederate, took up a pick-axe and struck Clark into the skull and killed him and buried him in another place. And so they became masters of the whole unsuspected, everyone concluding Clark was quite gone off with the goods he had borrowed. This happened fourteen years since. The *London Evening Post* for that date, September 9th, was to the same effect, but omitted the name of Arom.

IX

Polar Cold

FOR A period of six months, we know indeed where Eugene Aram was and even who was taking him in his dinners, but not with certainty what he did on any single day. We reasonably believe that on Tuesday, October 17th, he completed a panegyric on Justice Thornton and sent this to the *Gentleman's Magazine* over the pseudonym 'John Atkinson'. It is likely that he received a copy of the issue in which the poem appeared and that it was from the next page to that on which it ended that he learned of the death, on the Monday five weeks before, in an engagement upon the coast of Brittany, of a young baronet, shot through the head. Upon this young man also he wrote a panegyric.

He began a third poem. This, too, is largely panegyrical, but it begins and was to end personally enough. It bears no title, but an evocative epigraph from Virgil, *Insonuere cavae gemitumque dedere Cavernae.*

For these dread walls, sad sorrow's dark domain;
For cells resounding with the voice of pain,
Where fear, pale power, his dreary mansion keeps,
And grief, unpity'd, hangs her head and weeps;
What muse would leave her springs and myrtle shades,
The groves of Pindus and the Ionian glades?

The heroics followed, nevertheless, in the course of thirty-five patiently added couplets, again bringing in Justice Thornton and as full of local as of classical names.

> All these I see, as sailors see the shore,
> And sing, secluded, scenes I tread no more.
> Nor stars nor cheerful suns I now behold,
> Languid with want and pale with polar cold. . . .

He wrote both verse and prose. In the outside world, what could not yet be known as the Seven Years War had continued not only upon the coast of France but on others in the East and West Indies, Africa and the St Lawrence. In the land-fighting, twelve thousand Prussians and twenty thousand Russians had remained on the field at Zorndorf, while nine thousand of the former and seven thousand Austrians had fallen at Hochkirk. In three years, our Prussian allies had lost nearly eighty thousand men. In the mind of Eugenius Aram, the *Celtae* roamed and conquered.

The Lent assizes loomed. They were to be held on the northern circuit by Lord Mansfield and Sir Michael Foster. On March 6th, the *Leeds Intelligencer* announced the trial of Houseman, Aram and Terry and, on the 13th, its postponement, Philip Coates, the prosecutor in this cause, having, the previous Saturday, come before Foster to swear an affidavit, in which he made oath that by reason of the great length of time which had elapsed since the supposed murder was committed, in which no circumstantial proof appeared so as to charge Richard Houseman, Eugene otherwise Eugenius Aram and Henry Terry with being concerned in the said murder till the month of August last, so this deponent had not been able as yet to procure the several witnesses and proofs to be produced on this trial. The learned judge said, let them remain in gaol until the next assizes.

The case was a troublesome one. Of the fourteen witnesses bound over by Theakston or Thornton, none could prove much against Terry. If all three were indicted together, Anna Aram would be incompetent to testify, as also if either of the other two were indicted with her husband. She was indeed bound over in the sum of twenty pounds to appear at assizes, but, even if Aram had been acquitted as a principal, her evidence could only have been admitted against Houseman in so far as it did not jeopardise the former in any subsequent indictment as an accessory or in any private appeal of murder. It seemed impossible that she could appear against Houseman without implicating her husband. The conviction of Aram alone might, on the other hand, be secured if Houseman were admitted approver for the Crown.

What may have been decided in March is uncertain. What had been decided two months later was that Houseman should appear in evidence for the Crown. A conviction would be sought only against Aram. This dreadful fact was borne in upon him piecemeal. On June 2nd, we find him appending a question to a letter to a bookseller.

> Q. Whether Houseman, after his being apprehended and in custody and commitment upon a charge of murder, can possibly be admitted evidence for the King against me, as he says his counsel tells him he may: the fact with which he impeaches me being fourteen years ago and there being nothing against me but what he pretends to say. Whether is the power of admitting evidence invested in the judge or King's counsel, or both?

Had he had counsel of his own, he would not have needed to ask outside for confirmation of what Houseman's had told him. The second question was by then pedantic.

Though defending counsel was not in those days allowed to address the jury, what counsel could have done for Eugene Aram was advise him what line to follow in his own defence. Counsel could also have told him, what it seems he did not understand, that the question of Houseman's guilt would never be allowed to arise. The Crown lawyers would offer no evidence against Houseman, who would be at once acquitted. The only difficulty which faced Houseman's counsel was to keep his client from incriminating himself in the course of his evidence against Aram, and in this he would receive every assistance from the Crown, who no doubt had also assured themselves that Philip Coates, on behalf of Clark's family, would bring no appeal of murder against Houseman, but be content with the victim he was offered.

For in effect we may say that Aram had already heard sentence of death pronounced on him by Houseman, whose company he was in at York Castle. One thing might have prolonged Eugenius's life much beyond two months more. That was the death of Houseman.

Houseman knew that, to save his own neck, he must ensure the death of his former accomplice. He meant to do it. Perhaps Aram did not even know that. It does not appear, at any rate, that he made any attempt on Houseman's life. Apportionment of the guilt of fourteen years before is now impossible, but at that moment Aram was the less guilty.

He set himself down to compose his defence, which is in the Calendars from the beginning and which I shall print in full. It would read:

> My lord, I know not whether it is of right or through some indulgence of your lordship that I am allowed the liberty at this bar and at this time to attempt a defence, incapable and uninstructed as I am to speak, since, while I see so many eyes upon me, so numerous and awful a concourse, fixed with attention and filled with I know not what expectancy, I labour not with guilt, my lord, but with perplexity. For, having never seen a court but this, being wholly unacquainted with law, the customs of the bar and all judiciary proceedings, I fear I shall be so little capable of speaking with propriety in this place that it exceeds my hope if I shall be able to speak at all.
>
> I have heard, my lord, the indictment read, wherein I find myself charged with the highest crime, with an enormity I am altogether incapable of: a fact to the commission of which there goes far more insensibility of heart, more profligacy of morals than ever fell to my lot. And nothing possibly could have admitted a presumption of this nature but a depravity not inferior to that imputed to me. However, as I stand indicted at your lordship's bar and have heard what is called evidence adduced in support of such a charge, I very humbly solicit your lordship's patience and beg the hearing of this respectable audience, while I, single and unskilful, destitute of friends and unassisted by counsel, say something perhaps like argument in my defence. I shall consume but little of your lordship's time: what I have to say will be short, and this brevity, probably, will be the best part of it. However, it is offered with all possible regard and the greatest submission to your lordship's consideration and that of this honourable court.
>
> First, my lord, the whole tenour of my conduct in life

contradicts every particular of this indictment. Yet had I never said this, did not my present circumstances extort it from me and seem to make it necessary. Permit me here, my lord, to call upon malignity itself, so long and cruelly busied in this prosecution, to charge upon me any immorality of which prejudice was not the author. No, my lord, I concerted no schemes of fraud, projected no violence, injured no man's person or property. My days were honestly laborious, my nights intensely studious. And I humbly conceive my notice of this, especially at this time, will not be thought impertinent or unreasonable, but at least deserving some attention, because, my lord, that any person, after a temperate use of life, a series of thinking and acting regularly and without one single deviation from sobriety, should plunge into the very depth of profligacy, precipitately and at once, is altogether improbable and unprecedented and absolutely inconsistent with the course of things. Mankind is never corrupted at once. Villainy is always progressive and declines from right step after step, till every regard of probity is lost, and every sense of moral obligation perishes.

Again, my lord, a suspicion of this kind, which nothing but malevolence could entertain and ignorance propagate, is violently opposed by my very situation at that time with respect of health, for, but a little space before, I had been confined to my bed and suffered under a very long and severe disorder and was not able, for half a year together, so much as to walk. The distemper left me, indeed, yet slowly and in part, but so macerated, so enfeebled, that I was reduced to crutches and so far from being well about the time I am charged with this fact that I never, to this day, perfectly recovered. Could, then, a person in this condition take anything into his head so unlikely, so extravagant? I, past the vigour of my age, feeble and valetudinary, with no inducement to engage, no ability to accomplish, no weapon wherewith to perpetrate such a fact, without interest, without power, without motive, without means.

Besides, it must needs occur to everyone that an action of this atrocious nature is never heard of but, when its springs are laid open, it appears that it was to support some indolence or supply some luxury, to satisfy some avarice or oblige some malice. Yet I lay not under the influence of any one of these. Surely, my lord, I may, consistently with both truth and modesty, affirm this much. And none who have any veracity and know me will ever question this.

In the second place, the disappearance of Clark is suggested as an argument of his being dead. But the uncertainty of such an inference from that and the fallibility of all conclusions of such a sort from such a circumstance are too obvious and too notorious to require instances. Yet, superseding many, permit me to produce a very recent one, and that afforded by this castle.

In June, 1757, William Thompson, for all the vigilance of this place, in open daylight and double-ironed, made his escape, and, notwithstanding an immediate inquiry set on foot, the strictest search and all advertisement, was never seen or heard of since. If, then, Thompson got off unseen through all these difficulties, how very easy was it for Clark when none of them opposed him? But what would be thought of a prosecution against anyone last seen with Thompson?

Permit me next, my lord, to observe a little upon the bones which have been discovered. It is said (which perhaps is saying very far) that these are the skeleton of a man. It is possible, indeed, it may, but is there any certain known criterion which incontestably distinguishes the sex in human bones? Let it be considered, my lord, whether the ascertaining of this point ought not to precede any attempt to identify them.

The place of their *depositum*, too, claims much more attention than is commonly bestowed upon it, for, of all places in the world, none could have mentioned any wherein there was greater certainty of finding human bones than a hermitage, except he should point out a churchyard, hermitages in time past being not only places of religious retirement but of burial too. And it has scarce or never been heard of but that every cell now known contains or contained these relics of humanity, some mutilated and some entire. I do not inform, but give me leave to remind your lordship, that here sat solitary sanctity, and here the hermit or the anchoress hoped that repose for their bones, when dead, they here enjoyed when living.

All the while, my lord, I am sensible this is known to your lordship and many in this court better than to me. But it seems necessary to my case that others, who have not at all perhaps averted to things of this nature and may have concern in my trial, should be made acquainted with it. Suffer me then, my lord, to produce a few of many evidences that these cells were used as repositories of the dead and to enumerate a few in which human bones have been found, as it happened in this question, lest to some that accident might seem extraordinary and consequently occasion prejudice.

1. The bones, as was supposed, of the Saxon St Dubritius were discovered buried in his cell at Guy's Cliff near Warwick, as appears from the authority of Sir William Dugdale.

2. The bones thought to be those of the anchoress Rosia were lately discovered in a cell at Royston, entire, fair and undecayed, though they must have been interred for several centuries, as is proved by Dr Stukeley.

3. But my own county, nay, almost this neighbourhood, supplies another instance, for in January 1747 were found by Mr Stevin, accompanied by a reverend gentleman, the bones, in part, of some recluse, in the cell at Lindholm near Hatfield. They were believed to be those of William of Lindholm, a hermit who had long made this cave his habitation.

4. In February 1744, part of Woburn Abbey being pulled down, a large portion of a corpse appeared, even with the flesh on and which bore cutting with a knife, though it is certain this had lain above two hundred years, and how much longer is doubtful, for this abbey was founded in 1145 and dissolved in 1538 or 1539.

What would have been said, what believed, if this had been an accident to the bones in question?

Further, my lord, it is not yet out of living memory that a little distance from Knaresbrough, in a field, part of the manor of the worthy and patriotic baronet who does that borough the honour to represent it in Parliament, were found, in digging for gravel, not one human skeleton only but five or six deposited side by side with each an urn placed at its head, as your lordship knows was usual in ancient interments.

About the same time and in another field almost close to this borough was discovered also, in searching for gravel, another human skeleton. But the piety of the same worthy gentleman ordered both pits to be filled up again, commendably unwilling to disturb the dead.

Is the invention of these bones forgotten, then, or industriously concealed, that the discovery of those in question may appear the more singular and extraordinary, whereas in fact there is nothing extraordinary in it? My lord, almost every place contains such remains. In fields, in hills, in highway sides, in commons, lie frequent and unsuspected bones. And our present allotments for rest for the departed are but of some centuries.

Another particular seems not to claim a little of your lordship's notice and that of the gentlemen of the jury, which is that perhaps no example occurs of more than one skeleton being found in one cell; and in the cell in question was but one, agreeable in this to the peculiarity of every other known cell in Britain. Not the invention of one skeleton but of two would have appeared suspicious and uncommon.

But then, my lord, to attempt to identify these, when even to identify living men sometimes has proved so difficult, as in the case of Perkin Warbeck and Lambert Simnel at home and of Don Sebastian abroad, will be looked on perhaps as an attempt to determine what is indeterminable.

And I hope, too, it will not pass unconsidered here, where gentlemen believe with caution, think with reason and decide with humanity, what interest the endeavour to do this is calculated to serve, in assigning proper personality to those bones whose particular appropriation can only appear to Eternal Omniscience.

Permit me, my lord, very humbly to remonstrate that, as human bones appear to have been the inseparable adjuncts to every cell, even any person's naming such a place at random as containing them in this case shows him rather unfortunate than consciously prescient and that these attendants on every hermitage only accidentally concurred with this conjecture, a mere casual coincidence of words and things.

But it seems another skeleton has been discovered by some labourer, which was full as confidently averred to be Clark's as this. My lord, must some of the living, if it promotes some interest, be made answerable for all the bones that earth has concealed and chance exposed? And might not a place where bones lay be mentioned by a person by chance as well as found by a labourer by chance? Or is it more criminal accidentally to name where bones lie than accidentally to find where they lie? Here, too, is a human skull produced, which is fractured. But was this the cause, or was it the consequence, of death? If it was violence, was that violence before or after death? My lord, in May 1732, the remains of William, Lord Archbishop of this province, were taken up by permission in this cathedral, and the bones of the skull were found broken. Yet certainly he died by no violence offered to him alive, that could occasion that fracture there.

Let it be considered, my lord, that upon the dissolution of religious houses and the commencement of the Reformation the ravages of those times affected both the living and the dead. In search after imaginary treasures, coffins were broken up, graves and vaults dug open, monuments ransacked and shrines demolished. Your lordship knows that these violations proceeded so far as to occasion parliamentary authority to restrain them, and it ceased about the beginning of the reign of Queen Elizabeth. I entreat your lordship, suffer not the violence, the depredations and the iniquities of those times to be imputed to this.

Moreover, what gentleman here is ignorant that Knaresbrough had a castle, which, though now a ruin, was once considerable both for its strength and garrison? All know it was vigorously besieged by the arms of the Parliament: at which siege, in sallies, conflicts, flights, pursuits, many fell in all the places round it and, where they fell, were buried. For every place, my lord, is burial earth in war, and many, questionless, of these rest yet unknown, whose bones futurity shall discover.

I hope, with all imaginable submission, that what has been said will not be thought impertinent to this indictment and that it will be far from the wisdom, the learning and the integrity of this place to impute to the living what zeal in its fury may have done, what nature may have taken off and piety interred or what war alone may have destroyed, alone deposited.

As to the circumstances that have been raked together, I have nothing to observe but that all circumstances whatever are precarious and have been but too frequently found lamentably fallible. Even the strongest have failed. They may rise to the utmost degree of probability, yet they are but probability still. Why need I name to your lordship the two Harrisons, recorded by Dr Howell, who both suffered upon circumstances because of the sudden disappearance of their lodger, who was in credit, had contracted debts, borrowed money and went off unseen and returned a great many years after their execution? Why name the intricate affair of Jacques de Moulin, under King Charles II, related by a gentleman who was counsel for the Crown; and why the unhappy Coleman, who suffered innocent, though convicted upon positive evidence, and whose children perished for want because the world uncharitably believed the father guilty? Why mention the perjury of Smith, incautiously admitted King's evidence, who, to screen himself, equally accused Fainloth and Loveday of the murder of Dunn, the first of whom in 1749 was executed at Winchester; and Loveday was about to suffer at Reading had not Smith been proved perjured, to the satisfaction of the court, by the surgeon of Gosport hospital.

Now, my lord, having endeavoured to show that the whole of this process is altogether repugnant to every part of my life; that it is inconsistent with my condition of health about that time; that no rational inference can be drawn that a person is dead who suddenly disappears; that hermitages were the constant repositories of the bones of a recluse; that the proofs of this are well authenticated; that the revolutions in religion or the fortune of war have mangled or buried the dead—the conclusion remains perhaps no less reasonably than impatiently wished for.

> I, at last, after a year's confinement, equal to either fortune, put myself upon the candour, the justice and the humanity of your lordship and upon yours, my countrymen, gentlemen of the jury.

This might elicit high praise as a specimen of English prose composition. Delivered with a blend of firmness and modesty, it could only be thought a model of propriety in the deportment of a man on trial for his life. It would prove nothing so much to the point as with what perfect sincerity its author claimed to be wholly unacquainted with law, the customs of the bar and all judiciary proceedings.

The judges appointed to the Lammas assizes for the county and city of York were Henry Bathurst and William Noel, the former to sit at *nisi prius* and the latter on the Crown side. The Hon. Mr Bathurst we have seen prosecuting Mary Blandy eight years earlier. He was a man in his middle forties, who had formerly represented Cirencester in the House of Commons, would later be lord high chancellor, with a barony which has lasted, and four years after that would inherit his father's title as Lord Bathurst. An older man, a schoolfellow of Dr Johnson's in Lichfield, Noel was described by Horace Walpole as a pompous man of little solidity, but this view was not shared by other lawyers.

Precept to the sheriffs to hold a commission of *oyer* and *terminer* and general gaol delivery three weeks thence was issued by the two judges on July 4th. With them, to lead for the Crown, would be Fletcher Norton, K.C., caricatured as Sir Bullface Doublefee, whose art Lord Mansfield considered very likely to mislead a jury. 'With him,' the Scottish jurist and parliamentarian was to say, 'I felt it more difficult to prevent injustice being done than with any person who ever practised before me.' At the Lent assizes, the illustrious Mansfield would himself have been present, though not directly concerned with criminal actions.

The assize was formally opened on Saturday, July 28th. The judges adjourned to their lodgings and on Sunday heard a sermon in the Minster. On Monday, Bathurst and Noel proceeded to hear the civil and criminal pleas. Among the former, Bathurst had to consider the complaint of a Miss Redfern against William Bowes, Esq., for a breach of promise of matrimony. The inhabitants of the townships of Hook and Brayton were charged with not repairing highways, and true bills had been found by a grand jury against persons accused of larceny, murder, receiving and assault. Seven such were arraigned in the course of the week. Their names were Mason, Houseman, Aram, Terry, Goodsir, Walker and Rancey.

On Friday morning, Mr Justice Noel took his seat, and these seven were brought to the bar. Twelve jurors, all of the quality of gentlemen, were called. None was challenged. The twelve were sworn and empanelled.

The other prisoners being put back, George Mason was bidden to hold up his hand and indicted of stealing two pecks of malt, value one shilling and sixpence, and three of wheat, value twopence, the property of Richard Calverley. The jury found him guilty. He pleaded his clergy, was burnt in the hand and discharged.

Richard Houseman was then put to the bar. Mr Norton rose to ask for a verdict of not guilty, if the court was willing. Judge Noel replied that it was entirely a matter for counsel's discretion. He directed a verdict of not guilty, which the jury at once returned.

Houseman stood down. Aram was brought up again from the cells, set to the bar and bidden to hold up his hand, which he did. The clerk of the arraigns addressed the jury. A junior Crown lawyer opened the indictment, after which the Hon. Mr Norton spoke as should here have followed had his speech been preserved.

He then resumed his seat, to be followed by another junior, who proceeded to call Richard Houseman. Houseman spoke very low, and the judge had to ask counsel what the witness said.

Peter Moor was next put into the box, followed by Barnett and Beckwith, Tutin and Latham. John Barker described Aram's arrest. Mr Locock, the surgeon, was called. The last witness was the magistrate, Mr Thornton. He proved taking the prisoner's two examinations. These were put in and shown to the jury. The prisoner then read out the defence he had written.

Among those who listened, one at least was a schoolmaster. This was Mr Paley of Giggleswick, who had brought his gifted son, William, these forty miles east to study an occasion which so clearly reflected upon the profession of scholarship. It was making, that is certain, an impression on the mind of the future philosopher and divine, then sixteen, who a few years later in Cambridge would be heard uttering the undergraduatelike remark that Aram had hanged himself by his own cleverness.

When it came to the bones, Judge Noel would perhaps recall that as many as thirty years ago Samuel Gale had talked to him about Dr William Stukeley. If the judge had kept up his antiquarian studies, he would know, as the man in the dock apparently did not, that the bones at Royston had been anything but 'entire, fair and undecayed' and that others had not thought them those of Rosia. As to St Dubritius, he had been found not at Guy's Cliff but on Bardsey.

The story of William Thompson (not the one who had found the wrong bones in the present case, but the one who had vanished in his fetters from York Castle the year before last) had been a tale savoured over the port, but none of the lawyers would know any better than their hanged man that at that moment Thompson lay no more than three feet from the courthouse wall, having been killed by the fall, and that he would lie there undiscovered twenty years more in his rusting irons. They would know about *R.* v. *Coleman* and *R.* v. *Fainloth & Loveday* and what effect these unfortunate judicial errors had had on certain reputations, while any who had recently dipped into Howell might remember that it was not the Harrisons but the Perrys who had been hanged.

Mr Justice Noel resumed the evidence, we may believe with as much fairness as could be exhibited in the resumption of selected evidence. His charge to the jury has not been preserved.

We know that the jury's deliberation was brief. We suppose our twelve gentlemen not to have retired.

During the whole trial, the prisoner had behaved with great

steadiness and decency. He heard his conviction and received his sentence with profound composure and left the bar with a smile on his countenance.

Henry Terry was next put to the bar, indicted as an accomplice. No evidence was offered against him, and he was immediately discharged. Afterwards, he was seen to ride out of York in a triumphant and boasting manner, wearing a green cockade in his hat in contempt and derision of the malice of his prosecutors.

Four other cases were tried that day for the Crown. For receiving stolen goods, knowing them to have been stolen, John Goodsir was sentenced to be transported fourteen years. At *nisi prius*, Mr Justice Bathurst awarded Miss Redfern damages of fifteen hundred pounds against William Bowes, Esq., for perfidious breach of a promise of marriage. On Saturday morning, Noel, J., completed the cases for the Crown. Francis Weatherill and Stephen Byass also were sentenced to be transported fourteen years, for what offence the gaol book does not say. William and John Cockburn were sentenced to be hanged for burglary. An order was made for Eugene Aram otherwise Eugenius Aram, after execution, to be hung in chains on Knaresborough Forest near to the town of Knaresborough. After a hasty collation, the judges and Sir Bullface Doublefee took post for Newcastle.

Even in our own time, anything reported from the condemned cell or the scaffold must be treated with great reserve. It is, however, generally believed that Eugene Aram admitted the justice of his sentence, on Saturday, to Mr Collins, vicar of Knaresborough, and that, coming to knock off his chains on Monday morning, the executioner found him weak from loss of blood, having cut his arm in two places with a razor he had contrived to secrete. Rather less general belief is given to the report that, to Mr Collins or another clergyman, he gave as his motive for attacking Clark the discovery of his wife's infidelity with the pock-broke youth. On Sunday, he evidently found time to put his literary remains in order, most notably the *Essay towards a Lexicon upon an Entirely New Plan*, on which his intellectual reputation rests.

He was executed at Knavesmire, York, on August 6th, 1759. Conveyed to Knaresborough, his body was gibbeted next day, seventy or eighty yards along the right-hand side of the road to Plompton, south of the Low Bridge, opposite Thistle Hill. The gibbet was studded with nails to prevent it from being cut down.

An account of the recent trial at York appeared in London bookshops on Thursday, August 16th. That Saturday's *London Chronicle* and *Cambridge Journal* printed a letter from York which recounted how, the previous week, a mob had assembled about the house of Richard Houseman in Knaresborough and were with great difficulty prevented from pulling it down. They had carried Houseman about the streets in effigy, which was afterwards knocked on the head with a mason's pick, then hanged and burnt.

The magazines considered the verdict on Aram just. 'In his defence,' wrote Tobias Smollett in *The Critical Review*, 'which, however, seems to be as good as his cause admitted of, he does not confute anything here alleged against him.' He was, said the *London*, 'convicted on many concurrent proofs and a number of the strongest circumstances. . . . What this Eugene is remarkable for is having read a very extraordinary defence, which he had drawn up with very great art and in no inelegant style.' On his return from Newcastle, Mr Justice Noel is reported to have said that, though it could not avail him, this defence was so clever that Aram must have spent fourteen years preparing it.

X

Disciple and Master

IN THAT penultimate year of the reign of George II, the triple tree at Tyburn was demolished, and Thomas Turlis began his nineteen years' experiments with the new moving gallows, which had a primitive drop, the patient thus tending to die rather of a broken neck than by slow strangulation. One of the first to submit to this improved treatment was a forger, John Ayliffe, a servant of the unpopular paymaster, Henry Fox, whose political opponents accused him of having compassed the man's death to cover guilty secrets of his own. The treatment was bungled, the knot slipping from behind Ayliffe's ear.

A notable hanging in 1760 was that of Lord Ferrers, a backwoods peer who had murdered his steward. He was the last English nobleman to be hanged, and it was done with a silk rope, the new drop being draped with black baize, as was the beam.

The first we shall note in the new reign was that of Theodore Gardelle, the Swiss miniaturist, for slaughtering his landlady with a savagery less remarkable than his attempts to dispose of the body subsequently. He was launched into eternity not at Tyburn but in the Haymarket and thereafter gibbeted at Hounslow. Hanging people elsewhere than at Tyburn enjoyed a certain vogue that year and the next. For concealing part of his effects from his creditors, John Perrott was hanged in Smithfield, John Plackett for robbery in City Road.

The author of *Pamela* and *Clarissa* died of natural causes. A knighthood was conferred on the blind half-brother of his late rival, the author of *Jonathan Wild* and other works.

Among Scots drifting south in the autumn of 1762, James Boswell was more comfortably circumstanced and better-connected than most. Also, he had been to London before. He was twenty-two. His father, an Edinburgh lawyer, had been elevated to the bench and made Lord Auchinleck.

A week after his arrival, Boswell was admitted to the Beefsteak club, in a room over Covent Garden theatre. There he ate, drank and sang in the company of the amusing demagogue, John Wilkes, the elephantine poet, Charles Churchill, Wilkes's assistant on *The North Briton*, and the Earl of Sandwich, who was still their friend. Ten days later, he was in the theatre for the first night of Arne's *Love in a Village*. Twice before Christmas and again in January, he attended receptions at Northumberland House in the Strand. He met Goldsmith and Garrick, the latter of whom promised him that he should be a very great man.

On April 30th, a Saturday, for his attack on the King's speech in *The North Briton* a week before, Wilkes was committed to the Tower on a general warrant. The legality of general warrants was contested. Wilkes's arrest was, in any case, decided by Lord Chief Justice Pratt to have been a breach of privilege. On Tuesday, May 3rd, Boswell walked up to the Tower to see Wilkes come out.

The order for Wilkes's discharge had not arrived. Boswell decided that he ought to see prisoners of one kind or another, so went to Newgate. He stepped, he tells us, into a sort of court before the cells. They were surely most dismal places, he thought, three rows of 'em, four in a row, all above each other, with double iron windows and, within those, strong iron rails. In those dark mansions were the unhappy criminals confined.

The young Scot did not go in, but stood in the court, where

were a number of strange blackguard beings with sad countenances, most of them friends and acquaintances of those under sentence of death. He saw two of these pass by to chapel.

One was an Irishwoman, known to Newgate Calendar readers as Hannah Dagoe. Boswell records her surname as 'Diego'. It may have been either. Dagoes are known as such from that characteristic Spanish name, just as hooligans are from a characteristic Irish name. Hannah was the terror of her fellow-prisoners. Arrested for stripping a poor neighbour's room bare, she had succeeded in stabbing one of those who gave evidence against her. To Boswell she seemed a big, unconcerned being.

The other appeared a genteel, spirited young fellow, just as Macheath in *The Beggar's Opera*. He was dressed in a white coat and blue silk vest, with his hair neatly queued and a silver-laced hat smartly cocked. He walked firmly and with a good air, his chains rattling upon him. An acquaintance asked him how he was. 'Very well,' he said, quite resigned. He was Paul Lewis, the son of a clergyman, who had served with commissioned rank successively in both services before turning highwayman. James Boswell tells us that he really took a great concern for this young ruffian, of the same age as himself, and wished to relieve him.

In prison, Lewis had threatened the life of the chaplain or ordinary, the Rev. Stephen Roe, for denying him admission to the sacrament, unless he gave some proof of penitence, at the same time as another man under sentence of death whom Boswell did not see that day. This was John Rice, a broker, who, by forging letters of attorney, had defrauded a Yorkshirewoman of nineteen thousand pounds, fled the country when this was discovered and been extradited by the French. Able to pay garnish, he was accommodated in a private room.

That night, Mr Roe supped with him. A runner was heard to call to another that Mr Rice desired a boiled chicken.

'You need not,' said the first runner, 'be curious about the sauce, for you know he's to be hanged tomorrow.'

'True,' replied the other, 'but the Ordinary sups with him, and he's a hell of a fellow for butter.'

This was in due course recorded not by James Boswell but by another gossip of the day, George Selwyn, who, as a third, Horace Walpole, said of him, loved nothing upon earth so well as a criminal, except the execution of him. Boswell himself was at Tyburn next morning, however, his curiosity to see the melancholy spectacle of the executions being so strong that he could not resist it, although he was sensible that he would suffer much from it. As a boy in Edinburgh, he had read much about Tyburn in one of the earlier compilations, which he calls the *Lives of the Convicts*. He had a sort of horrid eagerness to be there. He also wished to see the last behaviour of the handsome Paul Lewis. He got upon a scaffold very near the fatal tree, so that he would clearly see all the dismal scene. There was a most prodigious crowd of spectators.

Two carts approached along the Oxford road. In the first were Lewis and Hannah Dagoe, in the second Rice, who had petitioned unsuccessfully to be allowed a carriage. He was occupied, the Calendars tell us, in prayer, his whole deportment so much that of the gentleman and the Christian that the spectators were greatly affected. On his arrival at the gallows, he stood up in the cart and made three low bows to the crowd, which seemed to entreat their prayers and pity.

Lewis had fainted in chapel and afterwards been prevented from committing suicide with a pen-knife he had concealed in his pillow. On his arrival at the fatal tree, he looked around him with a face of inexpressible anguish and addressed himself to the multitude in terms of which the Rev. Mr Roe cannot but have approved.

Hannah Dagoe, on the road to Tyburn, had shown little concern at her miserable state and paid no attention to the exhortations of the Romish priest who attended her. When the cart in which she was bound was drawn under the gallows, she got her hands and arms loose, seized Turlis the executioner, struggled with him and gave him so violent a blow on the breast as nearly knocked him down. She dared him to hang her, took off her hat, cloak and other parts of her dress, which should have been his perquisites, and, to spite him, flung them among the crowd. After much resistance, he got the rope about her neck, which she had no sooner found accomplished than, pulling a handkerchief bound round her head over her face, she threw herself out of the cart, before the signal given, with such violence that she broke her neck and died instantly.

James Boswell was most terribly shocked and thrown into a very deep melancholy. On Thursday morning, he awoke heavy, confused and splenetic. On Friday, he remembered a friend's prescription that, on arising, he should cut two or three brisk capers round the room, which he did and found attended with most agreeable effects. It expelled the phlegm from his heart, gave his blood a free circulation and his spirits a brisk flow, so that he was all at once made happy. He resolved to persist in the exercise. That morning, Wilkes was discharged from his confinement and followed to his house in Great George Street by an immense mob, who saluted him with loud huzzas while he stood bowing from his window.

In Russell Street, Covent Garden, a former actor, Thomas Davies, kept a bookshop. Samuel Johnson was his friend and came frequently to the house, where Davies more than once invited young Boswell to meet the great man, but some unlucky accident had so far prevented the meeting.

It was on Monday, May 16th, twelve days after the visit to Tyburn, that Johnson unexpectedly entered the shop while Boswell was sitting in Mr Davies's back parlour, after having drunk tea with him and Mrs Davies. Mr Davies, having perceived Johnson, through the glass door of the room in which they were sitting, advancing towards them, announced his awful approach somewhat in the manner of an actor in the part of Horatio, when he addresses Hamlet on the appearance of his father's ghost: 'Look, my lord, it comes!' Knowing Mr Johnson's mortal antipathy at the Scotch, Boswell cried to Davies, 'Don't tell where I come from!' But the bookseller did so.

Johnson was a man of a most dreadful appearance. He was a very big man, troubled with sore eyes, the palsy and the King's evil. He was very slovenly in his dress and spoke with a most uncouth voice. His dogmatic roughness of manner was disagreeable. Yet Boswell was highly pleased with the extraordinary vigour of his conversation and thought there was no ill nature in his disposition.

When the young man left, Mr Davies followed him to the door and said:

'Don't be uneasy. I can see he likes you very well.'

And so it was to turn out.

In consequence of a dispute with his landlord, Boswell in July went to Sir John Fielding's, the great seat of Westminster justice, in Bow Street. A more curious scene he never beheld. It brought fresh into his mind the ideas of London roguery and wickedness which he had first conceived by reading *The Lives of the Convicts* and other such books. There were whores, chairmen and greasy blackguards of all denominations assembled together.

The late novelist's blind half-brother had his court in a back hall. His clerk, who officiated as a sort of chamber counsel, heard all the causes and gave his opinion. As Boswell had no formal complaint to make, this clerk did not carry him in but told him that, as his landlord had used him rudely, although he had taken his lodging by the year, he was only obliged to pay for the time he had lived in the house.

Thereafter, for a month, the young man took lodgings in the Inner Temple, where Johnson also then had chambers and lived in literary state, very solemn and very slovenly, being, at fifty-three, in easier circumstances, the result of a pension awarded him that year. In August, Boswell set off to study law in Utrecht, and Johnson travelled with him to Harwich to see him on his way.

Dr Johnson's criminal involvement may be said to have begun when, at the time of his first arrival in London, he frequented Richard Savage. We cannot connect him more closely than at a third or fourth remove with any case we have considered since. Thomas Warton, his host there, tells the following anecdote of his visit to Oxford in 1754.

> About this time there had been an execution of two or three criminals at Oxford on a Monday. Soon afterwards, one day at dinner, I was saying that Mr Swinton, the chaplain of the gaol and also a frequent preacher before the University, a learned man but often thoughtless and absent, preached the condemnation-sermon on repentance, before the convicts, on the preceding day, Sunday; and that in the close he told his audience that he should give them the remainder of what he had to say on the subject the next Lord's Day. Upon which one of our company, a Doctor of Divinity and a plain matter-of-fact man, by way of offering an apology for Mr Swinton, gravely remarked that he had probably preached the same sermon before the University. 'Yes, sir, (says Johnson) but the University were not to be hanged the next morning.'

The reader may recall that the Rev. J. Swinton had collaborated with Mary Blandy on her *Own Account* and that he had conducted her to the place of execution. Such an experience might well leave a man absent-minded two years later. Thirty years later, John Lamb, clerk and servant-companion to Samuel Salt, a bencher of the Inner Temple, would tell his son Charles, not yet born, how mere distant awareness of that occasion had made the old man at once thoughtful and forgetful when dining with another lawyer, who must have been Mr Serjeant Stevens, of Doctors' Commons, brother of the late Mrs Blandy. As Charles Lamb would recall, forty years later still:

> He was to dine at a relative of the unfortunate Miss Blandy on the day of her execution; and [my father], who had a wary foresight of his probable hallucinations, before he set out schooled him with great anxiety not in any possible manner to allude to her story that day. S. promised faithfully to observe the injunction. He had not been seated in the parlour, where the company was expecting the dinner summons, four minutes, when, a pause in the conversation ensuing, he got up, looked out of the window, and pulling down his ruffles—an ordinary motion with him—observed it was a gloomy day and added, 'Miss Blandy must be hanged by this time, I suppose.'

Dr Johnson may also have given her a passing thought, but we have no warrant for saying that he did. We do know that, for a whole winter, of uncertain date, he had attended the office of another Westminster justice, Saunders Welch, to hear the examination of the culprits, but had found an almost uniform tenor of misfortune and profligacy. The year before his first meeting with Boswell, he had been much concerned with investigating the Cock Lane ghost. There was indeed a superstitious streak in Johnson, but he discovered the ghost to be spurious. It was as well that he did, for the ghostly manifestations had been promoted as part of a criminal conspiracy to implement charges of murder against a worthy citizen. The instigators of the plot, principally a sister of the woman said to have been murdered, never appeared in the dock, but all through 1763 and the following year the most active conspirator was in prison, except on three occasions when he was taken out to be stood in the pillory. He, John Parsons, had been the parish clerk of St Sepulchre's, a very drunken man.

As a parish clerk might also be the sexton, it is not in the least improbable that Parsons should in his time have appeared and been heard tolling and intoning under the archway outside the condemned hold of Newgate, the night before executions. By then, it seems, the night exhortation in prose had been versified, which perhaps made it easier to remember. It now went:

All you that in the condemned hold do lie,
Prepare you, for tomorrow you shall die.
Watch all, and pray, the hour is drawing near
That you before th' Almighty must appear.
Examine well yourselves, in time repent,
That you may not t' eternal flames be sent;
And when St Sepulchre's bell tomorrow tolls,
The Lord have mercy on your souls.

With all the other city gates, the Newgate archway (and all that stood over it) was pulled down shortly thereafter, so that succeeding bellmen had to position themselves elsewhere.

Dr Johnson's sole recorded appearance as a witness in a court of law took place the year before the foundation stone was laid for a new and commodious Newgate prison with adjacent sessions house in the Old Bailey. It was in the old sessions house that, in 1769, he gave evidence of character for an Italian resident, Giuseppe Marc' Antonio or Joseph Baretti, charged with murder. Johnson was in very good company. Also called for the defence were Garrick, Goldsmith, Burke and Sir Joshua Reynolds, as well as the Mr Beauclerk and Mr Fitzherbert who to us are background figures, of whom, as of Baretti himself, most of us are aware only in the pages of Boswell's *Life of Johnson*.

There we first meet him, long before Boswell did, in the year of Henry Fielding's death, teaching his native language, compiling an Italian–English dictionary and translating both ways. Though he spent the greater part of his life in England, Baretti has, one understands, considerable importance in Italian literary history, as a critic, as an editor and as an amusing commentator on European affairs. After richer beginnings than any literature in the world, the Italian had, it is true, settled down to a rather thin history. To the reasons for this depletion which we all know, Baretti added one in his conversations with Johnson. He was, he said, 'the first man that ever received copy-money in Italy'. This I take to mean that Italian publishers had never paid their authors, who were therefore amateurs. The tradition persists to this day.

At the age of fifty, having then been domiciled in this country for eighteen years, Baretti became the centre of an unpleasant street incident in a part of London long devoted to prostitution, though his purpose in it was respectable. The date was Friday, October 6th, 1769, the time about five o'clock in the afternoon. Baretti's own account of the incident is as follows.

> Going hastily up the Haymarket, there was a woman at a door . . . eight or ten yards from the corner of Panton Street, and she clapped her hands with such violence about my private parts that it gave me great pain. This I instantly resented, by giving her a blow on the hand, with a few angry words. The woman got up directly, raised her voice and, finding by my pronunciation that I was a foreigner, . . . called me several bad names, . . . among which damned Frenchman and . . . woman-hater were the most audible.

> I had not quite turned the corner before a man made me turn back, by giving me a blow with his fist and asking me how I dare strike a woman; another pushed him against me, and pushed me off the pavement; then three or four more joined them. I wonder I did not fall from the high step which is there. . . . A great number of people surrounded me presently, many beating me. . . .
>
> There is generally a great puddle in the corner of Panton Street, even when the weather is fine; but that day it had rained incessantly, which made it very slippery. I could plainly perceive my assailants wanted to throw me in the puddle, where I might be trampled on, so I cried out, 'Murder!' There was a space in the circle, from whence I ran into Panton Street. . . . I was in the greatest horror, lest I should run into some stones, as I have such bad eyes. I could not run so fast as my pursuers, so that they were upon me, continually beating and pushing me, some of them attempting to catch me by the hair-tail: if this had happened I had been certainly a lost man. . . . Somewhere in Panton Street, I gave a quick blow to one who beat off my hat with his fist.

In Baretti's hand, as he gave this blow, was unfortunately a weapon.

> A man almost blind could not but be seized with terror on such a sudden attack. . . . My knife was neither a weapon of offence or defence: I wear it to carve fruit and sweetmeats, and not to kill my fellow-creatures.
>
> It is a general custom in France not to put knives upon the table, so that even ladies wear them in their pockets for general use.

Baretti took refuge in a shop in Oxendon Street, where a constable and two other men arrested him and took him before Sir John Fielding, who allowed him to dispatch a man to the Royal Academy club in Gerrard Street to fetch Sir Joshua Reynolds and other gentlemen. The man struck with the fruit-knife, presumably a Welshman, since his name was Evan Morgan, had been taken to the Middlesex hospital, where he died.

Baretti's account is taken from his defence before autumn sessions at the Old Bailey, on October 20th. It is printed equally by Jackson and by Knapp & Baldwin, who, however, differ in other respects and here clearly did not depend on the same reports. Jackson also prints evidence for the prosecution.

Elizabeth Ward deposed that, between nine and ten at night on the 6th of October, she heard a woman, whom she had never seen before, ask the prisoner to give her a glass of wine, and at the same time take hold of him in a manner inconsistent with decency; that the prisoner proceeded forward, but, soon turning back, doubled his fist and struck this deponent a violent blow on the face; that, on her screaming out, three men came up and demanded 'how he could strike a woman' and, shoving him once or twice, pushed him off the pavement. At this time, she said, Baretti drew a knife, while the men followed him, calling out, 'Murder! he has a knife out!' and this deponent believed that the deceased was stabbed at this juncture.

The deposition of Thomas Patman was to the following effect, that he had been in company with a Mr Clark and the deceased on the night above-mentioned; that he saw Mr Baretti strike a woman, whom he did not know, on the head, and, on her screaming out, Morgan and Clark pushed Patman, though not with much violence, against Baretti, who gave him a blow on the left side, in consequence of which the blood ran down into his shoe; that he then called out he was stabbed; that Baretti retreated; that Morgan followed him about half way up Panton Street, where Morgan received a wound from the prisoner, in consequence of which he fell to the ground.

The testimony of John Clark confirmed, in several particulars, that of the preceding evidence; but, on his being cross-examined, he acknowledged that Patman did not know he was stabbed till Mr Baretti ran into Panton Street. He likewise owned that himself had sworn before the coroner 'that Morgan collared Baretti before he knew Patman was wounded; and that one of the women said the prisoner ought to have a knock over the head with her patten'.

The evidence of Mr Lambert, a tallow-chandler in Panton Street, was to the following effect. He said that Mr Baretti ran into a grocer's shop opposite his house; that Patman was standing at his door with the blood running down his shirt, and said a gentleman in the shop had stabbed him. Mr Baretti had at that time a knife in one hand, and a silver case over the blade, which was bloody. Mr Lambert, who at that time was in the office of constable, called to Baretti to surrender and, immediately running towards him, seized him and took him into custody, in order to convey him before a magistrate.

Morgan having been carried to the Middlesex hospital, one of the patients who had been there at the time declared that he had heard the deceased say that he saw a gentleman assault two women, on which without intending to give offence he went to assist them, when Baretti stabbed him in two places, and that he then turned round and stabbed him a third time; and that the third wound hurt him more than the two former.

The testimony of Mr Wyatt, the surgeon who attended Morgan, imported that the deceased had received three wounds, one of which, being in the belly, was the immediate occasion of his death. He further said that, while he was dressing Patman, Clark being present, and enquiring into what gave rise to the misfortune, Clark said that they saw a gentleman abusing a lady who was acquainted with Morgan; that Morgan pushed Clark against Patman and that Clark pushed him against the prisoner; that he was not struck by either of them, but he believed the woman damned him for a French *bougre* and said he ought to have his head cloven with a patten.

A short time after this, Mr Wyatt demanded of Clark whether the woman was of his acquaintance; and he replied in the negative and then denied that she was even acquainted with Morgan, though, not more than two minutes before, he had confessed that she was.

Apart from the significant difference in the time of day on which the first two witnesses insist, the picture here is of a man somewhat less provoked and reacting with far greater violence. The evidence of Clark, both before the court and as reported by the surgeon, was inconsistent. Other persons deposed to the frequency of similar outrages in the Haymarket.

Baretti was found to have acted in self-defence and so acquitted even of manslaughter. The following year, he returned to Italy, doubtless intending to stay there. He had, it may be noted, elected to be tried by an all-British jury. It was then already the case that a foreigner enjoyed the option of trial by a jury half-composed of his fellow-countrymen.

In the years between the Cock Lane ghost and the Baretti incident, a murderess peculiarly execrated in London had been Elizabeth Brownrigg, the sadistic midwife. An Edinburgh case which must have engaged Boswell's interest (he was practising there as an advocate not many months after her escape) was that of Catharine Nairn, which is full of romantic possibilities.

Boswell involved himself, a little later, with what is known as the Douglas Cause, a question of disputed inheritance. Neither during those years nor during the next six do I know of any case eliciting comment from Dr Johnson.

It is likely enough that he noticed a highway robbery in 1772, because of the man who was robbed, with whose later misfortunes he was to involve himself closely and whom it is probable that he had already at least seen and heard. This was Dr William Dodd, the fashionable preacher, then in his forties. He, too, had frequented the Cock Lane ghost, and he had first made his reputation as chaplain of Magdalen House, a home for reformed prostitutes run on lines which Johnson had recommended in *The Rambler.*

A name Johnson noted the following year was that of John Rann, a dandified highwayman famous for wearing a bunch of sixteen strings at the knees of his breeches, of whom Johnson said to Boswell: 'Sixteen-String Jack towered above the common mark.' The bearing of this remark is obscure to me, but it was intended in some way to illuminate the poetry of Gray. By the time Johnson made it, Dodd was in disgrace.

XI

The Unfortunate Dr Dodd

DODD'S FIRST APPEARANCE in literature which anyone still reads was Horace Walpole's brief portrayal of him preaching at the Magdalen in January 1760 before a party from Northumberland House, which included Prince Edward, not yet duke of York.

> The chapel was dressed with orange and myrtle, and there wanted nothing but a little incense to drive away the Devil—or to invite him. Prayers then began, psalms and a sermon: the latter by a young clergyman, one Dodd, who contributed to the Popish idea one had imbibed by haranguing entirely in the French style, very eloquently and touchingly. He apostrophised the lost sheep, who sobbed and cried from their souls—so did my Lady Hertford and Fanny Pelham, till I believe the city dames took them both for Jane Shores. The confessor then turned to the audience and addressed himself to the Royal Highness, whom he called Most Illustrious Prince, beseeching his protection. In short, it was a very pleasing performance, and I got the most illustrious to desire it might be printed.

It was printed, and so were many of Dodd's sermons, as well as a great deal of his bad verse.

He is also mentioned in one of Lord Chesterfield's letters to his adopted son, whose tutor Dodd was (and responsible for the publication of some of them in Edinburgh soon after their author's death). He was a royal chaplain. He had a chapel of his own, and at least one of his charities has survived, the Royal Humane Society, founded to promote the resuscitation of persons apparently drowned. The Magdalen itself has survived.

In spite of these many distinctions and benefactions and two small livings, Dodd had reached his forties without serious preferment and was living beyond his means, vain, smiling, plumply handsome, the maccaroni parson, an ecclesiastical fop, suspected even of debauchery, wrongly, I feel sure, for he was notably uxorious, his wife perhaps a greater liability than he knew. The man lacked gravity. He does not seem to have been unamiable.

The robber, William Griffiths, once a seaman, had already appeared in the dock at the Old Bailey in early 1772 for a robbery in the course of which (this he later confessed) he had discharged a pistol at a surgeon's wife in Highgate. One of his two accomplices, having been allowed to turn approver, had then denied in court the statement he had sworn before Sir John Fielding, and the case had fallen to the ground, leaving the accomplice to face a charge of perjury. His narrow escape did not discourage Griffiths.

> The Rev. Dr Dodd and his lady were returning from a visit they had been making to a gentleman at St Albans, but were detained on the way at Barnet, because a postchaise could not be immediately procured. While the doctor was waiting at Barnet for the chaise, it occurred to him that there might be danger on the road. Upon which he concealed most of his money, except two guineas which he put in his purse, with a bill of exchange.
>
> Night was hastily approaching when they left Barnet; but they proceeded unmolested until they came near the turnpike at the extremity of Tottenham Court Road, when three men called to the driver of the carriage and threatened his instant destruction if he did not stop. The post-boy did not hesitate to obey such summons; but no sooner was the carriage stopped than a pistol was fired, the ball from which went through the front glass of the chaise, but did not take any effect to the injury of the parties in it, though it terrified them in a very high degree. . . .
>
> . . . Griffiths opened the door of the chaise, on which the

> doctor begged him to behave with civility, on account of the presence of the lady. He then delivered the purse, with its contents, and likewise gave the robber some loose silver. Griffiths, having received the booty, departed with the utmost precipitation.
>
> Dr Dodd lost no time in repairing to Sir John Fielding's office, where he and his lady gave so full a description of the person of the principal robber that it was easily conjectured that Griffiths must have been the party; but who had been his associates in the business has never yet transpired.
>
> . . . Griffiths was soon taken into custody. On his examination before Sir John Fielding, Dr Dodd hesitated to swear positively to his person; but Mrs Dodd, who had regarded him with more attention, positively declared on oath that he was the person who had committed the robbery.
>
> The magistrate, therefore, committed Griffiths to Newgate; . . . and he was called down to trial at the next sessions at the Old Bailey. . . .
>
> Dr Dodd declared that it was with great reluctance he came into a court of justice on such an occasion, which he said he would not have done if the robbery had not been attended with circumstances of an aggravating kind; but that the firing of the pistol was a crime of so horrid a nature that his regard to the safety of others had induced him to commence a prosecution . . . abhorrent to the feelings of his own mind. He, however, would not swear to the identity of the prisoner's person.
>
> On the contrary, Mrs Dodd swore that he was the actual person that had committed the robbery. . . . This evidence was deemed so conclusive that the jury did not hesitate to find him guilty, in consequence of which he received sentence of death.

That Dodd's reluctance to see this happen had been genuine was clearly the view of Griffiths's mother, who solicited his good offices with the Secretary of State, to whom (this is not in the Calendars) he in fact, on December 19th, the day but one after her son's conviction (there was some abnormal delay about either the passing or the execution of sentence), addressed a letter, in which he said:

> For her sake and that of her family and in consideration of his youth, I humbly beg leave to recommend [Griffiths] to your lordship's attention. Transported for life, he may be useful to society; dying in his present state, he can be of no utility to others.

It is perhaps also worth noting here that in the course of the year Dodd had composed a sermon (its delivery also delayed) On the Frequency of Capital Punishment, in which he says:

> It may seem strange, if not incredible, that of all the nations upon earth the laws of England are the most sanguinary; there being in them, as I am credibly informed, over a hundred and fifty capital cases.

And he envisages a reformation which

> shall save from an ignominious end numbers of subjects and citizens, hurried into eternity in the very bloom and flower of life, with all their sins and imperfections upon their heads, and cuts them off at once from all . . . possibility of making amends to the state they have injured, to the friends they have alienated, and the God they have so daringly offended.

The number of capital offences had reached a hundred and sixty a few years previously* and was still being added to.

Griffiths was hanged, with others, on January 20th, 1773. The others were George Turner and William Simpson, for robbing a man on the highway of his silver buckles; Nathaniel Bailey, for robbing a man of his cane; and Benjamin Bird, for forging a bill of exchange. Of this last, Knapp & Baldwin record:

> When the melancholy procession of these criminals, as usual, stopped opposite St Sepulchre's church to hear the bellman repeat the warning, Bird, in the utmost agony of mind, threw his head on the shoulder of the clergyman who sat next to him, and, while he hid his face, his whole frame was agitated in a manner not to be described, which Dr Johnson denominates 'the utmost exacerbation of human misery.'

I have failed to discover where Johnson so denominates it or in what connection. It is not certain whether he ever noted Griffiths's name, let alone Bird's. The hangman on this occasion was no longer Turlis, but the Edward Dennis who figures so prominently, though with only the barest trace of historical foundation, in *Barnaby Rudge*.

* I have yet to meet anyone who had seen the whole list, but the figure comes from Sir William Blackstone's *Commentaries*, 1765–8, treated by lawyers as one of the most authoritative works of all time on any subject.

Newgate prison was being rebuilt. One punishment its new walls would never see was the *peine forte et dure*, the pressing a man, if necessary to death, for refusal to plead. Fifty years before, in the time of Jonathan Wild, a number of robbers had endured weights of up to four hundred pounds before changing their mind, the idea being that, if they did not plead, they could not be properly convicted, and their goods would not be forfeit. In 1772, it was enacted that refusal to plead should be treated as a plea of guilty. Torture was thus finally banished from the English penal system.

Other deplorable practices were not, as a member of the Royal Society, John Howard, discovered when he was appointed high sheriff of Bedford in the year in which Griffiths was hanged. That year, Elizabeth Canning died in Connecticut. That year also, died Lord Chesterfield and Evelyn Pierrepont, second duke of Kingston, leaving all he possessed to the Elizabeth Chudleigh whom he had married four years previously, on condition that she remain a widow. She, however, had married him bigamously. Her estranged husband, the Hon. Augustus John Hervey, was heir to the earldom of Bristol, to which he would succeed two years later. Boswell and Johnson were in the Hebrides.

In January 1774, its incumbent, Dr Moss, having been advanced to the bishopric of Bath and Wells, the rich living of St George's, Hanover Square, became vacant. It was in the gift of the lord chancellor, at that time Lord Apsley, who was none other than the Bathurst we have seen prosecuting Mary Blandy in Oxford and sitting at *nisi prius* in York. His wife, Tryphena, Lady Apsley, received an anonymous letter, offering her three thousand pounds down, with an annuity of five hundred pounds a year, if she would procure it for a person to be named later. The letter was traced to a law clerk, to whom it had been dictated by Mrs Dodd.

Dr Dodd disclaimed all knowledge of the officious zeal of his consort, but his name was struck off the list of royal chaplains. He went abroad and stayed in Geneva with his former pupil,

Philip Stanhope, who had succeeded to the earldom of Chesterfield and who made him very welcome, even, we are told by Horace Walpole, riding out several miles to meet him in weather so severe that he contracted frostbite. In London, Samuel Foote mounted one of his comedies, *The Cozeners*, into which he introduced a Dr and Mrs Simony, whom everyone recognized as the Dodds. The doctor also went to Paris and was reported at the races in the uniform of a musketeer.

Back in London, he found his reputation divided rather than black. He lost the chaplaincy of the Magdalen, but the new Lord Chesterfield presented him to a living in Buckinghamshire. The Methodists were on his side, and so were the Freemasons, who made him their grand chaplain at the same time as they laid the foundation stone of the hall in Great Queen Street. He took over *The New Morning Post*, a step described, it is true, as descending so low as to edit a newspaper. He contracted new debts.

It was 1775. That year, proceedings for bigamy were started against the duchess of Kingston, and forgeries were discovered in the interest of Robert and Daniel Perreau, twins from the Windward Islands, the former a highly regarded apothecary in Golden Square. He treacherously attempted to lay the blame on his brother's mistress, Mrs Rudd, an Irish courtesan of great reputed beauty. The American war of independence had started. In December, Mrs Rudd was tried and acquitted.

In January, the Perreau twins were tried, found guilty and hanged. In April, before the House of Lords, the duchess of Kingston was tried, found guilty and discharged. She went abroad and was to live contentedly around foreign courts for twelve years. In June, David Garrick gave his last performance at Drury Lane, in a play, *Wonder*, by the gifted Mrs Centlivre, so called by the name of her third husband, who had been Queen Anne's French cook. In December, an English partisan of American independence (his real name James Hill, but known as 'John the Painter') started a fire at Portsmouth docks, which burned out the rope house.

On February 4th, 1777, the Rev. William Dodd, LL.D.,

forged a bond for the sum of £4,200 in the name of Philip Stanhope, fifth earl of Chesterfield.

> The method adopted in this forgery is remarkable. He pretended that the noble lord had urgent occasion to borrow four thousand pounds, but did not choose to be his own agent and begged that the matter might be secretly and expeditiously conducted.
>
> The doctor employed one Lewis Robertson, a broker, to whom he presented a bond, not filled up or signed, that he might find a person who would advance the requisite sum to a young nobleman who had lately come of age. After applying to several persons who refused the business, because they were not to be present when the bond was executed, Mr Robertson, absolutely confiding in the doctor's honour, applied to Messrs Fletcher & Peach, who agreed to lend the money. Mr Robertson returned the bond to the doctor, in order to its being executed; and on the following day the doctor produced it as executed, and witnessed by himself. Mr Robertson, knowing Mr Fletcher to be a particular man and who would object to one subscribing witness only, put his name under the doctor's. He then went and received the money, which he paid into the hands of Dr Dodd. . . .

Knapp & Baldwin here omit, with confusing effect, a paragraph which I restore in part from Jackson.

> The money being thus in the doctor's possession, he gave Mr Robertson a hundred pounds for his trouble and paid some of his own debts with a part of the remainder. . . . The bond being left with Mr Manley (attorney for Messrs Fletcher & Peach), he observed, in the condition of the bond, a . . . blot in the first letter E in the word SEVEN. . . . He . . . did not suspect a forgery; yet he . . . advised [Mr Fletcher] to have a clean bond filled up and carried to Lord Chesterfield for execution.
>
> . . . Lord Chesterfield was surprised and immediately disowned it. Upon this, Mr Manley went directly to Mr Fletcher, to consult what steps to take. Mr Fletcher, a Mr Innis and Mr Manley went to Guildhall to prefer an information respecting the forgery against the broker and Dr Dodd. Mr Robertson was taken into custody, while Fletcher, Innis, Manley and two of the lord mayor's officers went to the house of the doctor in Argyle Street.
>
> On their opening the business, he was . . . very much struck and affected. Manley told him that, if he would return the money, it would be the only means of saving him, and he instantly

> returned six notes of five hundred pounds each, making three thousand pounds; he drew on his banker for five hundred pounds; the broker returned one hundred pounds, and the doctor gave a second draft on his banker for two hundred pounds and a judgment on his goods for the remaining four hundred pounds. All this was done by the doctor in full reliance on the honour of the parties that the bond should be returned to him cancelled; but, notwithstanding this restitution, he was taken before the lord mayor and charged. . . . The doctor declared he had no intention to defraud Lord Chesterfield or the gentleman who advanced the money. . . . He was pressed, he said, exceedingly, for three hundred pounds to pay some bills due to tradesmen; and took this step as a temporary resource, and would have repaid it in half a year. 'My Lord Chesterfield,' added he, 'cannot but have some tenderness for me, as my pupil. I love him, and he knows it. There is nobody wishes to prosecute. I am sure my Lord Chesterfield don't want my life. I hope he will show clemency to me. . . .' Clemency, however, was denied; and the doctor was committed to the Compter, in preparation for his trial.

The lord mayor of the day was Sir Thomas Halifax, later M.P. for Aylesbury, himself a banker, a member of the firm which is now Williams & Glyn's Bank. He is described by Hugh Childers as vacillating in his political views but by Birkenhead as an active member of the Court party against Wilkes, with whom Dodd was thought to be intimate, having recently entertained him at dinner.

It was February 8th. The doctor was marched on foot from Guildhall to Wood Street, and the populace jeered loudly. It was no doubt this fact which upset Dr Johnson. In his eyes, the man's character was bad. No more than Fielding did Johnson oppose capital punishment in principle or the wide range of its application at that time. What shocked him was the prospect of a clergyman of the established Church being drawn to Tyburn in a cart and there hanged before a mob largely hostile to the clergy. We must perhaps allow for some possible influence from Wilkes, with whom Johnson had recently established amicable relations. We may also invoke the example of Voltaire, with his proclaimed indignation at the infamous Calas case and his derision at our execution of Admiral Byng.

The year before, Johnson had interested himself in the case of a Scottish clergyman, the Rev. James Thomson, with whom Boswell was concerned professionally in Edinburgh. The action against Thomson was for defamation from the pulpit in connection with the Douglas Cause, and, to Boswell on one of his London visits, Johnson had dictated an eloquent Argument in Support of the Right of Immediate and Personal Reprehension from the Pulpit. He was, we may say, ripe for Dodd's appeal to the service of his pen.

Dodd was found guilty on February 22nd by a reluctant jury, which also put in a strong recommendation to mercy previously prepared. The young earl of Chesterfield had testified against him, as no doubt he had been bound to do. There had been an irregularity in the manner in which Robertson's evidence was procured against the doctor, and the legality of the conviction had to come before the judges, as it did in May. On the 14th of that month, Dr Dodd was put to the bar and told that he must prepare for sentence. Dodd was now in Newgate, almost completely rebuilt, in a private room, under a humane keeper, Akerman, writing hundreds of lines of generally deplorable (but intermittently relieved, as when he wrote of 'the dear, pale face' of his father, late vicar of Bourne in Lincolnshire) blank verse under the title of *Thoughts in Prison*. His appeal to Johnson was made through the countess of Harrington.

Johnson first provided a speech to the Recorder of London, to be read out by Dodd on May 26th, when he appeared for sentence. The Calendars reproduce it in full, with no mention of its source, as Jackson does part of a sermon written by Johnson for Dodd to preach to his fellow-convicts on Friday, June 6th (for this, Knapp & Baldwin substitute the account of Dodd's last days by the Rev. John Villette, then Ordinary of Newgate). Boswell, not at the time in London, was to be thorough in listing and quoting Dr Johnson's further efforts on behalf of Dr Dodd. There were letters to Bathurst, to the future Lord Liverpool and in Dodd's name to Lord Mansfield, thought by Horace Walpole to have been the most vindictive of those who might have led George III to reprieve Dodd and (this was Johnson's hope) let him leave the country. There were letters from Dodd to the King and from Mrs Dodd to the Queen. There was a mass petition, which collected over twenty thousand signatures and was presented by Lord Percy, and there was one on behalf of the City. Letters were exchanged between Johnson and Dodd himself. What Johnson never did was visit Dodd in prison. It would, he said, have done himself more harm than it did Dodd good.

His last service was the composition of an address to the people from the scaffold, designed to be read in Dodd's name by the Ordinary. This (reproduced by Knapp & Baldwin, but not by Jackson) was not in fact so read, 'as it seemed not possible to communicate the knowledge of it to so great a number of persons as were then assembled'. The size of the crowd seems also to have frustrated an attempt at resuscitation. The story is (and it is better founded than many such stories) that at an undertaker's in Goodge Street a hot bath was kept waiting for Dr Dodd's body and that the surgeon in attendance was none other than John Hunter, at that time much concerned with the problems of the Royal Humane Society, with which the clergyman had also been involved. It is said that Hunter worked on the body, but that the carriage which brought it had taken too long to get through the crowd.

A further story, palpably absurd, is that the attempt was successful and that Dodd was presently found living contentedly in Provence. One of our authorities for believing that he was in fact buried at Cowley, in Middlesex, is Horace Walpole. He further intimates that he was one of those who saw to it that Mrs Dodd did not become destitute, though she is represented as living on for seven years, at Ilford, in great corporal and mental inanity.

Johnson himself is an authority for plans there had been to rescue Dodd from Newgate, one of them by leaving a wax image in his place. The story was told, at tea in Derby, that September. It was on the same occasion that Boswell quoted to Johnson one of those observations for which the latter has since been most often quoted: 'Depend upon it, Sir, when a man knows he is to be hanged in a fortnight, it concentrates his mind wonderfully.' This had been made to a man who suspected Johnson of having composed Dodd's sermon to his fellow-convicts, on the ground that it had a great deal more force of mind in it than anything known to be Dodd's.

A little inconsistently, we may feel, Johnson, at tea in Derby, had, a moment before, expressed disapproval of Dr Dodd's leaving the world persuaded that *The Convict's Address to his Unhappy Brethren* was of his own writing. On the other hand, he commended Dodd for his reply to pious friends who had tried to console him by saying that he was going to leave a wretched world. Dodd had had honesty enough not to join in the cant. 'No, no,' he had said, 'it has been a very agreeable world to me.' 'I respect Dodd,' said Johnson, 'for thus speaking the truth.' But then added, we must suppose censoriously: 'For, to be sure, he had for several years enjoyed a life of great voluptuousness.'

The following April, dining at Thrale's, to a clergyman asking whether Dodd's sermons were not addressed to the passions, Johnson said that ('be they addressed to what they may') they were nothing. A few days later, Boswell, then much around, found Dr Johnson sitting at home on a Sunday, an unread copy of Dodd's *Thoughts in Prison* lying upon the table. Boswell, to whom the poem appeared to be an extraordinary effort by a man who was in Newgate for a capital crime, picked up the book and read a passage aloud. Johnson said: 'Pretty well, if you are previously disposed to like them.'

> I read another passage, with which he was better pleased. He then took the book into his own hands, and, having looked at the prayer at the end of it, he said, 'What *evidence* is there that this was composed the night before he suffered? *I* do not believe it.' He then read aloud where he prays for the King, &c., and observed, 'Sir, do you think that a man the night before he is to be hanged cares for the succession of a royal family? Though he may have composed this prayer then. A man who has been canting all his life may cant to the last. And yet a man who has been refused a pardon after so much petitioning would hardly be praying thus fervently for the King.

But Dr Johnson never pretended to have thought other than poorly of the man whose life he had made such admirable efforts to save. Those efforts stand all the more to his credit.

A younger clergyman, the Rev. James Hackman, was in love (whatever that may mean) with the earl of Sandwich's *maitresse en titre*, Martha Ray or Reay, who seems to have been an extraordinarily pleasant and intelligent young woman, then in her thirties, highly musical, whom, a stay-maker's daughter, Sandwich had picked up in St James's Park when she was eighteen and sent abroad to be educated. In April 1779, she went to Covent Garden with an Italian woman friend to attend a performance of Arne's *Love in a Village*, often revived. At the close of the performance, as she was about to step into the coach, Hackman appeared with two pistols, one of which he discharged at her, which killed her on the spot, and the other at himself, without effect. He then beat himself with the butt end on his head, but after some struggle was secured, his wounds dressed, and he was carried before Sir John Fielding.

Nine days after the murder, three before Hackman's execution, Boswell attended his trial. He dined with Johnson and friends who included the quarrelsome Topham Beauclerk.

> Johnson . . . was much interested by my account of what passed, and particularly with [Hackman's] prayer for the mercy of heaven. He said, in a solemn, fervid tone, 'I hope he *shall* find mercy.'
>
> . . . In talking of Hackman, Johnson argued, as Judge Blackstone had done, that his being furnished with two pistols was a proof that he meant to shoot two persons. Mr Beauclerk said, 'No; every wise man who [intends] to shoot himself [takes] two pistols, that he [may] be sure of doing it at once. Lord [Charles Spencer's] cook shot himself with one pistol, and lived ten days in great agony. Mr [Delmis] who loved buttered muffins, but durst not eat them because they disagreed with his stomach, resolved to shoot himself; and then he ate three buttered muffins for breakfast before shooting himself, knowing that he should not be troubled with indigestion: *he* had two charged pistols; one was found lying charged upon the table by him, after he

> had shot himself with the other.' 'Well,' said Johnson with an air of triumph, 'you see here one pistol was sufficient.' Beauclerk replied smartly, 'Because it happened to kill him.' And either then or a very little afterwards, being piqued at Johnson's triumphant remark, added, 'This is what you don't know, and I do.' . . . A little while after this, the conversation turned on the violence of Hackman's temper. Johnson then said, 'It was his business to *command* his temper, as my friend, Mr Beauclerk, should have done some time ago.'

Johnson's petulance with Beauclerk had its own personal history. In terms of criminal history, Johnson and Blackstone seem to have been right. Near Grenoble, almost fifty years later, the scene of this *crime passionnel* was to be almost exactly reproduced in a church and to provide the basis for a very great crime novel indeed, *Le Rouge et le Noir*. Unlike his real-life prototype but like Stendhal's criminal hero, the Rev. James Hackman had been torn between the Army, *le rouge*, and the Church, *le noir*. Unlike Julien Sorel, he had tried *le rouge* before settling for *le noir*.

He occurred just too late for inclusion in the last of the original five volumes of *The Newgate Calendar*. The following year, incited in the first place against Roman Catholicism, the London mob burned prisons and other judicial buildings, including the house in Bow Street. Nineteen rioters were hanged in London and Middlesex, on Tower Hill and in Bishopsgate Street, Coleman Street, Bow Street, High Holborn, Oxford Street, Bethnal Green, Whitechapel, Old Bailey, Old Street, Moorfields and Bloomsbury Square, seven more, of whom three were women, in the borough of Southwark, where the riots had started. Though he indeed received sentence of death for looting in Holborn, Edward Dennis, the hangman, was released to play his part in the hanging and flourished six years longer. Lord George Gordon himself was acquitted of constructive treason, at which Dr Johnson declared himself glad.

In 1783, the journey to Tyburn was to be abolished, and hanging thereafter done for the most part in front of Newgate prison. This Johnson deplored.

'The age,' said he, 'is running mad after innovation; all the business of the world is to be done in a new way; men are to be hanged in a new way; Tyburn itself is not safe from the fury of innovation. . . . No, Sir, . . . it is *not* an improvement. . . . Sir, executions are intended to draw spectators. If they do not draw spectators, they don't answer their purpose. The old method was most satisfactory to all parties; the public was gratified by a procession; the criminal was supported by it. Why is all this to be swept away?'

It was true that Dr Dodd had not, as Johnson feared, been jeered at by a mob hostile to clergymen. Nor had he been precisely carted to Tyburn, he and Hackman both being allowed coaches.

On April 18th, which in 1783 was Good Friday and warm, Johnson talked of Dodd.

'A friend of mine,' said he, 'came to me and told me that a lady wished to have Dr Dodd's picture in a bracelet and asked me for a motto. I said I could think of no better than *Currat Lex:** I was very willing to have him pardoned, that is, to have the sentence changed to transportation: but, when he was once hanged, I did not wish he should be made a saint.'

Boswell records that here Mrs Burney, wife of his friend Dr Burney, came in and that Johnson seemed to be entertained with her conversation. She, we may care to recall, was not the first Mrs Burney, mother of Fanny, James and the others, but, at the time of Eugene Aram's arrest, had been Mrs Stephen Allen, a wine-merchant's wife in King's Lynn. Johnson admired *Evelina.* James had done well in the Navy.

At that moment, the engraver, William Wynne Ryland, was in hiding, under an assumed name, at Stepney, where he claimed he had gone, as an invalid, for the country air. Though he is mentioned in Mrs Thrale's autobiography, it does not appear that Dr Johnson knew him. A younger man, William Blake, never much given to reading newspapers but just then somewhat in blue-stocking society, acquainted with the Mrs Montagu whom Johnson so esteemed and with so busy a gossip as 'Nollekens' Smith, may have been startled to learn how near his prophecy of twelve years ago was to fulfilment. For, at fourteen, Blake

* Let the law take its course.

had been taken by his father to Ryland's studio as a possible apprentice and, as they left, had said: 'Father, I do not like the man's face. It looks as if he will live to be hanged.' For on the Monday of Holy Week, an advertisement had appeared in the newspapers offering a reward for Ryland's apprehension on charges of counterfeiting two bills of exchange for £7,114 with intent to defraud the United East India Company.

The reward was claimed by his landlady, a cobbler's wife, when Mrs Ryland took one of her husband's shoes down to be mended and the cobbler spotted the name 'Ryland' inside.

> When the officers of justice went to apprehend Ryland, they found him in a corner of the room on his knees and heard a noise like a guggling in his throat, which was occasioned by his having cut it. He had a razor in his hand, and a basin stood before him.

Though it did not prove fatal, the wound delayed his trial, which came on in late July. He was convicted on expert evidence, that of a paper manufacturer, Mr Waterman of Maidstone. The forgery itself was so perfect that only a highly skilled engraver could have done it. It had been done on paper made later than the date shown.

After sentence, Ryland was allowed a month to complete a set of plates for the benefit of his wife and children (a rich man, he had contracted gambling debts). He was executed on Friday, August 29th, in a thunderstorm. It is said, no less by Blake's biographer, Alexander Gilchrist, than by Knapp & Baldwin, that he was the last man to be hanged at Tyburn, but it appears that this was not quite so, Bleackley having established that one Richard Austin was executed there on November 7th.

In June the following year, Boswell exposed himself to the shocking sight of fifteen men executed before the debtors' door at Newgate and went straight round to Johnson's to proclaim his view that human life could not be machinery, since it contained so many instances of the wickedness and misery which just then clouded his mind. Broadly, Johnson agreed. He also said that unhappy convicts might do better to be attended by a Methodist preacher or a Popish priest than one of the regular clergy, a view which Methodists were to be heard quoting with triumph after the publication of Boswell's *Life*.

Mrs Dodd died the following month, Johnson five months later. If we care for such coincidences, we may therefore note that what is agreed to have been an age in literary history ended very little more than a year after the close of the far longer age of Tyburn.

XII

A Change of Century

ANDREW KIPPIS, LL.D., F.R.S., was classical and philological tutor at the nonconformist academies of Hoxton and Hackney. At the former, his most fervent and brilliant pupil was William Godwin, who in 1778 became minister of a congregation at Ware in Hertfordshire.

That year, Kippis published the first two volumes of his *Bibliographia Britannica*. Among the important erudite, he included Eugene Aram. This inclusion of a convicted murderer was warmly attacked in *The Gentleman's Magazine*, ignorant or careless of the fact (or just possibly because it was not a fact) that 'John Atkinson' had been, as Dr Kippis was, one of its contributors. Kippis as warmly replied.

In *The Newgate Calendar*, Aram's was simply one name among the first six hundred. It was Kippis who ensured that he would be remembered.

Also that year, that the Yorkshire scholiast might share immortality of another kind with Jonathan Wild and two others was made possible, in the first place, by a young physician of Knaresborough's response to the news that gibbets standing on it would be removed when the whole of Knaresborough Forest, along with other common lands, was enclosed. Inspired no doubt by the great example of Hunter, Dr Hutchinson had started his own little museum of anatomical specimens and already possessed the skull of Adam de Thirsk, last abbot of Fountains, hanged for his refusal to acknowledge the ecclesiastical supremacy of Henry VIII. One night, accompanied by his nephew, a boy called Effingham Wilson, Dr Hutchinson took out a ladder, set it up against the gibbet off the Plompton road and succeeded in detaching, if not the entire skull, the cranium from the rusted iron, in the process sawing off the tip of one of the sharp mastoid processes.

It was an unusually small cranium for a man. Exposed to nineteen winters, it needed no maceration. For some reason, Dr Hutchinson caused a local craftsman, one Pickard, to saw it in two along the median line and join it with two neat hinges. When the gibbet itself came down, the great, studded upright was purchased by a joiner for use as a baulk or beam in building a new inn, the Windmill.

Mrs Aram, we may care to note, had been dead these four years. Richard Houseman had died the year before. This dreadful scoundrel had more than once tried to hang himself and been cut down by his stepdaughter. He died still so shunned by the townsfolk that, in case it should be torn in pieces, his body was secretly conveyed for burial to Marton in Cleveland, the birthplace of Captain Cook, then in Tahiti.

On July 27th, 1784, from Saville Row, another learned gentleman wrote to Bishop Percy, of the *Reliques*, to say that a woman had called on him to offer some MSS of Eugene Aram's *Celtic Dictionary*. She had given him to understand that these had once been in the bishop's hands, and he supposes that they would have remained there had his lordship thought them of any value. It is likely enough that the woman was Sally Aram, who had married an innkeeper in London and of whom no more is heard.

Two others of Aram's children were then still alive and not at all ready to die. Joseph Aram, a saddler and Methodist lay preacher, lived at Hammerton on the road between Knaresborough and York, himself father of a son, Matthias, and two daughters. Elizabeth Aram lived at Northallerton, wife of a tramp currier called York.

At college, William Godwin had been a Sandemanian, more Calvinist than either his teachers or his parents. In his second ministry, however, at Stowmarket in Suffolk, he read the French *philosophes* and came to describe John Glas, Sandeman's Scottish father-in-law and founder of the sect, satirically, as 'a celebrated north-country apostle who, after Calvin had damned ninety-nine in a hundred of mankind, . . . contrived a scheme for damning ninety-nine in a hundred of the followers of Calvin'. Godwin left his third ministry, at Beaconsfield in Buckinghamshire, and settled in London to save the world by his pen, sponsored by Dr Kippis but gradually dropping the part of a clergyman and enunciating such principles as that God Himself had no right to be a tyrant.

The French followed the American revolution and roused Utopian enthusiasm in England, but soon turned to horror. Adopting our jury system, the French reserved their principal enthusiasm for Dr Guillotin's improved decapitator. While the heads fell and the hags knitted, Godwin wrote and published his *Enquiry concerning the Principles of Political Justice and its Influence on General Virtue and Happiness*, so becoming a founding father both of anarchism and of English romanticism, for not only Shelley later but, for a while, even Wordsworth sat, figuratively, at his feet, while Coleridge and Southey dreamed of an ideal community on the Susquehanna.

The *Enquiry* appeared in February 1793, the month in which, very shortly after the execution of Louis XVI, Britain declared war on France. That year, at Hackney theological college, a new pupil of the aging Dr Kippis was William Hazlitt, the son of Unitarian parents, who had spent three years of his boyhood in America. It may be supposed to have been at Hackney and because of Kippis that Hazlitt, like Godwin at Hoxton, first became aware of the learned murderer, Eugene Aram, in whom both retained an interest.

A marked divergence between Calendars is that Knapp & Baldwin omit the English treason trials of the following year, to which Jackson devotes a hundred and sixteen pages, with twenty more to a Scottish case of that same autumn and rather less to an Irish case the following year, both of which Knapp & Baldwin do cover. Almost ninety pages of Jackson are devoted to the case of Thomas Hardy, which came to trial on October 28th (at, our more leisurely lawyers may care to note, eight o'clock in the morning). That of John Horne, known as Horne Tooke (he had adopted the name of a benefactor), followed on November 17th and that of John Thelwall on December 1st. All three were found not guilty. These were not the only members of the Constitutional Society put on trial at the time, before Lord Chief Justice Eyre, sitting with four commissioners.

Godwin was closely interested in these trials. He was himself considered for indictment (the suggestion was rejected in the privy council by Pitt, on the ground that *Political Justice* cost three guineas and could thus do little harm among those who had not three shillings to spare), and he designedly affected the proceedings by publishing anonymous *Remarks on Judge Eyre's Charge to the Jury*, presumably in the case of Thomas Hardy. Hazlitt records that Horne Tooke later kissed Godwin's hand at dinner, saying that it was the hand which had saved his life. Horne Tooke was noted for his wit. His life had been saved, like Hardy's earlier, by a jury directed by Judge Eyre.

That year also, Godwin published a novel, *Things As They Are, or the Adventures of Caleb Williams*. It tells, in the first person, the story of a young man, the orphaned son of poor parents who have nevertheless contrived to give him some education, discovering that his employer and benefactor once committed a murder. He is imprisoned on a false charge and, escaping, pursued by the agents of this former employer and benefactor, until the two finally come face to face again. The employer and benefactor, Mr Falkland, dies in consequence of this confrontation, and Caleb is overwhelmed by a sense of guilt, feeling that he is himself a murderer.

To summarise it thus can give little idea of the sombre power of a book which some critics place among the great English novels, but which seems not to be widely known, even although one of the paperback companies reprinted it less than ten years ago. It is variously interpreted, in terms alike of political justice and of residual Calvinist theology. It is seen also as a precursor of such moderns as Franz Kafka. Its interest for us here must be confined to what Godwin was to say, almost forty years later, in the preface to a reprint, about what he does not precisely admit as sources but lists as books he was reading of set purpose while he wrote one or another of the three parts of his novel. Three such books seem to concern us.

> I turned over the pages of a tremendous compilation, entitled *God's Revenge against Murder*, where the beam of the eye of Omniscience was represented as perpetually pursuing the guilty, and laying open his most hidden retreats to the light of day. I was extremely conversant with the *Newgate Calendar* and the *Lives of the Pirates*.

A more minute scholar than I will have to answer the question whether *God's Revenge against Murder* could be the compilation revised by Henry Fielding, to which he added the names of Mary Blandy and Elizabeth Jeffries. *Lives of the Pirates* was no doubt Captain Charles Johnson's 1734 compilation, regarded as one of the Newgate Calendar family and dealing also with criminals other than pirates. The *Newgate Calendar* in question can hardly have been other than the original five volumes which take us up to February 1779, with the conviction of an Irishman for practising extortion by threatening to accuse Charles Fielding, a son under age of Lord Denbigh, of an unnatural crime. We ought, however, to bear in mind the fact that, by the time Godwin wrote his preface, Jackson, Wilkinson, and Knapp & Baldwin would all have appeared, as well as the compilation under a different title attributed to George Borrow, so that *The Newgate Calendar* had already come to mean almost anything in that field.

What I should have liked to determine is whether, with *Caleb Williams*, William Godwin could be said to have been the first of those whom, after Thackeray, we call 'the Newgate novelists'. To determine this formed no small part of what led me to my first *Newgate Calendar*, the 1932 abstract of Knapp & Baldwin. Among the two hundred cases in this thousand-page omnibus volume, I could find none which might have been thought to provide the plot of Godwin's novel or even of the sub-plot of the Hawkins father and son whom Falkland had allowed to be hanged for the murder committed by himself. I did feel, however, that the case of Dr Johnson's friend, Joseph Baretti, might have suggested elements of the personality and past history of Falkland.

Falkland is represented as having spent some years in Italy. And why not? It was a country unknown to Godwin, but he might well find in what he had read about it an explanation of the not-quite-English sense of honour and instinct for revenge which characterise a man otherwise distinguished from our native squirearchy only by his addiction to learning and the company of men of letters, unless it were also by the fact that he was of small stature, a fact inessential to his character as portrayed elsewhere by Godwin, but relevant to the murder, an act of compulsive revenge upon a big oaf, also a member of the squirearchy, who had knocked Falkland down in a public place. The totally unexplained thing about Falkland is that, long before he went to Italy, his parents had blessed him with an Italian Christian name, 'Ferdinando'. It was, I presently noted, the Christian name of the only other Italian whose case figures in the unabridged Calendars. This was Paleotti, a *marchese* of unattractive disposition, brother-in-law of the late duke of Shrewsbury, who was, however, hanged at Tyburn as a common malefactor in 1718 for running his manservant through when the latter, having suffered previous rebuffs, declined to go out attempting to borrow further money on behalf of his master.

These are trifling points, but they are all that I can discover in the way of specific debts contracted by Godwin in *Caleb Williams* to the *Newgate Calendar* with which he was to describe himself as 'extremely familiar'. In a more general way, he no doubt picked up from it some of his prison detail, while the gang of thieves into whose hands Caleb first falls after his escape may remind us of the Hampshire smugglers. This is not much. It is not enough to make Godwin one of the Newgate novelists.

He might have become their leader if he had carried out a plan he apparently nurtured for many years. This was to base a novel on the case of Eugene Aram. The fact was not to transpire until a lesser writer had done just that, after taking his turn at Godwin's feet.

Although the English treason trials that year resulted in no capital convictions, the Calendars record a more than average number of hangings in 1794. All the murder cases were, however, tried at county assizes, in Dorchester, Winchester, Bury St Edmunds, Portsea, York and Gloucester. Four were of murderesses. These were Elizabeth Marsh, a girl of fifteen, who battered her grandfather to death while he was alseep and who declared that, until since her confinement, she had been wholly unacquainted with the difference between good and evil; Anne Scalberd, who put arsenic into her mother-in-law's milk; and two Hannahs, Limbrick and Webley, who battered young children to death, in the one case a stepdaughter, in the other her own bastard child, in a manner still apparently common in working-class households. There were hangings for robbery at Salisbury and Radnor, and, of those on the drop before the debtors' door at the new Newgate, one was a forger, a native of Glasgow, another, on the same day, a letter-sorter at the General Post Office, who had stolen a Bank of England note for £15 from one of the letters passing through his hands.

A peculiar horror at the beginning of the next year was the rape at a house in Great Portland Street of a Scottish girl aged seven by an Irishman, who into the bargain infected the child with venereal disease. At the level of literacy, three forgers were executed that year, one of these at Bristol, while another was saved by a flaw in the indictment. A Jew, charged with forgery and bearing the odd name of Isdwell Isdwell, was first sprung from Clerkenwell and then murdered by those who had effected his escape.

That year and the next, two soldiers were shot at Brighton, five sailors hanged on board the *Defiance*, for mutiny. Two Americans of colour and a Spaniard suffered at Execution Dock for piracy and murder aboard an American ship in the Channel, and 1796 also had its forgers. A parricide of the greatest literary interest that year was executed with a knife by Mary Anne Lamb, a mantua-maker aged thirty-one, who first pursued a little girl, her apprentice, around the room, and then her invalid mother calling her to desist, turned on the latter with loud shrieks and stabbed her to the heart, also gashing her father's forehead. This dreadful scene is unmentioned in any Calendar, and it seems that no case was ever brought against Mary Lamb, who was not even confined in Bedlam but allowed to remain in the care of her younger brother, Charles, a clerk in the East India House, who had published sonnets in the *Morning Post* and who had himself been briefly in an asylum after an unhappy first love affair.

In the dawn of a new literary age, a significant event before the end of the eighteenth century was the marriage of William Godwin to Mary Wollstonecraft, blue-stocking author of *A Vindication of the Rights of Women*. Another, a purely literary matter, was the publication of *Lyrical Ballads* by Samuel Taylor Coleridge and William Wordsworth. When, by most people's reckoning, the century turned, Wordsworth had gone to live in the Lake District, where a few months later Coleridge joined him, living near Keswick. There, two summers later, he was visited by his friend since their schooldays, Charles Lamb, and Lamb's sister Mary, whose nervous troubles were for the moment over.

In London, the following winter, the Lambs made the acquaintance of Captain James Burney, a naval officer retired from active service, who, between hands of whist, was writing the first volume of a *History of the Discoveries in the South Sea*. Twenty-four years previously, he had seen Captain James Cook hacked to death by savages on the beach in Hawaii and afterwards, a young lieutenant, had sailed *Discovery* home. Forty-five years ago, a boy of eight, he had seen Eugene Aram arrested or, at least, had been a pupil of Aram's at the school in King's Lynn where the arrest took place.

Neither of these stories would seem particularly suitable for Mary Lamb's ears, and, while the first might be a matter of public repute, we do not even know that Captain Burney then thought the second worth telling, unless it arose in conversation with the unhappy William Godwin, only nine years before so famous, remarried and setting up as a bookseller. If we think it worth noting, it is here we should note the death, at Hammerton on the York road from Knaresborough, a few weeks before the first meeting of the Lambs and those particular Burneys, of Joseph Aram, the saddler and Methodist lay preacher. His son, Matthias, his widow and two daughters shortly thereafter emigrated to America, where it is possible there are Aram descendants.

Another who might have been interested in the story was young William Hazlitt, also a dissenter, who seemed unable to make up his mind what to interest himself in, but who, the following year, was painting Charles Lamb's portrait as a Venetian senator. The year after that, we may note that the last of the Aram children died, again in January, Elizabeth, not of the cold but of cancer, in the workhouse at Northallerton.

XIII

The Bride of Buttermere

THE CHAR is a hill trout. At the sign of the Char in Buttermere, the beauty of the landlord's daughter, Mary Robinson, had been noted by a traveller, Joseph Budworth, when she was only fourteen and put by him in a successful book, *A Fortnight's Ramble to the Lakes in Westmorland, Lancashire and Cumberland.* The poor little pot-house became a tourist resort. Poems were written on its whitewashed walls, and artists drew the girl's portrait.

She must have been twenty-two before Coleridge and Wordsworth, as the latter puts it in Book VII of *The Prelude*, first

> Beheld her serving at the cottage inn;
> Both stricken, as she entered or withdrew,
> With admiration of her modest mien
> And carriage, marked by unexampled grace.

She was twenty-four when Colonel the Hon. Alexander Augustus Hope, M.P. for Linlithgowshire, came to stay at the Queen's Head in Keswick. He was a splendid-looking man in his early forties, fresh-complexioned, black-browed but fair-haired, dressed with a fashionable simplicity, tall, strongly built, full of wit and energy, courtly in his manners. He was, into the bargain, own brother to the Earl of Hopetown. He was fond of fishing for char and, to indulge this pastime, would ride as far as the lake of Buttermere, nine miles away.

Also staying in Keswick were Colonel Moore, who had been member for Strabane while there was still an Irish parliament, and his ward, a young lady of fortune. A Mr Crump, a Liverpool merchant residing at Grasmere, presented with a boy child, called it Augustus Hope Crump after Colonel Hope, but presumably had no marriageable daughter at the moment. Colonel Hope proposed marriage to Colonel Moore's ward and was accepted. On the 1st of October, from Buttermere, the former sent a letter by hand to the latter, saying that business called him to Scotland and requesting the guardian of his betrothed to cash the enclosed draft for £30, drawn on Mr Crump. Colonel Moore did so and sent back a further £10 for the expenses of the journey.

Next day, Colonel Hope indeed left for Scotland, but took with him the fair maid of Buttermere, to whom he had been secretly married that morning by the Rev. John Nicholson at Loweswater. With the news of this romantic elopement, other rumours began to circulate in the neighbourhood. That this was so was communicated by Mr Nicholson to Colonel Hope. It did not at once come to the ears of Coleridge, whose article 'A Romantic Marriage' appeared in the *Morning Post* for October 11th. The poet and metaphysician had in fact found Colonel Hope's grammar faulty and thought him rather common.

Next day, Colonel Hope returned with his bride to Buttermere. The day after that, he went into Keswick with the Rev. Mr Nicholson and called at the Queen's Head. There, he was invited to the room of a new tourist, Mr Harding, a barrister and, in his own district, a justice of the peace. He knew the member for Linlithgowshire and accused our Colonel Hope of being an impostor.

It might have been thought that the correct procedure was for a local magistrate to order his arrest on Mr Harding's evidence. It appears, however, that, Colonel Moore and the postmaster being at hand to give evidence that the supposed Colonel Hope had franked letters under that name, using a parliamentary privilege, Mr Harding procured a warrant from a local magistrate and gave the impostor into the charge of a constable.

Together with most of the common folk, the constable was still deluded by the false Hope and allowed him to go fishing on the lake while dinner was preparing at the Queen's Head. A boatman rowed him across Derwentwater into the gathering darkness, and Keswick saw him no more. That, at any rate, is what Bleackley makes of the muddle. It does not consound at all points with the Calendars.

The man's real name was John Hatfield or Hadfield. He had been married once to an illegitimate daughter of Lord Robert Manners and was currently married in Devonshire. He was an absconding bankrupt, and the draft on Crump had been forged.

Coleridge wrote two further articles for the *Morning Post* under the title 'The Fraudulent Marriage'. The false Colonel Hope evaded capture for two months, but was eventually taken by Bow Street officers near Swansea, lodged for a fortnight in Brecon gaol and taken to London.

It became known that the fair maid of Buttermere was expecting a child and that her parents were in poverty, the impostor having obtained their savings. Money was collected for them. Ballads were sung about the fair maid, and in April 1803 a burletta called *Edwin and Susan*, based on her story, was played at Sadler's Wells. Wordsworth saw it on a visit to London:

> . . . too serious theme for that light place—
> I mean, O distant Friend! a story drawn
> From our own ground,—the Maid of Buttermere,—
> And how, unfaithful to a virtuous wife
> Deserted and deceived, the Spoiler came
> And wooed the artless daughter of the hills,
> And wedded her, in cruel mockery
> Of love and marriage bonds. These words to thee
> Must needs bring back the moment when we first,
> Ere the broad world rang with the maiden's name,
> Beheld her. . . .

Hadfield was still in Newgate. Committed for trial at Carlisle, he did not reach that town until May 25th, nor was arraigned till August 15th, before Sir Alexander Thompson. He was defended by Holroyd, whom also we shall meet again as a judge, and James Scarlett, afterwards Lord Abinger, appeared for the Crown. Convicted that day, the false Colonel Hope was sentenced the next. Wordsworth and Coleridge were in Carlisle and sought an interview with him. He received Wordsworth, but refused to see Coleridge. He was hanged on September 3rd, a Saturday.

Mary Robinson's child, born in June, had not lived.

> We since that time not unfamiliarly
> Have seen her—her discretion have observed,
> Her just opinions, delicate reserve,
> Her patience, and humility of mind
> Unspoiled by commendation and the excess
> Of public notice—an offensive light
> To a meek spirit suffering inwardly.
>
> . . . She lives in peace
> Upon the spot where she was born and reared;
> Without contamination doth she live
> In quietness, without anxiety:
> Beside the mountain chapel, sleeps in earth
> Her new-born infant, fearless as a lamb
> That, thither driven from some unsheltered place,
> Rests underneath the little rock-like pile
> When storms are raging. Happy are they both—
> Mother and child!

Five years later, she was properly married and became Mrs Richard Harrison, wife of a small landowner (a Cumberland 'statesman'), to whom she was to bear seven children, of which five lived. Married, she did not at first leave her parents' house and was probably still there when, the following year, Thomas De Quincey returned to Grasmere, a young man of twenty-four who wrestled more successfully than Coleridge with the opium habit.

In the course of a life long and comfortable enough to have allowed him to write far more than he did, De Quincey was to touch on a fair number of murder cases. News of the one which lodged most effectively in his memory reached Dove Cottage,

Grasmere, a little over two years after his settling there. The scene of the crime was the Ratcliffe Highway, never a law-abiding neighbourhood, in dockland, north of the Thames, east of London Bridge and the Tower. What remains of it is now simply The Highway. The date was December 7th, 1811. The Knapp & Baldwin account* cannot much differ from those which first reached the Lakes.

> On a dark evening, . . . about the time when tradesmen are shutting up their shops, Mr Marr, a respectable draper, sent his servant-maid to purchase some oysters for the family supper. Mr Marr was in the act of placing goods, which had been exposed to the view of customers on the counter, upon their shelves. The girl left the shop door a-jar, expecting to return in a very few minutes; but unfortunately the nearest place of sale for oysters had disposed of the whole, and she therefore went further on her errand. Meantime two or more ruffians entered the shop [and] shut the door. . . .
>
> . . . The girl returned with the oysters, and finding the shop door shut, rang the bell; but no person answered. At this instant a watchman, passing on his round, asked what she did there; and he pulled the bell with violence, which so much alarmed the villains that they made a precipitate retreat through a window of the back part of the house, across some mud and along an intricate way which no one that had not previously reconnoitered the situation could have readily found.
>
> The watchman, finding the bell still unanswered, went to the next door neighbour and gave an alarm. Some three or four men collecting together, it was determined to scale the wall which divided Mr Marr's back premises from those of the adjoining house. This was done without much loss of time, and there was presented one of the most woeful scenes that ever disgraced human nature. The body of Mr Marr and his shop-boy, the latter of whom appeared, from evident marks, to have struggled with the assassins, near each other; that of Mrs Marr in the passage and the infant in its cradle, all dead, but yet warm and weltering in their blood. The horrible scene for a moment petrified those who first entered, and they naturally feared the murderers might still be in the house, plundering the property therein. They opened the street door and called out an alarm of 'Murder!' which spread with such rapidity that the neighbourhood was very soon in an alarm. The nightly watch mustered

* That in Jackson is longer and more circumstantial.

> and the drum [beat the melancholy call] to arms—in fine, though now near midnight, so great a crowd assembled that it was necessary to shut the doors, while some one explained the cause of the alarm to those in the street.

Twelve days later, a massacre on a comparable scale took place at another house in the neighbourhood, clearly, it was felt, the work of the same men. Several were arrested on suspicion, and it was at the examination of one of these that another first spoke of knocking at a door, the door, in fact, of the inn, the Pear Tree, at which both lodged, not that of the scene of either crime. De Quincey's mind seems to have run the two suggestions together. (He would later insist that, as, unlike those of other cities, all London doors had both bells and knockers, there must also have been knocking at the Marrs' door.) It reminded him of the knocking at the gate in *Macbeth*, so eloquently soliloquised on by a drunken porter shortly before the murder of Duncan is discovered.

Coleridge was in London at the time. When they next met, De Quincey asked him about the alarm verging on panic which the massacres were said to have spread throughout the metropolis. Coleridge said that he had not been alarmed.

In the end, one man, a ginger-whiskered Irish seaman called John Williams, was thought by everyone, including De Quincey, to have single-handed committed all the murders. To this belief he gave colour by hanging himself in Coldbath Fields prison. There was, in consequence, no trial. Williams had cheated the gallows, the judiciary and the public. A splendid procession was organised, however. Taking part in it were several hundred constables, with their staves, clearing the way; the newly formed mounted patrol, with drawn cutlasses; another body of constables; the parish officers of St George's, St Paul's and Shadwell, on horseback; peace officers on horseback; more constables; the high constable of the county of Middlesex, on horseback; the body of Williams extended at full length on an inclined platform, erected on a cart, about four feet high at the head and gradually sloping towards the horse, giving a full view of the body, which was dressed in blue trousers and a white and blue striped waistcoat, the fatal maul and ripping-chisel with which the murders were understood to have been perpetrated exposed to view, respectively to the left and right of the head; and a strong body of constables bringing up the rear. Though with less practice, the county of Middlesex, it was clear, could, when it chose, do things in as much style as the city of London or the royal and parliamentary precincts of Westminster.

> . . . The countenance of Williams was ghastly in the extreme, and the whole had an appearance too horrible for description.
>
> The procession advanced slowly up Ratcliffe Highway, accompanied by an immense concourse of persons eager to get a sight of the murderer's remains. When the cart came opposite to the late Mr Marr's house, a halt was made for near a quarter of an hour. The procession then moved down Old Gravel Lane, along Wapping, up New Crane Lane and into New Gravel Lane. When the platform arrived at Mr Williamson's late house, a second halt took place. It then proceeded up the hill and again entered Ratcliffe Highway, down which it moved into Cannon Street and advanced to St George's turnpike, where the New Road is intersected by Cannon Street. There, a grave about six feet had been prepared, over which the main water-pipe runs. Between twelve and one o'clock, the body was taken from the platform and lowered into the grave, immediately after which a stake was driven through it; and, the pit being covered, this solemn ceremony concluded.

A nice surprise, one imagines, for some gang of navvies within the past hundred and fifty years.

That Williams was guilty at all has recently been questioned. Also in question is whether he committed suicide or was murdered in prison by some, his accomplices or not, who feared that on trial he might bring out the truth.

XIV

King Ludd

GEORGE III had betrayed symptoms of insanity twenty-three and even forty-six years before. In 1811, he retired to permanent seclusion, mad and blind. We had thus entered the period of nine years' Regency. We had entered the age of gaslight four years previously, in Pall Mall if not yet in Ratcliffe Highway. The Gas Light & Coke Co. was incorporated in 1812.

In March of that year, *The Examiner* printed a poem ('The Triumph of the Whale') by Charles Lamb, in which 'the Regent of the Sea' or 'Prince of Whales' is portrayed not only as hugely fat and having 'oily qualities' but as a drunkard, a lecher, avoided by 'every fish of generous kind' and treacherous to sailors, but surrounded by crooked dolphins, doglike seals, sharks and miscellaneous flat fish. This unusual act of political aggression in verse passed officially unnoticed, though when Leigh Hunt, in the next issue of *The Examiner*, spelled out its charges in prose, it was to result in him spending two years in prison.

Some sailors had been treacherous to the Prince Regent or to his father. Two, of a saddeningly large number, former prisoners of the French, were hanged that month for having accepted an offer of release if they took up arms against their countrymen. It was, in general, a year of naval triumph. That Britain ruled the waves had become true.

The industrial revolution was meeting with opposition. First appearing in Nottinghamshire, the Luddites were dedicated to the destruction of machine looms. They operated in masked bands at night. They had a General, known as King Ludd or as Ned Ludd, who may have been mythical or may have been a real man, and, in so far as a whole class of individuals ever has, they had real grievances.

For the most part, they were content with rioting, the destruction of property and a bit of theft. Things came to a worse pass, however, in a neighbourhood, to the south-west of Huddersfield and a little way up the Colne valley, once familiar to the present writer. On the night of April 11th, a large number of men assembled in a field and, formed in lines of ten each, marched off to attack the mill of Mr William Cartwright, at Rawfords. There was a musket company, a pistol company and a hatchet company. The musket company was led by George Mellor, of Longroyd Bridge, a Colne crossing long within the bounds of Huddersfield.

> Mr C., being apprehensive of an attack being made upon his mill, procured the assistance of five soldiers, and retired to rest about twelve o'clock, and soon afterwards heard the barking of a dog. Mr C. arose; and, while opening the door, heard a breaking of windows, and also a firing in the upper and lower windows, and a violent hammering at the door. Mr C. and his men flew to their arms; a bell, placed at the top of the mill for the purpose of alarming the neighbours, being rung by one of his men, the persons inside the mill discharged their pieces from loop-holes. The fire was returned regularly on both sides. . . . The attack continued about twenty minutes. The fire slackened from without; and they heard the cries of the wounded. The men that were wounded were taken care of. They afterwards died.

Their number did not include Mellor.

He was to be quoted as saying:

'There's no way to break the shears but shoot the master.'

It appears that his desire for revenge was not specifically directed at Mr Cartwright of Rawfolds but could be satisfied by the death of any millowner. On April 28th, Huddersfield market was attended by William Horsfall, who owned a mill at Marsden, four or five miles up the Colne valley, along the Manchester road.

Horsfall stopped at an inn called Warren House in Crosland Moor. That might well be where the Griffin inn stood later, as the plantation to which he came a quarter of a mile farther on may well have been what was still a plantation in the author's boyhood, hacked down and built up with council houses (but of local stone, which made them seem less awful) in the early 'twenties. If this is so, then it seems likely that Horsfall meant to ride to Marsden not along the Manchester road but over the moors by way of Blackmoorfoot. To reach the nearest point in Crosland Moor, he would have to ride past Longroyd Bridge, where, it may be remembered, Mellor lived.

The landlord at Warren House was John Armitage. (Fifty years ago, the neighbourhood was still full of Mellors, Cartwrights, Horsfalls and Armitages.) Nine months later, he would testify at York that

> Mr Horsfall had . . . called at witness's house about a quarter past six in the evening, and got a glass of rum and water, treated two persons who were there, paid his reckoning, and rode away. Did not stop twenty minutes at witness's; nor did he get off his horse.

Another witness, Benjamin Walker, an accomplice, would state that Mellor, who had a loaded pistol, had told him and two others, William Thorp and Thomas Smith, to go with him to shoot Mr Horsfall.

> . . . Witness heard Mellor say Mr Horsfall was coming, and soon after heard the report of a pistol; they waited at a short distance till the job was done.

I shuffle various fragments of other evidence into a consecutive narrative, first that of Henry Parr, who

> was upon the road between Huddersfield and Marsden; and, after he had passed the Warren House, heard the report of firearms. Saw a person riding before him. Report seemed to come from . . . plantation—saw smoke arising at the same time, and four persons were in the plantation in dark-coloured clothes. The person who was before witness on horseback, after the report, fell down on the horse's chine, and the horse turned round as quick as possible. Mr Horsfall raised himself by the

> horse's mane, and called, 'Murder!' As soon as he called out murder, one of the four men got on the wall with one hand and two feet, . . . and he (Parr) set off to Mr Horsfall at full gallop. Mr H. said, 'Good man, you are a stranger to me; I'm shot.' Mr Horsfall grew sick, and blood began to flow from his side. Mr H. desired witness to go to Mrs Horsfall's.
>
> About seven o'clock, [John Armitage] heard that Mr Horsfall had been shot. Witness and the two persons whom the deceased had been treating went out together, and found Mr Horsfall about twenty or thirty yards below the plantation, sitting on the roadside, bleeding very much. They got him down to Warren House as soon as they could. Mr Horsfall died there.
>
> Mr Horton, surgeon, . . . extracted a ball from the deceased, and found several wounds in his body, and had no doubt they were the cause of his death.

This evidence was to be heard in court at York a little over eight months later, a series of cases against Luddites being held by special commission from the 5th to the 12th of January, 1813, before Sir Alexander Thompson, who had tried the false Colonel Hope at Carlisle almost ten years before. Of the four in the plantation, three, Mellor, Thorp and Smith, stood in the dock, Walker having been admitted Crown evidence.

The three were hanged on Friday, the 8th, behind York Castle. Every precaution had been taken to render a rescue impracticable. Two troops of cavalry were drawn up near the front of the platform, and the avenues of the castle were guarded by infantry. Fifteen more were hanged, in two batches, one in the morning, one in the afternoon, on Saturday the 16th, four for the attack on Cartwright's mill, the rest for burglary and theft. None of those found guilty of administering an unlawful oath received a capital sentence. Six men were to be transported for seven years. Sixteen were discharged on bail and sixteen more without bail.

A fortnight after the murder of Horsfall, there had taken place the 'assassination' (the term has no place in English law, and words cognate with it mean simply murder in other languages) in the House of Commons of the first Regency prime minister, Spencer Perceval, by a madman, who was nevertheless hanged. For three years after the York trials, industrial action of the Luddite type ceased.

During those three years, murderers in the private sector were hanged, and so were pirates, river pirates, forgers and, at Cambridge, a punter for nobbling racehorses, twice with fatal effect. The Hunterian collection of anatomical specimens was opened to the public at the new home of the Royal College of Surgeons of England in Lincoln's Inn Fields. The battle of Waterloo brought the Napoleonic wars to an end.

Police corruption was discovered both in the city of London and in Middlesex. Men were found to have been hanged on evidence manufactured to obtain rewards, much in the old style of Charles Hitchin and Jonathan Wild. Three Irishmen, convicted of theft but seen to have been led astray by *agents provocateurs*, were pardoned and sent home with money, with which they bought small farms. Of two Elizabeths hanged for poisoning, it seems probable that one was innocent. The crowd thought so. Luckily this time without fatal effect, the violence inherent in a literary family was again betrayed when John Lamb, elder brother of Charles and Mary, knocked Hazlitt down in a dispute over colour in Holbein and Vandyke.

It is usual to attribute the disorders of the years which followed to unemployment among discharged soldiers. A discharged soldier, Jeremiah Brandreth, certainly headed a recrudescence of activities, partly of Luddite type, which again spread north from Nottingham.

On December 2nd, 1816, London saw tumult on a larger scale than any since the Gordon riots, thirty-six years before. A figure vocally prominent that Monday was Henry ('Orator') Hunt (no relation to Leigh Hunt), a rich agitator, as popular champion of an ill-defined Liberty something of a successor to Wilkes and rival to Cobbett. A voice from the recent grave much heard was that of Thomas Spence, advocate of land nationalisation. The active rioting was conducted by two James Watsons, father and son, both medical men, Arthur Thistlewood, Preston, Hooper, all convinced Spenceans but great fools, and an *agent provocateur*, John Castles, a petty criminal professing revolutionary principles.

The day's principal activity was raiding gunsmith's shops. At one of these, in Snow Hill, young Watson, who had earlier stood on a wall to address indifferent soldiery in the Tower, discharged a pistol and wounded a customer who had tried to restrain him, the day's only serious casualty. An Irish sailor was hanged in March the following year for his conspicuously enthusiastic part in the looting. In June, the Watsons, Thistlewood, Preston and Hooper were tried for high treason, Castles appearing in evidence against them, Orator Hunt to discredit Castles's evidence. The five were acquitted. That is the last we hear of the Watsons or, indeed, of Preston and Hooper.

The following year, Thistlewood challenged the home secretary, Lord Sidmouth, to a duel. For this he received a year's prison sentence. He was released in May 1819, but does not appear to have accompanied Hunt to Manchester in August, when the latter's voice was heard again, contributing to the unhappy occasion known as 'Peterloo'. Hunt, on the other hand, was in prison at Ilchester when Thistlewood placed himself at the head of a conspiracy to kill all the ministers of the Crown at once.

This would become known as the Cato Street conspiracy, from the location of premises taken as a base for the operation, chosen by reason of their proximity to the house of Lord Harrowby, where a cabinet dinner was to be held on February 23rd, 1820. An *agent provocateur*, George Edwards, had again been planted among the conspirators, who might have been arrested without much trouble if Thistlewood himself had not met the first of the Bow Street patrol with a drawn sword and run him fatally through This made those with him (who, indeed, offered resistance) not only parties to a treasonable conspiracy but accessories to murder. Thistlewood and ten more were brought to trial, he and four others hanged.

The Cato Street conspiracy, like Luddite machine-breaking, the violent death of Spencer Perceval, the extraordinary behaviour of the mounted yeomanry in Manchester and the condonation of it by Westminster, has been much studied by general historians, who account variously for the remarkable extent of political agitation during the Regency. A criminal historian can only note its criminal aspects and with relief revert to crime in the private sector. The Regency itself had ended and the reign of George IV begun while the conspirators were being rounded up.

XV

Appeal of Murder and Wager of Battle

IN MAY 1817, Thistlewood, with the Watsons, Preston and Hooper, was still in prison awaiting trial for his part in the riots the previous December. Eugene Aram's cranium, together with the skull of Adam de Thirsk, was in the hands of the Lambeth phrenologist, J. K. Spurzheim, who thought it that of a woman. It belonged to a Dr Richardson of Harrogate, second husband of the widow of the adventurous Dr Hutchinson of Knaresborough, to whom he returned it with his report on the 22nd of the month.

On the 26th, in the evening, a very pretty girl, at twenty still a virgin, Mary Ashford, went dancing at an inn, the Tyburn House, a few miles out of Birmingham. By five o'clock in the morning, she was neither a virgin nor alive. A trail of blood and trampled grass led to a pond, from which her body was dragged with a rake.

A young man of exceptional strength, a bricklayer, Abraham Thornton, was arrested. He and another young man had walked Mary and her friend to the latter's home, where Mary had changed for the dance and left her ordinary clothes and whence, having changed again, she would have to walk home to her uncle's. He was reported to have said that he had been intimate with Mary's sister and would have Mary if he died for it.

A great deal of evidence was found, of kinds we do not much read about in old cases. Thornton's shoes were taken and matched with footprints on the ground, as were hers when they were found.

> These footmarks, which exhibited proofs of running and struggling, led to a spot where a distinct impression of the human figure, and a large quantity of coagulated blood, were discovered; in the same place were seen the marks of a man's knees and toes. From that spot, the blood was distinctly traced . . . towards the pit where the body was found, and it appeared plainly as if a man had walked along the footway carrying a body. . . . At the edge of the pit, her shoes, bonnet and bundle were found, but only one footstep could be seen there, and that was a man's. It was deeply impressed, and seemed to be that of a man who thrust one foot forward to heave the body he had in his arms into the pit.

Thus Knapp & Baldwin. Wilkinson is far more detailed, both about what could be deduced from marks on the ground and about other evidence, provided by Thornton's clothes and hers and by the dead body, opened up. Despite the many signs of sexual and other violence, death had been by drowning. Water and even duckweed were found in Mary Ashford's stomach. The evidence of time was bedevilled by a remarkable discrepancy between clocks, one of which was forty minutes fast.

The case was heard at Warwick on August 8th, before Sir George Holroyd (fourteen years before, leading defence counsel at the trial of John Hadfield, forger and bigamist, the false Colonel Hope). To everyone's astonishment, locally and in London, Abraham Thornton was acquitted of murder, and the Crown presented no evidence of rape.

It is what followed which was to make legal history.

> Subscriptions to defray the expense of a new prosecution were entered into. On an investigation of the circumstances, the secretary of state granted his warrant to the sheriff of Warwick to take [Thornton] into custody on an *appeal of murder*, to be prosecuted by William Ashford, the brother and heir at law of the deceased. He was accordingly lodged in Warwick gaol, until removed to London by *habeas corpus*, the proceedings on

> the writ of appeal being held in the court of King's Bench in Westminster Hall.
>
> On the 6th of November, the appellant, attended by four counsel, appeared in court, when, the counsel for Thornton stating that they had not had time to prepare for a case of such importance and novelty, the proceedings were adjourned to the 17th, on which day the prisoner, availing himself of a barbarous privilege extended to him by the antiquated and absurd law under which he stood appealed, demanded trial by *wager of battle*.

The picturesque rules for such a trial were as follows.

The appellee's right to this privilege being allowed and the judges having fixed a day and place for the combat, a piece of ground was to be set out, sixty feet square, enclosed with lists. A court was to be erected for the judges and a bar for the serjeants at law. Proclamation being made, the parties, each armed with a staff an ell long and a four-cornered leather target for defence, were to be introduced into the area (it would have been Tothill Fields) by the proper officers. The combatants would be bare-headed and barefoot, the appellee with his head shaved. He, having pleaded not guilty, would throw down his glove and declare he would defend the same by his body, the appellant, taking up the glove, that he was ready to make good the appeal, body for body. The appellee, taking the Bible in his right hand and in his left the right hand of the appellant, was then to swear thus:

> Hear this, O man whom I hold by the hand, who callest thyself [John] by the name of baptism, that I, who call myself [Thomas] by the name of baptism, did not feloniously murder [thy father, William by name], nor am in any way guilty of the said felony. So help me God and the saints; and this I will defend against thee by my body, as this court shall award.

To which the appellant should reply, holding the Bible and his antagonist's hand:

> Hear this, O man whom I hold by the hand, who callest thyself [Thomas] by the name of baptism, that thou art perjured, because that thou feloniously didst murder [my father, William by name]. So help me God and the saints; and this I will prove against thee by my body, as this court shall award.

Both were then to take an oath against sorcery and enchantment.

> Hear this, ye justices, that I have this day neither eaten nor drunk, nor have upon me neither bone, stone nor grass; nor any enchantment, sorcery or witchcraft, whereby the law of God may be abased or the law of the devil exalted. So help me God and His saints.

The battle was then to begin, and the combatants were bound to fight till the stars appeared in the evening. If the appellee were so far vanquished that he could not or would not fight any longer, he should be adjudged to be hanged immediately. But if he killed the appellant, or was able to maintain the fight from sunrise till the stars appeared in the evening, he should be acquitted. So also, if the appellant became recreant and pronounced the word 'craven' he, the appellant, should lose his *liberam legem* and become infamous, while the appellee should recover his damages and be for ever quit.

There were cases where the appellant might counterplead and oust the appellee from his trial by battle. These were vehement presumption or sufficient proof that the appeal was true or where the appellant was under fourteen or above sixty years of age or a woman, a priest, a peer or a citizen of London, because the peaceful habits of these citizens were supposed to unfit them for battle. Mary Ashford's brother was none of these, but he was physically delicate, no match for the powerful Thornton.

This latter threw down a gauntlet, with which his clever counsel, a Mr Reader, provided him. It was not picked up. At least, it was not picked up by Ashford. It was picked up by an officer of the court. It was taken into the custody of the court. That was on the 17th of November. The hearing took place before Lord Ellenborough, otherwise best known for his successful defence of Warren Hastings in the House of Lords twenty-five years before. The subscriptions had provided William Ashford with four counsel, led by a Mr Clarke.

'It would appear to me extraordinary indeed,' said Clarke, 'if the person who has murdered the sister should, as the law exists in these enlightened times, be allowed to prove his innocence by murdering the brother also.'

View of last Newgate Jail before demolition in 1904

The SURREY COUNTY GOAL, *in* Horse Monger Lane, *near Stones end*, Southwark *and the new manner of Executing Criminals thereon*.

View *of the* New SESSIONS HOUSE, Old Bailey.

John Thurtell
After a pencil sketch by William Mulready, R.A.

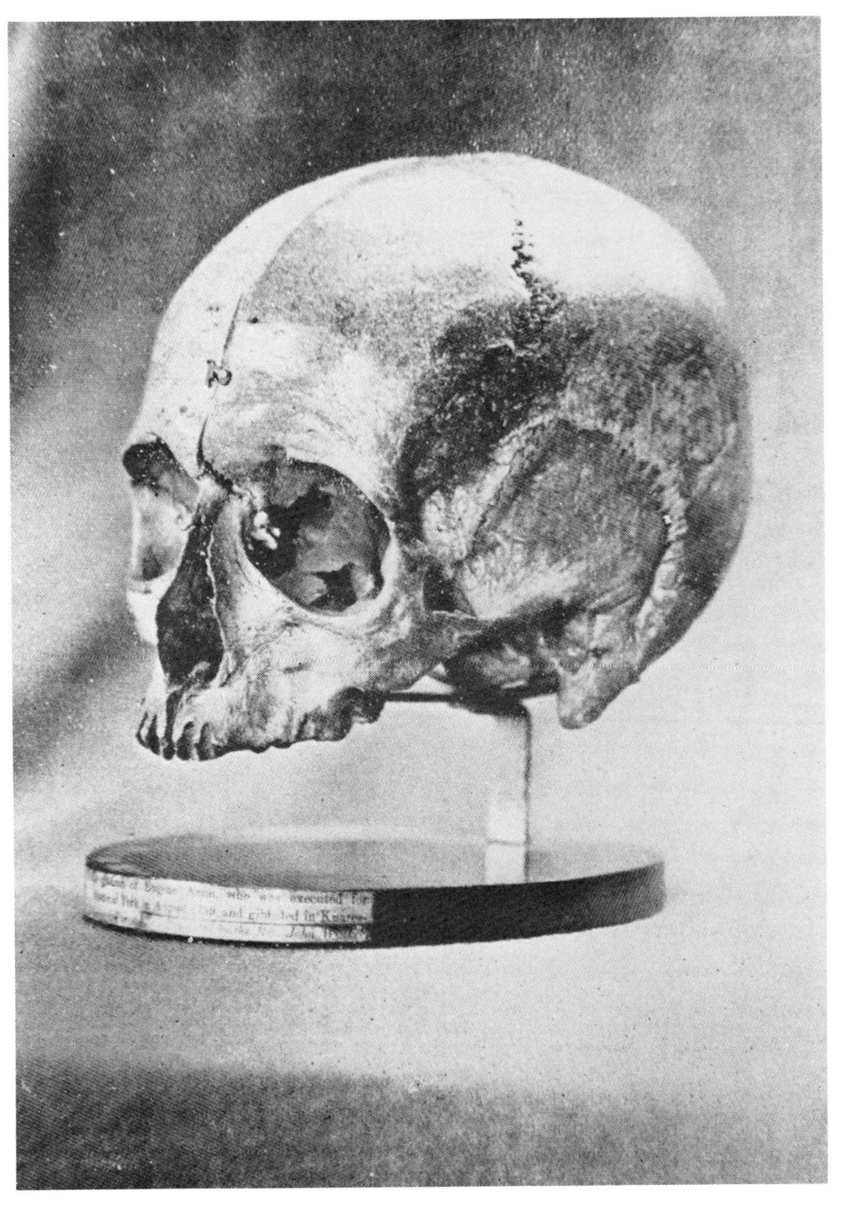

The cranium of Eugene Aram in the Royal College of Surgeons' Museum, as it was before wartime damage

H. FAUNTLEROY.

DR. DODD

Wilson Pinx.
Ryley Fecit
Miss Blandy
Now confin'd in Oxford Goal on Suspicion
of Poisoning her Father

'It is the law of England, Mr Clarke,' said Ellenborough. 'We must not call it murder.'

Further hearing of the case was postponed, at first until November 22nd, then until the 24th of January, 1818, again till the following Thursday, till February 6th, April 16th and, finally April 20th. The judges delivered their opinions *seriatim*, the substance of which was that, sitting there to administer the law, not as they wished it to be but as they found it, they considered the defendant entitled to claim trial by a wager of battle. The decision of the court was that there be trial by battle unless the appellant show reason why the defendant should not depart without day.

The prisoner departed.

> Nothing could remove from the public mind the conviction of his atrocity, . . . which . . . his own conduct and gloomy broodings, after he was set at liberty, served to strengthen and confirm. A wretched outcast, shunned and dreaded by all who knew him—his very name became an object of terror in the neighbourhood of his family—he, in a few months, attempted to proceed to America; but the sailors of the vessel in which he was about to embark refused to go to sea with such a character on board. He . . . succeeded in a subsequent attempt by disguising himself. . . .

On June 22nd, 1819, the royal assent was given to an act which abolished appeals of murder and trial by battle as oppressive and unfit to be used.

If it had been regularly maintained, the publication in weekly parts of *The New and Complete Newgate Calendar*, by William Jackson, Esq., of the Inner Temple, assisted by other gentlemen, must by then have been half way through the double Volume VI and be dealing with trials and executions not yet of the current century. The initial volumes of *The Newgate Calendar Improved*, by George Theodore Wilkinson, also appeared that year.

They contained little that would be new to William Godwin, then aged sixty-three, apparently in good health but financially straitened. He was not quite forgotten. In 1807, he had published, under an assumed name, the Lambs' *Tales from Shakespeare*, and the Lambs continued to see him, as did some of their circle. He received money now and then from Shelley, who, after four years at his feet, had eloped, three years before, with his daughter by Mary Wollstonecraft. The year before, Mary Shelley had herself enjoyed, with *Frankenstein*, more literary success than her father counted on any longer, though he continued to write.

This was more than could have been said for Charles Lamb over the past eight years, though Lamb was only forty-four. The two volumes of his *Works*, last year, had seemed to mark the culmination of a short literary career of only modest distinction, though Lamb would always enjoy the consolations of a genius for friendship. That in 1820 he would start writing again was due, as much as anything, to the extraordinary capacity for editorship of John Scott, a man not yet forty.

XVI

Men of Letters

THE FIRST ISSUE of the new *London Magazine*, under Scott, appeared in the last month of the Regency, the month of the Cato Street conspiracy. The first 'Elia' essay was printed in August (this was 'Recollections of the South Sea House'). The same issue included the first part of 'On the Conversation of Authors' by William Hazlitt, who had first appeared in the March issue with an article on small theatres.

The one fully professional man of letters among contributors to the *London*, Hazlitt, at forty-two, was a critic at the height of his powers, though under constant attack from what we should nowadays (by analogy with the arrangement of seating in the semicircular French Chamber of Deputies) call the Right. With Scott's own, his was the powerful, guiding mind. And yet his life was in disorder. He lived separated from his wife and was known to be in love with the landlord's daughter at his lodgings in Southampton Buildings. Although Hazlitt and Lamb had been friends these twenty years, relations between them were a little strained that summer by the presence in London of the Wordsworths. They called often at the Lambs' in Russell Street (next to a secondhand bookseller, between Covent Garden and Drury Lane theatres, with Bow Street court nearby), and Wordsworth, at no more than fifty, had pompously taken to accepting invitations only after an assurance that the miscreant Hazlitt would not be there.

In the September issue, the continuation of Hazlitt's 'On the Conversation of Authors' described an unshadowed evening at Lambs' some six years before, when they were living in the Inner Temple. Leigh Hunt had been there, but most of those present had not been authors. There was, for instance, Lamb's first schoolmistress, a Mrs Reynolds. Admiral Burney might be considered an author, since he had spent fourteen years writing his *History of the Discoveries in the South Sea* in five volumes and had also published a book on whist. But even Mrs Reynolds had known Goldsmith, who had lent her his own copy of *The Deserted Village*.

The conversation had turned on persons then dead whom those present would have wished to have seen. Names canvassed had been those of Locke and Newton, Sir Thomas Browne and Fulke Greville, Sir Philip Sidney, Pope, John Bunyan, Oliver Cromwell, Garrick, Hogarth and Handel. Mrs Reynolds had reminded the company that she *had* seen Goldsmith ('everyone turned round to look at Mrs Reynolds, as if by doing so they could get a sight at Goldsmith'). Lamb had inquired if there was anyone that was hanged that Hazlitt would choose to mention.

'And I answered, "Eugene Aram. . . ." '

It does not appear how, if at all, Burney had then reacted to his old teacher's name. He is on record only as having murmured about Columbus.

In September 1820, when the article appeared, Mary Lamb's behaviour was giving rise to anxiety again. In November, the Edinburgh magazine, *Blackwood's*, returned to its attacks on the Cockney school. This time, it was Elia's essay 'On Christ's Hospital' which aroused Scotch contempt. John Scott replied in the *London* for January 1821.

It was Lockhart who issued the challenge to a duel, but a better marksman, his friend, a lawyer, Christie, who appeared on Primrose Hill with pistols on February 16th. A week later, the young poet on whose behalf the duel would increasingly seem to have been fought died in Rome. John Scott lingered four more days, then succumbed to his intestinal wound.

The shadow of these two deaths persisted, but so did the magazine, with different publishers, Taylor & Hessey, who had been Keats's. John Taylor himself was titular editor. For April, Hazlitt wrote the editorial notes. Taylor's active deputy was a boy not yet quite twenty-one, a promising engraver, who had also achieved a discreet literary merit by revising Helen Maria Williams's translation (still excellent, but already a quarter of a century old and now seeming here and there quaintly expressed) of the durable French romance, *Paul and Virginia.* He had not yet published or, so far as anyone knew, written anything of his own, but he was clever and reliable. He was a bookseller's son.

An April bride, at St Margaret's, Westminster, was Admiral Burney's daughter, Sarah, who married her cousin. The admiral was in fine wig and buckle on this occasion, a striking contrast to his usual neglect of personal appearance. He did not once, Lamb noted, shove up his borrowed locks to betray the few grey stragglers of his own beneath them. Though he knew it displeased the old ladies, Lamb himself was in black, as always.

In May, he dined with Coleridge in Highgate. In June, he and Mary were in Margate, which, sixty years before, had been the unfortunate Dr Dodd's favourite watering place. At some point during that spring or early summer, Lamb took Thomas Hood to see the admiral, fifty years his senior, who told him the story of how, sixty-three years ago, he had seen Eugene Aram arrested and that he was beloved by the boys and used to discourse to them of murder, not occasionally but constantly.

It was in May that a tall and splendidly handsome youth just eighteen, George Borrow, articled to a solicitor in Norwich, was sent with a thousand pounds to a magistrate, Mr Petre, of Westwick House, North Walsham. He walked, as he was to spend a great part of his life doing. His way lay due north, for thirteen miles, to Aylsham, where a demand to be told whether he knew where the fight was likely to be was shouted out to him by a short, thick fellow in brown top-boots and bareheaded, who stood with his hands in his pockets at the door of an alehouse.

> Now, as I knew nothing about the fight, and as the appearance of the man did not tempt me greatly to enter into conversation with him, I merely answered in the negative, and continued my way.

He bore left.

> One mile, two miles, three miles were speedily left behind; and now I came to a grove of birch and other trees, and opening a gate I passed up a kind of avenue, and soon arriving before a large brick house, of rather antique appearance, knocked at the door. . . . I found his worship a jolly red-faced gentleman, . . . dressed in a green coat, white corduroy breeches, and drab gaiters. . . . When [he] had received the money, and signed and returned a certain paper which I handed to him, he rubbed his hands, and looking very benignantly at me, exclaimed,—
>
> 'And now, young gentleman, that our business is over, perhaps you can tell me where the fight is to take place?'

They drank Madeira. The magistrate asked young Borrow whether he could box.

> 'A little.'
>
> '. . . Boxing is . . . a noble art—a truly English art; may I never see the day when Englishmen shall feel ashamed of it, or blacklegs and blackguards bring it into disgrace! I am a magistrate and, of course, cannot patronise the thing very openly, yet I sometimes see a prize-fight: I saw the Game Chicken beat Gulley.'
>
> . . . But here we heard a noise, like that of a gig driving up to the door, which was immediately succeeded by a violent knocking and ringing, and after a little time the servant who had admitted me made his appearance in the room.
>
> 'Sir,' said he, with a certain eagerness of manner, 'here are two gentlemen waiting to speak to you.'
>
> 'Gentlemen waiting to speak to me! who are they?'
>
> 'I don't know, sir,' said the servant; 'but they look like sporting gentlemen, and—and'—here he hesitated; 'from a word or two they dropped, I almost think that they come about the fight.'
>
> 'About the fight,' said the magistrate. 'No! that can hardly be; however, you had better show them in.'
>
> Heavy steps were now heard ascending the stairs, and the

servant ushered two men into the apartment. . . . Both of them were remarkable looking men, but to the foremost of them the most particular notice may well be accorded: he was a man somewhat under thirty and nearly six feet in height. He was dressed in a blue coat, white corduroy breeches, fastened below the knee with small golden buttons; on his legs he wore white lamb's-wool stockings, and on his feet shoes reaching to the ankles; round his neck was a handkerchief of the blue and bird's eye pattern; he wore neither whiskers nor moustaches, and appeared not to delight in hair, that of his head, which was of a light brown, being closely cropped; the forehead was rather high but somewhat narrow; the face neither broad nor sharp, perhaps rather sharp than broad; the nose was almost delicate; the eyes were grey, with an expression in which there was sternness blended with something approaching to feline; his complexion was exceedingly pale, relieved, however, by certain pock-marks, which here and there studded his countenance; his form was athletic, but lean; his arms long. In the whole appearance of the man, there was a blending of the bluff and the sharp. You might have supposed him a bruiser; his dress was that of one in all its minutiae; something was wanting, however, in his manner—the quietness of the professional man; he rather looked like one performing the part—well—very well—but still performing a part. His companion!—there, indeed, was the bruiser—no mistake about him: a tall massive man, with a broad countenance and a flattened nose; dressed like a bruiser, but not like a bruiser going into the ring; he wore white-topped boots and a loose brown jockey coat.

As the first advanced towards the table, . . . he doffed a white castor from his head and made rather a genteel bow; looking at me, who sat somewhat on one side, he gave a kind of nod of recognition.

'May I request to know who you are, gentlemen?' said the magistrate.

'Sir,' said the man in a deep but not unpleasant voice, 'allow me to introduce to you my friend, Mr [Painter], the celebrated pugilist'; and he motioned with his hand towards the massive man with the flattened nose.

'And your own name, sir?' said the magistrate.

'My name is no matter,' said the man; 'were I to mention it to you, it would awaken within you no feeling of interest. It is neither Kean nor Belcher, and I have as yet done nothing to distinguish myself like either of those individuals, or even like my friend here. . . .'

'In what can I oblige you, sir?' said the magistrate.

'Well, sir; the soul of wit is brevity; we want a place for an approaching combat between my friend here and a brave from town. Passing by your broad acres this fine morning, we saw a pightle which we deemed would suit. Lend us that pightle, and receive our thanks; 'twould be a favour, though not much to grant: we neither ask for Stonehenge nor for Tempe.'

My friend looked somewhat perplexed; after a moment, however, he said, with a firm but gentlemanly air, 'Sir, I am sorry that I cannot comply with your request.'

'Not comply!' said the man, his brow becoming dark as midnight; and with a hoarse and savage tone. 'Not comply! why not?'

'It is impossible, sir; utterly impossible!'

'Why so?'

'I am not compelled to give my reason to you, sir, nor to any man.'

'Let me beg of you to alter your decision,' said the man, in a tone of profound respect.

'Utterly impossible, sir; I am a magistrate.'

'Magistrate! then fare ye well, for a green-coated buffer and a Harmanbeck.'

'Sir!' said the magistrate, springing up with a face fiery with wrath.

But, with a surly nod to me, the man left the apartment; and in a moment more the heavy footsteps of himself and his companion were heard descending the staircase.

'Who is that man?' said my friend, turning towards me.

'A sporting gentleman, well known in the place from which I come.'

'He appeared to know you.'

'I have occasionally put on the gloves with him.'

'What is his name?'

And here the record, in *Lavengro*, published thirty years later, is abrupted.

A harmanbeck was a constable, the harmans being the stocks. The name of the sporting gentleman, well known in Norwich, was John Thurtell. Then in his late twenties, the spoilt son of a prosperous father, he had, for five years, between the ages of fifteen and twenty, held a commission in the marines. Set up by his father as a bombasine-manufacturer, he had failed earlier in the year. To be found more often in London than in Norwich, his frequentations, among the sporting Fancy, were of men who were his inferiors in all but cunning and who cheated him.

On some other pightle or enclosed field in North Walsham, the fight between Ned ('Flatnose') Painter and Tom Oliver was fought on Tuesday, July 17th.

> It was soon over; some said that the brave from town, who was reputed the best man of the two, and whose form was a perfect model of athletic beauty, allowed himself, for lucre vile, to be vanquished by the massive champion with the flattened nose. One thing is certain, that the former was suddenly seen to sink to the earth before a blow of by no means extraordinary power.

Thus *Lavengro*. In *The Romany Rye*, however:

> Ned Flatnose fairly beat Tom Oliver, for though Ned was not what's called a good fighter, he had a particular blow, which if he could put in he was sure to win. His right shoulder . . . was two inches farther back than it ought to have been, and consequently his right fist generally fell short; but if he could swing himself round, and put in a blow with that right arm, he could kill or take away the senses of anybody in the world.

The more expert had perceived that, when Painter followed Oliver to the ropes, the latter had received a tremendous blow to the temple. Later, he was to say that it had operated on him like a shock of lightning, rendering him totally insensible. At any rate, when time was called, he did not appear at the scratch.

There was much grinding of teeth amongst the fighting men from town.

'Tom has sold us,' said they, 'sold us to the yokels. Who would have thought it?'

For many weeks, the weather had been of the most glorious description. That day, too, had dawned gloriously and so continued till some two hours after noon. The fight was fought beneath a glorious sky of deep blue, with a big, fierce sun in the midst of that blue, not a cloud to be seen, only in the far west, just on the horizon, something like the extremity of a black wing.

That was only a quarter of an hour ago, and now the whole northern side of the heaven was occupied by a huge, black cloud, and the sun was only occasionally seen amidst masses of driving vapour. Another fight was hardly started when there was a rush and a roar overhead, a wild commotion. The tempest was beginning to break loose. And now the storm was at its height. The black thundercloud had broken into many, which assumed the wildest shapes and the strangest colours, some of them unspeakably glorious. The rain poured in a deluge, and more than one waterspout was seen at no great distance. An immense rabble was hurrying all in one direction, a multitude of men of all ranks, peers and yokels, prizefighters and Jews, a wild confusion of hail and rain, men and horses, carts and carriages. All hurried in one direction, through mud and mire. The town of Aylsham was only three miles distant. It was soon reached and soon filled, it would not contain one third of that mighty rabble. But there was another town farther on, the good old city, only twelve miles.

In the midst of all that mad throng, at a moment when the rain gushes were coming down with particular fury and the artillery of the sky was pealing as he had never heard it peal before, George Borrow felt someone seize him by the arm. He turned round and beheld Mr Petulengro.

'I can't hear you, Mr Petulengro,' he said, for the thunder drowned the words the gipsy appeared to be uttering.

'Look up there, brother!' said Mr Petulengro, pointing.

Borrow looked up. Among the clouds were some of vivid green, others of the brightest orange, others as black as pitch. The gipsy's finger was pointed to a strange kind of cloud which looked something like a stream of blood.

'Whose bloody *dukkeripen* does that foreshadow?' Borrow asked.

'Who knows?' at first said the gipsy.

But down the way, dashing and splashing and scattering man, horse and cart to the left and right, came an open barouche, drawn by four smoking steeds, with postilions in scarlet jackets and leather skullcaps. Two forms were conspicuous in it, that of the successful bruiser and that of his friend and backer, whose stern features wore a smile of triumph as he nodded in the direction of where Borrow stood with Mr Petulengro.

Pointing, as the barouche hurried by (dashing through the rain gushes), at Thurtell, the gipsy then said:

'His!'

Or so if we are to believe the later Borrow.

John Lamb died, Elia's burly elder brother. Admiral Burney died, leaving his family ill-provided. Messrs Taylor & Hessey gave monthly dinners for contributors to the *London*.

Hood was not the only Tom on the paper. There were also Thomas Noon Talfourd and Thomas Griffiths Wainewright, both men in their twenties. Thomas De Quincey, whose *Confessions of an English Opium Eater* startled the readers monthly, was thirty-five.

Talfourd was a barrister, called that year. A great future in law and politics awaited him. He was to do a great deal for authors' copyright, so that after him no compilation like *The Newgate Calendar* would be able to come into existence in the same way. He does not concern us otherwise, though he did not disgrace literature.

After a year in the Army, Wainewright had commenced painter, like Hazlitt, but had been in the new magazine from the beginning, writing mainly on art under pseudonyms of which 'Janus Weathercock' seemed likeliest to stick. He was a grandson of the Dr Griffiths who had founded the *Monthly Review* and conducted it for over fifty years. This link with the age of Johnson had perhaps been Wainewright's sufficient *entrée* to the *London*. He was also related, not too distantly, to the Burneys and had been a pupil of the rear-admiral's brother, the great classical scholar, Charles like his father.

The only time De Quincey and Wainewright met was at the November dinner. Lamb and Hazlitt were there. So were Hood, Talfourd and three contributors not so far mentioned here or to be mentioned again, John Hamilton Reynolds (in the magazine 'John Corcoran'), Bryan Waller Proctor (a Yorkshireman, in the magazine 'Barry Cornwall' for anagrammatical reasons) and the giant Scot, a deserter from *Blackwood*, Alan Cunningham, tangy with wet sheet and flowing sea, a wind that followed him fast.

De Quincey, a very small man, who, moreover, was feeling off colour that day, found Wainewright's appearance better suited to express the dandyism which overspread the surface of his writing than the unaffected sensibility which, this nevertheless made clear, lay in his nature. Hazlitt also found Wainewright's manner precious, though his perceptions were often sound. Hazlitt and Wainewright had crossed swords in the magazine a year and a half before, on the subject of little theatres.

Hazlitt wanted to see a prize fight, and in December he drove out to one on Hungerford Downs between Bill Neat and Tom ('Gas') Hackman. Before him on the box of the coach to Reading sat a trainer with whom he exchanged civilities and whose name was John Thurtell. When, on the coach out of Reading, Hazlitt sat inside, he found Thurtell there also, who slept much of the time but presently started out of his sleep, swearing he knew how the fight would go, for he had had a dream about it.

In the essay ('The Fight') which he was presently to publish not in the *London* but in the *New Monthly*, Hazlitt makes fun of Thurtell's conversational powers. 'Tom Turtle' he calls him.

> He was confined in his topics to fighting dogs and men, to bears and badgers. . . . The whole art of training (I, however, learned from him) consists in two things, exercise and abstinence, abstinence and exercise, repeated alternately and without end.

In Borrow, we see Thurtell blustering, whether angry or triumphant. In Hazlitt, he seems depressed, for reasons of which we may discover more than one. Although his essay was to keep up a sprightly tone, we know that Hazlitt was depressed at the time. Any possible contact between their two depressions was inhibited by the presence in their coach from Reading of a third party, a stout valetudinarian sporting the white beaver of the Fancy, himself perhaps also depressed, though convalescent.

Even Thurtell's dream had misled him. The Gasman was beaten by the local favourite. Like many others of the London Fancy, John Thurtell returned to town with pockets to let.

The eminent critic drove back with Peter George Patmore, father of the poet. Patmore had been John Scott's second in the duel with Christie, and his management of the affair was criticised. At first, Christie had not returned Scott's fire.

For much of the following spring and early summer, Hazlitt was in Edinburgh. The Lambs were in Paris and Versailles all summer. Hazlitt was in Scotland, they in France, when murderous fishermen capsized Shelley off the Italian coast. A few days before, the trustees of his grandfather's will had converted Thomas Griffiths Wainewright's five thousand pounds of 5 per cent into five and a quarter thousand of new 4 per cent stock. He studied their signatures. Before Shelley's ashes were buried in Rome and before Hazlitt returned to London divorced, 'Janus Weathercock' had copied the signatures on a power of attorney and cashed two and a quarter thousand pounds of his capital.

It deprived nobody, but it was a dangerous thing to do. Counterfeiting bank-notes had become so common that the Old Bailey was choked with Bank of England prosecutions. (For some reason, the Lancashire assizes were even worse.) To obviate the spectacle of rows of hanged men beyond even the taste of the time, thus also saving the courts' time, the Bank had adopted a practice of pressing only non-capital charges if the culprits would plead guilty. Even so, three men had been hanged for forgery four years before. It was longer since a person of note had been found guilty of forgery on a large scale, but the penalty of death still stood for forging a power of attorney (indeed, for other forms of forgery, too). This would be discovered to his cost by a gifted financier, Henry Fauntleroy, whom eight years' success at the craft had made reckless at much the same time.

Thomas Griffiths Wainewright did it for love. He wanted to marry Eliza Abercrombie, a beautiful but penniless young woman who lived with her mother and two little sisters at Mortlake. On the capital he had realised, they married. They went first to a Griffiths uncle at Turnham Green, then set up on their own, for a while at Twickenham but presently in Great Marlborough Street, where they entertained lavishly. It had been the actress Sarah Siddon's house.

Life had ebbed from *The London Magazine*. By September 1823, Charles Lamb was writing to Bernard Barton, the Quaker poet, that he lingered 'among the creaking rafters, like the last rat'. Three buttresses which he said had already been pulled down were Hazlitt, Proctor, and 'their best stay, kind, light-hearted Wainewright, their Janus'. But De Quincey was even then writing for the *London* a contribution which would turn out to be one of its most durable monuments, his essay on the knocking at the gate in *Macbeth*.

De Quincey had, he tells us, been puzzled for years by the remarkable effect of this knocking, when there occurred the Ratcliffe Highway murders, twelve years previously.

> Now it will be remembered, that in the first of these murders (that of the Marrs), the same incident (of a knocking at the door, soon after the work of extermination was complete) did actually occur, which the genius of Shakespere has invented. . . . The murderers and the murder must be insulated—cut off by an immeasurable gulf from the ordinary tide and succession of human affairs—locked up and sequestered in some deep recess; we must be made sensible that the world of ordinary life is suddenly arrested—laid asleep—tranced—racked into a dread armistice; time must be annihilated; relation to things without abolished. . . . The knocking at the gate is heard; and it makes known audibly that the reaction has commenced; the human has made its reflex upon the fiendish; the pulses of life are beginning to beat again; and the re-establishment of the goings-on of the world in which we live, first makes us profoundly sensible of the awful parenthesis that had suspended them.

All this part of the essay is admirable. The manner in which De Quincey writes of the murders themselves is different.

> Mr Williams made his *début* on the stage of Ratcliffe Highway, and executed those unparalleled murders which have procured for him such a brilliant and undying reputation. On which murders, by the way, I must observe, that in one respect they have had an ill effect, by making the connoisseur in murder very fastidious in his taste, and dissatisfied by anything that has been since done in that line. All other murders look pale by the deep

> crimson of his; and as an amateur once said to me in a querulous tone, 'There has been absolutely nothing *doing* since his time, or nothing that's worth speaking of.' But . . . it is unreasonable to expect all men to be great artists, and born with the genius of Mr Williams.

I find this manner quite insufferable. It was to spoil everything De Quincey wrote subsequently about other cases, notably about a something which, albeit on a smaller scale, was certainly doing, in what then was rural Hertfordshire, towards the end of the month in which the *Macbeth* essay appeared.

In a lane near Radlett on the evening of Friday, October 24th, a shot was heard, followed by groans. On Saturday morning, a small pen-knife and a pistol were found, the latter with brains and hair inside the barrel. Of three men presently in gaol at Watford charged with murder, one was John Thurtell. He had been arrested by a robin redbreast or Bow Street runner at a London tavern off Bond Street. The victim, found in a sack in a stream outside Elstree, is correctly named and domiciled in a well-known stanza which, however, is at fault with respect to the nature and source of his injuries.

> They cut his throat from ear to ear;
> His brains they battered in:
> His name was Mr William Weare;
> He dwelt in Lyon's Inn.

These lines, which have been attributed to Theodore Hook, were greatly admired by Sir Walter Scott, as was the murder itself. De Quincey did not think much of it.

XVII

Rex versus *Thurtell and Hunt*

THERE ARE similarities between the cases of Eugenius Aram and John Thurtell. In both, a man of (this is not perhaps so obvious with Thurtell) superior endowment was involved in a criminal conspiracy with uneducated riff-raff, who yet contrived to outwit him. In each case, if we accept the findings in court, it was he alone who struck the actual blows which deprived the disreputable vicitim of life (for, despite the 'Mr' and the good address, Weare had been no more than a waiter turned professional gambler, doing well at it, cheating Thurtell among others, returning from Doncaster races flush with money the latter considered his). In both cases, an accomplice was allowed to escape prosecution by turning Crown witness or approver. In each case, the accused man's speech in his own defence is regarded as a classic of its kind, a kind common in days when, among lawyers, only those for the Crown were heard in court, except on points of law.

Thurtell's defence was more than twice as long as Aram's had been, even without the extracts from books which Mr Justice Park allowed the defendant to read in court at a length certainly not less than forty minutes, however fast he gabbled. These extracts (cases, mainly, in the previous century, of false conviction on circumstantial evidence) were preceded by what must have been an improvised examination, from notes made in court, of the evidence heard for the Crown. The exordium and peroration, the former itself lengthy, were composed pieces, learnt by heart. The preparation of all this was remarkable in a man never of studious habit, the more so if we consider that he was only ten weeks, whereas Eugene Aram had been a whole year, in prison awaiting trial. Its delivery was to be in part magnificent, in part tedious. It was heard on January 7th, 1824, the second day of the trial at Hertford assizes.

Borrow and Hazlitt apart, of Thurtell in the flesh we have a more complete impression than we can ever hope to form of Aram. There is a profile of him from the pencil of the young I.R.A., William Mulready. There are the reminiscences of Pierce Egan, the sporting journalist and author of *Life in London*, and from the pen of a Mr Herbert, of whom no more is known but who wrote well and was to sell his account to the *London*, we have a verbal description, wholly consonant with the graphic image, of

> the murderer, complete in frame, face, eye and daring. . . . He was dressed in a plum-coloured frock coat, with a drab waistcoat and gilt buttons and white corded breeches. His neck had a black stock on, which fitted . . . stiffly to the bottom of the cheek and end of the chin, and which therefore pushed forward the flesh on this part of the face so as to give an additionally sullen weight to the countenance. The lower part of the face was unusually large, muscular and heavy, and appeared to hang like a load to the head and to make it drop like a mastiff's jowl. The upper lip was long and large, and the mouth had a dogged appearance. His nose was rather small for such a face, but it was not badly shaped. His eyes were too small, and buried deep under his protruding forehead, so indeed as to defy you to detect their colour. The forehead, extremely strong, bony and knotted, and the eyebrows were forcibly marked, though irregular, that over the right eye being nearly straight and that over the left turning up to a point, so as to give a very painful expression to the whole face. . . . His frame was exceedingly well-knit and athletic. . . . I have observed that Thurtell seldom looked at the person with whom he conversed, . . . but . . . straight forward.

In the Mulready profile, it appears that the mouth must be very full of large teeth, but from another, incontrovertible source we shall learn that Thurtell had lost a good many and must have suffered both from toothache and from the crude ministrations of the dentists of his day, which might in part account for the raised eyebrow and pained expression, as well as for some recorded behaviour. There is repeated evidence to the fact that he was tall, an inch or two short of six feet. This being so, we may deduce from that other incontrovertible source that Borrow's observation or his memory was at fault when he described Thurtell's arms as long. The proportions of his frame were in fact the reverse of simian, in that his legs were long in relation to his arms. This would be an advantage in some sports, but not in the one he had chosen, boxing.

In the earlier part of the trial, Thurtell's bearing was alert and at moments effectively theatrical. When called upon to speak in his own defence, he (according to the same Mr Herbert) seemed to retire within himself for half a minute and then, slowly, the crowd being breathlessly silent and anxious, drawing in his breath and gathering up his frame and looking very steadfastly at the jury, spoke in a deep, measured and unshaken tone, accompanying what he first said with a rather studied and theatrical action.

He began:

'My lord and you, gentlemen of the jury, under the pressure of greater difficulties than perhaps it has ever before fallen to the lot of man to sustain, I now appear before you to vindicate my character and preserve my life. . . .'

The difficulties to which he alluded were real enough. There was, first, the nature of the evidence brought against him for the Crown. This, it is true, was of the same order as that which had fallen to the lot, over sixty years before, of Eugenius otherwise Eugene Aram, *viz.*, in the main, that of an accomplice formally put to the bar and acquitted, guaranteeing his own immunity by giving his evidence as the Crown lawyers wished it to be given. It is a mean and despicable part to play, and in the earlier case Houseman had at least had the grace to look ashamed. William Probert, a big Welshman and a cleverer man than Houseman, with some presence, had displayed an effrontery which might impress some of the jury and had, moreover, been backed up by a wife hardly less deeply involved in the murder of Weare and the disposal of his body.

At a time, too, when public comment on matters *sub judice* did not automatically constitute contempt of court, extraordinary prejudice had been created in this case before the trial, by newspapers, among which *The Times* was a chief culprit, and on the stage. At the Surrey theatre, a play had been mounted which represented the supposed events of the night of October 24th last, and to give it greater verisimilitude the actual gig hired by Thurtell had been purchased and was used in performance, the bald-faced horse that went with it, whose puzzled eyes had seen all (if only it could have spoken), being also exhibited. An injunction to restrain these performances during the trial was indeed in force, but the damage had been done.

To these and other libels Thurtell referred in his exordium, as also to his gallant service in the Marines, ending with a little vote of thanks to the sheriff and magistrates during his imprisonment. He then proceeded, from notes he had made, to analyse Probert's evidence. His audience lost interest. He stammered, blundered and seemed confused throughout. Then followed the protracted reading, and he read badly. When he had finished his books and laid his papers aside, he seemed, however, to return with joy and strength to his memory and to muster up all his might for the peroration.

'. . . If you bring in a verdict of guilty,' he said, 'the law afterwards allows no mercy. . . . Cut me not off in the midst of my days. . . . I ask not so much for myself as for those respectable parents whose name I bear and who must suffer in my fate. I ask it for the sake of that home which will be rendered cheerless and desolate by my death. Gentlemen, I am incapable of any dishonourable action, . . . much less of the horrid crime with which I am now charged. . . . I say, in the language of the Apostle, "Would to God ye were altogether such as I am, save these bonds."

'Gentlemen, I have now done. I look with confidence upon

your decision. I hope your verdict this day will be such as you may ever after be able to think upon with a composed conscience and that you will also reflect upon the solemn declaration which I now make. So help me God, I am innocent!'

The solid, slow and appalling tones in which he wrung out these last words can never (I again quote Mr Herbert) be imagined by those who were not auditors of it. The final word 'God!' was thrown up with almost gigantic energy, and he stood after its utterance with his arms extended and his face protruded and his chest dilated, as though he dared not move lest he should disturb the still echoing appeal. Such a performance, for a studied performance it surely was, has seldom been seen on the stage, and certainly never off. Thus to act in the very teeth of death demands a nerve which not one man in a thousand ever possessed.

The second accomplice, Hunt, who had failed to be allowed King's evidence and had sat throughout in the dock with Thurtell, was so nervously prostrated that he could not read his own defence. An officer of the court read it for him. Mr Justice Park resumed the evidence and delivered his charge to the jury, who retired at half-past three and were out for twenty minutes, finding John Thurtell guilty of murder and Joseph Hunt guilty as an accessory before the fact. 'Thurtell shook not to the last,' says Herbert. 'Hunt was broken down, gone. He sobbed aloud in the wildness of his distress.' The sentence passed upon Thurtell, in the usual form, was that he be taken to the place from whence he came and from thence that he be taken on Friday, the 9th instant, to a place of execution and there hanged by the neck until he was dead and that his body be taken down and given to the surgeons for dissection. While these last words were spoken, he took snuff. The same sentence was passed upon Hunt, but without specified date or notice of dissection. His sentence was in fact commuted to one of transportation.

Crowds drove out from London to witness Thurtell's execution, and the pickpockets were busy. It was the first time Hertford had seen a gallows with the new drop. Gratifyingly, the patient's neck went off like a pistol.

After two hours' exhibition to the learned and privileged in

Hertford, the corpse was put into yet a third gig and driven to St Batholomew's hospital in London, where it was found that a finger had been cut off one hand. For some weeks, dissection was publicly performed at St Bartholomew's by the famous surgeon, Abernethy, until, even in that weather, the odour became offensive. The skeleton was then stripped, macerated, articulated and delivered into the keeping of the students' demonstrator of anatomy, Thomas Wormald.

The *Medical Adviser* for January 17th contained an article by a physician who had witnessed the execution and inspected the body when it was first exposed in Hertford. 'Criminals,' he said, 'who are, in general, the victims to peculiar passions, . . . become objects of phrenological interest.' His own observations, he found, had not been shared by a colleague who was present. He himself had found the organ of destructiveness to be very slight indeed and that of benevolence well developed. That his colleague did not agree should not, he thought, be opposed to the system of phrenology, but rather held to prove 'that the unfortunate culprit did the murder under an irritation of feeling and revenge. We could perceive in his countenance, when he was upon the fatal platform, that the feeling of irritation was working upon his breast. His brow, his fierce eye, his contracted lip, his firm step—all showed that he was in such a state of mind, that if he had then been storming a town, he would have laid many an enemy prostrate. Cool and deliberate murderers are generally cowards; but he proved by the manner in which he deported himself on the scaffold . . . that he was a courageous man, one that could meet death in any shape.' A writer in the next issue ridiculed phrenology, and George Combe wrote an indignant letter.

Mr Herbert's account of the trial appeared in the *London Magazine* for February. That month Hazlitt remarried, and at Missolonghi Lord Byron had a fit which deprived him of speech but not of motion.

On May 17th, with a forged power of attorney, Thomas Griffiths Wainewright obtained possession of his remaining capital, a sum of three thousand pounds with which he continued to entertain lavishly in Great Marlborough Street. It was a picture of his, *The Milkmaid's Song*, at that year's Royal Academy exhibition, which Blake so admired, describing it to young Samuel Palmer as 'very fine'. In September, Henry Fauntleroy, himself a banker, who had successfully negotiated forged powers of attorney for the past eight years, was arrested upon the discovery of one of these by the trustees.

On October 30th, he was brought to trial. On November 30th, he was hanged outside Newgate before a crowd estimated at over a hundred thousand. Next day, Charles Lamb wrote to Bernard Barton:

> The fate of the unfortunate Fauntleroy makes me . . . cast reflecting eyes around on such of my friends as by a parity of situation are exposed to a similarity of temptation. I tremble . . . when I think that so many poor victims of the Law at one time of their life made as sure of never being hanged as I in my presumption am too ready to do.

It is not known whether Wainewright trembled. If he did, he might have found reason to do so again the following year when, in Bristol, on April 4th, Henry Savary, a banker's son, was sentenced to death for forging a bill of exchange for a mere £500, but may have breathed more easily again when the sentence was commuted to transportation.

The Probert whose evidence had hanged Thurtell was himself hanged that year for stealing a horse from a fellow-countryman, a farmer called Meredith. His bearing at the end elicited less admiration than that of his former accomplice. His hair had turned white in prison, and at the place of execution 'his limbs were completely palsied, his agitation dreadful'. The date was June 20th, 1825, the place Old Bailey, before the debtors' door of Newgate Prison.

Knapp & Baldwin's *Newgate Calendar* ends there and then, apart from a statistical postscript. In this, they say that the offences made capital by the laws of England then amounted to 'about 223'. They point out that, of these, six had been made so in the course of the century and a half from Edward III to Henry VII, thirty in the next century and a half from Henry VIII to Charles II and the rest on the last century and a half, most of them under the Georges.

> More offences were made capital during the single reign of George III than during the reigns of all the Plantagenets, Tudors and Stuarts, put together. There are persons now living at whose birth the number of capital offences did not exceed 70, and during whose lives such offences have been multiplied more than threefold. If we inquire whether, with this increasing severity, crime has been kept under, the answer is very much the reverse. But the fact is . . . that this severity is more nominal than real—that out of an average 1,110 on whom the awful sentence is annually passed in England and Wales, the number executed does not quite average 83. . . . The punishment usually substituted is transportation for life, one which . . . is not unfrequently anticipated with delight.

Throughout the period, it is difficult to discover more than a couple of dozen offences for which anybody was in fact hanged. A breakdown for the past seven years shows the highest figures for burglary, murder, robbery on the person and forgery, in that order.

The last execution for forgery was to take place four years later. For murder, I shall, if I may, extend the catalogue in the last *Newgate Calendar* proper by two cases which may be said to fall within the Newgate Calendar period, since even the later was tried in the year in which Knapp & Baldwin's fourth and last volume was published.

In the late spring of 1826, two Scottish brothers, Michael and Alexander M'Kean, murdered a woman at an inn a few miles outside Manchester in circumstances sufficiently robust to appeal even to De Quincey, who, twenty-eight years later, would devote eight pages to the crime, compared with his sixty on the Ratcliffe Highway murders. Already, the following year, when he published his first paper 'On Murder considered as one of the Fine Arts' in *Blackwood's Magazine*, De Quincey spoke of the recent case of the M'Keans as 'far beyond the vaunted performance of Thurtell' and indeed as 'bearing that relation . . . to the immortal works of Williams which the *Aeneid* bears to the *Iliad*'. Apart from the fact that no less a person said this, the case need not detain us.

On May 18th, 1827, three months after the appearance in *Blackwood* of De Quincey's unengaging nonsense, a young tenant farmer in Polstead, Suffolk, murdered a village beauty, Maria Marten. As a melodrama based on this case has proved exceptionally durable, some elements of the story may be supposed to be generally known, as, for example that Maria's body was buried in a building known as the Red Barn and that the fact was revealed to her stepmother in a dream, perhaps also that at the time of her murder she was dressed in man's clothes ready to elope with her murderer, generally presented as the young squire, a vile seducer. No copy of more than a fragment of the original play is extant, but versions have been put together by later hands at various times and for different theatrical occasions.

The mole-catcher's daughter had, indeed, borne a child to William Corder, as also previously to his older brother, since deceased. Both these children had died, while a child she had borne between the two survived. The father of this middle child was the young squire of Polstead, but he had behaved with some decency, financially speaking.

The body remained undiscovered beneath the floor of the Red Barn exactly a year, during which Corder went away and married and with his wife set up a school at Ealing. When, on May 19th, 1828, the body was dug up and an inquest held, Maria's stepmother spoke of dreams of where it lay, but at the time of the young woman's disappearance there had been circumstances pointing very suspiciously to the Red Barn, and there was to be no mention of dreams at Corder's trial.

We may note here that, the week after the discovery of the body of Maria Marten, Sir Walter Scott, on his way out of London at the start of a return journey to Scotland, paused at Radlett to inspect the scene of the Thurtell murder and described the remains of Probert's cottage in his diary (souvenir collectors had been at work, as they presently were at the Red Barn). On his next arrival in Edinburgh, he would hear there of the murder of Mary Paterson, the second of three women dispatched that year by Messrs Burke and Hare.

William Corder was brought to trial at Bury St Edmunds on Thursday, August 7th. He was a small man, wearing spectacles, aged twenty-three. On Sunday the 10th, convicted and sentenced, he wrote out a confession. Cut down next day, his body was removed to a private room in the shire hall, where the county surgeon made a longitudinal incision along the chest as far as the abdominal parts and folded back the skin so as to display the muscles of the chest to public view. The body was then removed to the *nisi prius* courtroom, where it was placed upon the large table, still wearing its trousers and stockings. The public were admitted by one door and, passing by one end and along one side of the table, made their egress at the other, constables having been stationed to cause the visitors to keep moving.

At six o'clock, the doors were closed, and two artists, Mr Mizotti of Cambridge and Mr Child of Bungay, commenced their preparations for making casts of the head and face of the murderer. These were of course shaved before the plaster of Paris was applied. The countenance did not appear much changed, except that the under lip was drawn down. This exposed the teeth in the upper jaw. It also had the effect of somewhat obliterating an indentation which in life had been very observable at the top of the chin. About the neck and throat was a considerable effusion of blood occasioned by the pressure of the rope during strangulation.

When the artists had completed their work, the body was removed to the county hospital in a state of perfect nudity, the trousers and stockings having been claimed by the hangman from London, Foxton.* His rope was sold at auction for as much as a guinea an inch. Large sums were offered for the pistol and dagger supposedly used in the murder, but these were claimed by the

* Since Dennis, there had been William Brunskill, John Langley and James Botting. John Foxton or Foxen may be regarded as the last of the Georgian hangmen. His successor, William Calcraft, was indeed to serve a year under George IV, but his exceptionally long reign was to extend beyond that of William IV into the thirty-eighth of Victoria.

sheriff and afterwards transmitted to the curator of the Moyse's Hall museum in Bury.

That August, in Paris, died Franz Joseph Gall, founder of the science of phrenology, whose lectures had been prohibited in Vienna as dangerous to religion and who had never been allowed to lecture in London. On his return from the funeral, Dr Spurzheim found a cast of the head of William Corder awaiting him and wrote to Mr Child of Bungay to thank him for this and offer the artist some observations on the propensities of the late murderer. A copy of Spurzheim's letter was sent by the county surgeon to James Curtis, *The Times* correspondent at the trial, who was preparing a book on the case. A copy of this book, when it appeared, was bound in skin taken from Corder's body and deposited with the curator of the Moyse's Hall museum, together with the pistol and dagger and the dead man's scalp.

After maceration, his skeleton was exhibited at the hospital, where it was placed in a recess beneath a glass case. Beside it stood a box into which the silver put by visitors was applied to the wants of necessitous patients. By the operation of an ingenious spring, the arm of the skeleton pointed towards the box as the visitor approached it.

XVIII

The Newgate Novelists

AS IT HAPPENS, the last of our murders to be committed was the first to give rise to imaginative literature which has survived. Melodramas based on the Red Barn case were put on at several London theatres and as far afield as Weymouth. The one at the Pavilion, Mile End Road, was seen by Curtis, who, having also seen all but one of the characters *in propria persona*, was full of praise for the lifelike performances of the actors who portrayed Corder himself, the victim's father and her sister, criticising the actress who played Mrs Marten only on the ground that her 'attitude' was too 'aspiring'. The author of the play was a West Digges who can hardly have been the actor of that name whom James Boswell had known, seventy years before, in Edinburgh. Curtis obtained a copy of the play and reproduced several scenes from it in his book on the case. And so we have that much of the original.

A summary account of the case of Thurtell & Hunt occurs in a novel published that year, *Pelham*, the second by Edward Bulwer, a man of twenty-five who had commenced novelist when his mother had cut off his allowance because he had contracted against her wishes a marriage which was to turn out as disastrous as she had thought it would. He had somewhat taken

Shelley's former place as the young poet at the feet, and financial helper, of William Godwin, a man of seventy-two who still wrote, as did his gifted daughter, Shelley's widow. He had just finished a *History of the Commonwealth*. After a further glimpse into the future, *The Last Man*, she was looking into the past with a novel to be called *The Fortunes of Perkin Warbeck*.

In a popular annual, *The Gem*, for the following year, appeared a poem of more than two hundred lines, *The Dream of Eugene Aram*, by Thomas Hood. It was prefaced with the note:

> The late Admiral Burney went to school at an establishment where the unhappy Eugene Aram was usher, subsequent to his crime. The Admiral stated that Aram was generally liked by the boys and that he used to discourse to them about murder, in something of the spirit attributed to him in this poem.

The poem recounts how, while the other boys are playing cricket, Aram comes upon one reading *The Death of Abel* and tells him of a dream he had last night. It is the dream of a quite imaginary murder, of a victim quite unlike Daniel Clark, whose corpse would not remain buried.

> That very night, while gentle sleep
> The urchin's eyelids kiss'd,
> Two stern-faced men set out from Lynn
> Through the cold and heavy mist,
> And EUGENE ARAM walk'd between,
> With gyves upon his wrist.

The poem was reprinted in the course of the year, in *The Mirror*. We may, I think, suppose that both William Godwin and Edward Bulwer read it and perhaps also that the former then or not long thereafter disclosed to his young friend that he had long nursed the intention of writing a novel based on the story of Eugene Aram. If we knew this to be so, we might be tempted to think poorly not of what Bulwer did but of what he said later.

The future Lord Lytton had a family link with the Aram story, though, again, we do not know when he discovered it, for it was tenuous. Edward was the third and youngest son of General William Earle Bulwer of Heydon Hall and Wood Dalling in the county of Norfolk, two of whose sisters are believed on fair authority to have been among the little girls in the neighbourhood (barely of reading age) who, in 1758, were privately tutored by the usher from King's Lynn free school. Both Edward and the second son, Henry, had been born in London, however, and, the general dying when Henry was seven and Edward four, their mother appears to have severed all connection with Norfolk, the seat of her own family, the Lyttons, being at Knebworth in Hertfordshire and she herself preferring to live in London. It was after the appearance of Hood's poem that Edward Bulwer took what appears to have been a first holiday in Norfolk.

At seventy-four, it must have appeared unlikely that William Godwin would yet write his *Eugene Aram*, though frequently his vigour seemed undiminished, and, in 1830, he did in fact complete a new novel, *Cloudesly*. What Bulwer did that year (in which, let us note, the Georgian epoch ended) was begin to write a tragedy in blank verse about Eugene Aram. To this, more particularly in view of the publication of Hood's poem, there could hardly be much objection even had the master communicated to the disciple his own continuing intention of writing a novel on the same subject. The tragedy was not, in any case, to be finished.

The fragments of *Eugene Aram, A Tragedy* have commonly been printed with *Eugene Aram, A Tale* and will have been glanced at or not, according to their inclination, by most of those who have read the latter. The play, they may well have noted, was to open with a scene reminiscent of the first of *Doctor Faustus*, though with different harassment and another tempter. Great emphasis is placed on Aram's poverty. No wife is mentioned. The murder of the counterpart of the real-life Clark is suggested by a counterpart of the real-life Houseman (both are given other names, to be abandoned in the novel). It ensues. Aram insists that the blow was not struck by him. Ten years elapse between the first and second acts. We are shown Aram betrothed to a Madeline whose surname is not yet what it was to be in the novel. His provenance is unknown. The people in the neighbourhood love him. In a dialogue between Madeline's father and a neighbour, his obsession with poverty is again stressed, as it is in an unfinished scene with a poor woodman. A burden of guilt has also twice been hinted at, once in a first scene with Madeline herself. And that is all we have.

That, at the time of Clark's murder, Eugenius Aram had been esteemed very poor is on record. William Godwin had experienced great financial difficulties, in his middle sixties had been declared bankrupt, would no doubt, had he written his *Eugene Aram*, have laid stress on the scholiast's poverty and the impediment it may be to genius. Such an obsession would not come naturally to Bulwer, who since Aram was to be his hero, would yet welcome any consideration tending to prove his essential innocence. For to most men's minds actual hunger will at least excuse the theft of food, though hardly murder for goods not quickly disposed of.

Mention of *Doctor Faustus* may prompt the reflection that the harassed and tempted scholar there was old and is thereafter young. Not so in *Eugene Aram, A Tragedy*, where, in the second act, to be in love and meet a dreadful fate, he has put on ten years (in real life, it was thirteen). The lover is older than the harassed scholar. In real life, Aram, in his forty-first year at the time of the murder, was fifty-four when it came to light, a bit old for a lover on the stage. In the novel, Bulwer was to make him thirty-five at the time of his betrothal to Madeline Lester, so that at the time of the murder he was only twenty-five, a bit young for a harassed scholar. But in the novel Bulwer was to start, as it were, with the second act and show us Aram only at thirty-five, with a dark past, which is just about credible. In so far as Rowland Lester was to be Justice Bulwer and his daughters aunts of Edward Bulwer, their ages in real life had to be increased.

In the novel, Bulwer does not of course present the Lester girls as his aunts, but was merely to hint elsewhere that they were. In the novel, they are simply fictitious characters, whose ages might be whatever the author chose. They are shown, however, in their dealings with a real-life figure, and it is to that extent a historical novel. For the purposes of a historical novel, Bulwer would have done better with the real-life Miss Lidderdale, who had obligingly died quite young and who was the right age.

That it was in part Bulwer's intention to write or to be thought to have written historically is indicated by the use he makes of documents, principally of Aram's concluding speech in his own defence, printed in our ninth chapter, but also, in later editions, of an essay ('The Melsupper and Shouting the Churn') which Aram wrote in York castle. That he knocks almost twenty years off its protagonist's age is the great weakness of *Eugene Aram, A Tale*, not only as a historical novel but also as a study, in fictional form, of a real murderer, which the novel was certainly meant to be. Its other principal tampering with recorded fact is in the part it makes Houseman play in the intervening years, interesting as this may be in the way of speculation on those years, which to us are lost.

Although, in the present volume, I conceive myself to be writing literary as well as criminal history. I do not feel that I ought here to do much more than that in the way of literary criticism, a craft for which I nevertheless consider myself equipped. Rather as historian than as critic (but the dividing line is not always clear), I would like to claim for *Eugene Aram, A Tale* true originality as the first English novel in which sympathy is solicited for a real-life murderer whether by name or under a penetrable fictional disguise. For a murderer wholly fictitious as far as we know, the distinction belongs to *Caleb Williams*. For a disguised murderer, it belongs internationally to Stendhal's *Le Rouge et le Noir*, published a little over a year before *Eugene Aram, A Tale*.

Thereafter, it will be sympathy extended to the murderer which most obviously and increasingly distinguishes serious novels in which a murderer figures from murder mysteries or crime fiction. In the theatre, a parallel distinction might already have been made between melodrama and numerous tragedies in which murder is committed. The serious novelist and playwright have rarely been on the side of conventional morality or even of legal justice. The claim that serious creative writers act in the interests of a higher morality might, I have no doubt, sometimes be upheld, but would, upon examination, often crumble to reveal a shameful complicity, sometimes with no less sensation-seeking than is commonly found in the work of mere entertainers.

This statement might, I would say, be applied with greater force to writers who are in general treated more seriously than Edward Bulwer. About him, let us merely note for the moment that, whatever his understanding with Godwin, *Eugene Aram, A Tale* was written in the course of 1831 and, a few days before Christmas, dedicated not to the latter but to Sir Walter Scott.

By neat coincidence with its publication, on January 7th, 1832, *The Literary Gazette* printed Spurzheim's report on the skull he had taken for that of a woman, together with an account of how the adventurous Dr Hutchinson had originally obtained it. A fortnight later, the same paper first gave currency to one of the stories originating in King's Lynn about Aram's time there, suggesting further criminal intentions on his part. With the speed characteristic of theatrical enterprises in those days, the Surrey theatre had mounted an adaptation of Bulwer's novel, the work of Wm. T. Moncrieff, by February 9th.

It was a great year for reformers. The much-debated Reform Bill became law. This was not concerned with criminal law, but a great many felonies had in the past few years been removed from the capital list, and that year a bill abolishing the death penalty for all forms of forgery got as far as the House of Lords, which amended it to exempt from its provisions all persons convicted of forging wills or letters of attorney for the transfer of stock. An insurance company having made difficulties about the death of his sister-in-law, Helen Abercrombie, Thomas Griffiths Wainewright was in Boulogne.

A further piece of legislation which came into force that year was the Anatomy Act, 2 & 3 William IV, c. LXXV. This was only indirectly concerned with criminal law, but it greatly affected criminal practice. For centuries, the surgeons in London had been limited to four bodies of hanged malefactors a year, legally and compulsorily supplied. This limitation had given rise to the horrid trade of the resurrection men, which often included murder. It was in Edinburgh that, four years before, the fact had been most glaringly publicised, but it was as bad or worse in London. (The body of one of our principal characters, Jonathan Wild, had not reached Dr Thomas of Windsor by legitimate means. It was at present in the keeping of a Dr Frederick Fowler, who had inherited Dr Thomas's practice.) Body-snatching on a large scale ceased when it was enacted that the remains of any who in life had been maintained at the public charge and had died in workhouses or hospitals should, unless claimed within a certain period of time by next of kin, be made available to medical schools.

Hazlitt was dead. Coleridge and Lamb died in 1834. A highly successful publication of that year was *Rookwood*, by William Harrison Ainsworth, a young man from Manchester who would come to seem the archetypal Newgate novelist. The Calendar story which had first stimulated his imagination was that of Richard Turpin, hanged in 1739 for horse-stealing, a butcher turned cattle-thief, smuggler and member of a gang, centred on Epping Forest, which made a speciality of raiding houses when only the womenfolk were at home. One of the exploits for which he was famous in his time was blindfolding an old woman and sitting her on the fire until she divulged the whereabouts of her savings. That gang was no doubt among those on which Godwin had based his portrayal of the one into whose hands Caleb Williams falls after his escape from prison.

It is difficult to see what in the Calendar record of such a man's career would appeal to a young novelist. He was, it is true, described as having been (though pockmarked) 'distinguished by the comeliness of his appearance'. He had behaved with a swagger at the place of execution, flinging himself from the ladder instead of waiting to be turned off. He had, for a while, played highwayman in the traditional style, with a better-known gentleman of the road, King, whom he shot by accident. There was a wide variety of real-life episodes to choose from, including an escape by the window from an inn and the hiding, like Charles II, in an oak, while bloodhounds passed underneath. The epic ride to York on a mare called Black Bess, pathetically expiring at the conclusion of her superequine efforts, was wholly Ainsworth's invention or at least attribution.

In pre-Calendar days, a similar feat on a bay mare had been credibly ascribed to a more attractive figure, John Nevison, a Yorkshireman by birth, known as 'Nicks' and also as 'the Claude Duval of the North'. He had served with a volunteer regiment in the Dutch wars, and, when on his return he took to the road, Robin Hoodlike propensities and a way with the ladies had been part of his legend, while nothing on his record is as disgusting as much on Turpin's. He was, moreover, an accredited gaol-breaker, which might have been expected to appeal to Ainsworth in view of his later attraction to Jack Sheppard (the details are not unamusing, feigning plague being their essence). He was hanged at York on May 4th, 1685. His record of horsemanship had been a consecutive ride of very little under two hundred miles from Gravesend in fifteen hours.

It could be that Ainsworth never heard of Nevison. It seems more likely that he thought 'Dick Turpin' a better name for the hero of a novel than 'Jack Nevison' and that he felt safer with the detail of the eighteenth than of the seventeenth century, although this had been a better century for highwaymen, as for pirates, or, rather, a century for better highwaymen.

I do not suppose that schoolboys read *Rookwood* now. They did fifty years ago. There was also, I recall, a silent film (called, I fancy, *Dick Turpin's Ride to York*) featuring (this then meant what 'starring' was later to mean) a famous stage actor, Matheson Lang. The idea of Dick Turpin's ride to York might, I imagine, be found in the minds of many who never read *Rookwood*.

Thomas Griffiths Wainewright was still in Boulogne. In the summer of 1835, a case originally brought by him against the Imperial Life Insurance Company was tried in his absence at the Court of Exchequer. In the course of the proceedings, before Lord Abinger, it was strongly suggested by two witnesses and counsel that Wainewright had poisoned Helen Abercrombie, his sister-in-law. At a second trial in December, this suspicion was played down, but much evidence of forgery with attempt to defraud was heard. In the summer of 1837, Wainewright was reckless enough to come to London. He was spotted by a Bow Street runner, arrested and charged. He was in Newgate when, on June 20th, the reign of Queen Victoria began. On a visit to the prison a week later with three young friends, the actor Macready saw a man reading and delivered himself impromptu of the line: 'My God! there's Wainewright!' The prisoner, it appears, stared back defiantly but said nothing. One of the friends was Charles John Huffman Dickens, who, at twenty-five, author of *Sketches by Boz* and *The Pickwick Papers*, took a close interest in prisons and had visited Newgate before.

In early July, Wainewright appeared at the Old Bailey and pleaded guilty to two charges of non-capital forgery, no evidence being offered in respect of other charges still for the moment understood to be capital. He was, as he would have been in any case, sentenced to transportation for life and thereafter disappears from the London scene, though we know a fair amount about his fifteen subsequent years in Tasmania. He was never tried for murder, presumably because the Crown lawyers had no case to present. He is known to literature mainly by an essay on him ('Pen, Pencil and Poison') in Oscar Wilde's *Intentions*. On the circumstantial evidence, we convict him or not, as we please, at the assizes of our own minds. One thing appears to be certain. The remark for which he is most famous, that his reason for poisoning Helen Abercrombie was her thick ankles, was first attributed to him after his death many thousands of miles away and deserves little credit.

His forgeries were discovered too late for *The Newgate Calendar*. He concerns us because he had concerned or was to concern other writers. The first to write about him was De Quincey, who for the past ten years had been living in Edinburgh and whose *London Reminiscences* appeared the year after Wainewright's trial, sentence and departure. Dickens, at the time, was busy with *Oliver Twist*, which is very much a Newgate novel, though I cannot find any specific Calendar case on which its story could be thought to have been based.

In 1838, the British Association for the Advancement of Science held its eighth annual meeting in Newcastle. Mr Richardson, surgeon, of Harrogate, a founding member, arranged that the cranium of Eugene Aram should be exhibited before the medical section by a physician, a younger man, James Inglis, M.D., who, first, identified it by tracing its history and pointing out indications upon the bone of the iron hooks by which the hangman's victim had been gibbeted. He argued that the evidence against Aram had not clearly established the proof of his guilt, while an examination of the head on phrenological principles suggested that he was not guilty. In the discussion which followed, one of the Scotch phrenologists, on the other hand, contended that the skull was that of a person very likely to have been of a criminal character. If a person known to him had died of a blow on the head, it was very likely to have come from the person to whom the skull belonged.

Here we may note that, at some time within the next four years, upon the demise of Mr Richardson of Harrogate, this skull came into the possession of the adventurous Dr Hutchinson's grandson, a young clergyman, the Rev. John Walker, at Malton. There, at no great distance from either Harrogate or Knaresborough, it was to remain for the next quarter of a century and more.

Also in 1838, Edward Bulwer, M.P. for Lincoln, was created a baronet. In the next two years were published, none of them by him, three Newgate novels of which two had their plots based on specific Calendar cases, that of the other being set against events largely described in the Calendars. These were *Jack Sheppard* by W. Harrison Ainsworth, *Catherine* by William Makepeace Thackeray and *Barnaby Rudge* by Charles Dickens. Thackeray, it is true, was to describe what to us is a not insubstantial novel as 'a satirical story, . . . intended to ridicule a taste then prevalent for making novel heroes of Newgate malefactors', and ascribed it to an imaginary author, Ikey Solomons, Esq., Junior.

The origin of *Catherine* was the case of Catherine Hayes, unintentionally, the reader may remember, burnt alive in 1726 for the murder of her husband. Thackeray had no doubt chosen it for its extreme and grotesque bloodiness, but he must have been fairly conversant with one or another of the Calendars to find it. Despite Thackeray's moral squirming, it remains a Newgate novel, and we may recall with satisfaction that it was no less accused of immorality than the novel by Ainsworth whose huge success Thackeray deplored. Ainsworth did not ask us to 'expend our sympathies on cut-throats and other such prodigies of evil'. Jack Sheppard had cut nobody's throat, though Blueskin once had, ineffectually. To Blueskin, it is true, Ainsworth attributes a murder which is not on record, but then it can hardly be said that his readers were asked to expend their sympathies on Blueskin. *Jack Sheppard* is a novel we may admire without moral or too much aesthetic misgiving.

I shall not enter the crowded field of Dickens criticism in respect of *Barnaby Rudge*, but repeat that its principal real-life character, Dennis, was not in real life hanged, though briefly caught up in the Gordon riots. In the year of publication of *Barnaby Rudge*, there was a new edition of *Eugene Aram, A Tale*, to which Sir Edward Bulwer, then in Brussels, wrote a new preface. In this, he says:

> My regret . . . is not that I chose a subject unworthy of elevated fiction, but that such a subject did not occur to someone capable of treating it as it deserves; and I never felt this more strongly than when the late Mr Godwin (in conversing with me after the publication of this romance) observed that 'he had always thought the story of Eugene Aram peculiarly adapted for fiction, and that he had more than once entertained the notion of making it the foundation of a novel'. I can well conceive what depth and power that gloomy record would have taken from the dark and inquiring genius of the author of *Caleb Williams*.

Three years later, Sir Edward Bulwer became Sir Edward Bulwer-Lytton, thus fulfilling the terms of his mother's will and acquiring her family seat of Knebworth. On May 3rd, 1845, died Eugene Aram's other principal literary advocate, Thomas Hood, then rising forty-six, who had been in poor health for some years but not a bore about it, a very nice man. The following year, Sir Edward Bulwer-Lytton published *Lucretia*, a novel in which the villain is clearly based on Thomas Griffiths Wainewright and which Wainewright is believed to have read in Tasmania.

He would be seven years dead and not read the portrait of himself in the story ('Hunted Down') which Dickens was eventually to write on receiving a handsome offer of £1,000 from a New York publication, while at work on *A Tale of Two Cities*. Meanwhile, Dickens witnessed the execution of two of the earlier Victorian murderers, Frederick and Maria Manning, and put the latter, as Hortense, into *Bleak House*, into which also, with Inspector Bucket, he was prompt to introduce a member of the detective force recently formed on the Parisian model. Thackeray, who had witnessed the same double execution, for *Henry Esmond*, went, on the other hand, back, with no satirical purpose, to *The Newgate Calendar* for the unusually savage and doubly fatal duel between a duke of Hamilton and Lord Mohun.

XIX

A Kind of Immortality

ON JUNE 18th, 1847, Dr Frederick Fowler of Windsor wrote to the Royal College of Surgeons of England that he begged to offer for their acceptance the skeleton of the celebrated Jonathan Wild, which had been in the possession of himself and his predecessors upwards of fifty years. The peculiar character of the letters and figures on the coffin plate which accompanied it would, he said, be an additional proof of the authenticity of the skeleton. His offer being accepted, the skeleton arrived in Lincoln's Inn Fields in a state of excellent preservation, but with one serious defect. For no obvious reason, upon an unknown occasion, the posterior part of the vault of the skull had been removed by two saw-cuts, one vertical and transverse, the other horizontal.

To a phrenologist, this precluded all estimate of the self-esteem and love of approbation, the cautiousness and firmness of the late Jonathan Wild and seriously impeded reliable judgment of his concentrativeness, adhesiveness, secretiveness and acquisitiveness. M. Paul Broca, of Paris, then in his early twenties, had not, on the other hand, yet provided osteologists with the terminology they still use for the parts of the head or with alternative insights into the localisation of mental faculties. The surgeons of England may have noted that the brow was broad and low, with well-developed ridges; the face short and square, the lower jaw wide and rounded, with broad but not prominent chin; the man in his lifetime some five feet seven tall, with good teeth, though only three of these remained in the skull. The skeleton made an unimpressive showing beside that of the Irish giant, a young man called O'Brien or Byrne, who, towards the end of the eighteenth century, having produced near eight feet of bone, had come to London to exhibit himself for gain but, not living long thereafter, had become one of Hunter's own last preparations.

The amateur criminologist will hardly need me to tell him what were to be the most famous cases of the next twenty-two years. A murder of some literary interest was committed in New England in November 1849 by a professor of Harvard upon the person of a learned colleague, and Oliver Wendell Holmes appeared as an expert witness at the trial the following year, during which Mrs Gaskell recorded a murder in Manchester. A murder in Norwich the year after that, of his wife by a tailor, William Sheward, may be thought to bear in two ways on the story of Eugene Aram, in the first place because it was to go even longer undiscovered than his.

Despite the calamitous and shameful end to which real life and *Eugene Aram, A Tale* had brought him, there could be no doubt that Sir Edward Bulwer-Lytton's most successful fiction had invested a murderer with the interest proper to a hero. As people continued to say so and as a further new edition was called for that year, Sir Edward made one alteration to his novel more important than mere verbal correction. In a new preface, he wrote:

> On going, with maturer judgment, over all the evidences on which Aram was condemned, I have convinced myself that, though an accomplice in the robbery of Clark, he was free from both the premeditated design and the actual deed of murder. The crime, indeed, would still rest on his conscience, . . . but, finding my conviction, that in the murder itself he had no share, borne out by the opinion of many eminent lawyers, . . . I have accordingly so shaped his confession.

The following year, having thus purged himself from a long-standing reproach, Sir Edward returned to politics, from which for eleven years he had been absent.

The case of William Palmer in 1856 is of twofold literary interest, in that Dickens that year wrote about him and Thurtell in *Household Words* and in that a living poet, incredibly, once wrote a book in support of his innocence. In the same year, a boy of fifteen, Thomas Hardy, saw Elizabeth Martha Brown hanged in Dorchester for battering her husband's brains out. He was to write:

> I remember what a fine figure she showed against the sky as she hung in the misty rain, and how the tight black gown set off her shape as she wheeled half-round and back.

We cannot doubt that the memory was to play its part in the creation of *Tess of the D'Urbevilles*. We may suppose that the pseudonymous Marian Evans was even then at work on a novel not without some resemblance to *Tess* and perhaps importantly its predecessor, her *Adam Bede*, basing her story on that of a girl to whom a Methodist aunt had ministered on the eve of her execution for destroying the fruit of her shame.

The crimes of the eighteen-sixties do not concern us, but we may note that in 1862 the town of Knaresborough received publicity as the birthplace of Mother Shipton, the Tudor prophetess. This was due to a reprint of an old book, into which the publisher, Charles Hindley, had introduced, among other forgeries, a prophecy of the end of the world in 1881. In 1866, Sir Edward Bulwer-Lytton was raised to the peerage as Baron Lytton of Knebworth. Two years later, public executions were abolished in England and Wales.

After Christmas, William Sheward, for long the popular landlord of the Key and Castle Sun inn in Norwich, went visiting in London. On New Year's Day, 1869, maudlin with drink, loneliness and belated remorse, he walked into Walworth police station and insisted on telling the desk sergeant how, eighteen years before, in the course of a drunken quarrel, he had stabbed his first wife, who was much older than he was, with a pair of tailoring shears and thereafter spent miserable days disposing piecemeal of the body. Once he had sobered up, he denied all, but he was charged and sent back in a carriage to Norwich, where on April 20th he was hanged inside the Castle.

That year, the skull of Eugenius Aram moved, with the Rev. John Walker, from Malton in Yorkshire to Great Yarmouth, where it was installed in Bradwell rectory. There, it aroused little interest. Yarmouth is indeed in the same county as King's Lynn, but very much closer to Norwich, which lies between. Norwich, that year, had a very good murderer of its own, had had him (had it known this) for the past eighteen years. The story there, new to the young (and, indeed, to their elders, whose only genuine knowledge was that a Mrs Sheward had left her husband, as she had often threatened to do, and that bits of flesh still pickled in spirits of wine at the Guildhall had been thought to be those of a young girl), was of how mine host at the Key and Castle Sun had long ago put his wife's head in a saucepan on the fire, broken it up and dropped bits of it here and there about Thorpe; replaced it in the saucepan with guts and emptied these in the cockey in Bishopsgate Street; and cut her long hair into small pieces, which had blown away as he walked about streets known to them all.

The Walkers decided to get rid of their old skull. In a letter dated December 9th, the Rev. John offered it to the Royal College of Surgeons of England. It was accepted by William Flower, conservator for eight years past of the Hunterian collection. It travelled its last hundred and twenty miles in a box. Fowler took it out and numbered it 337. He noted that not only the mandible but also the right maxilla and nasal bone were missing. Though hinged, the cranium proper was intact, save that the tip of the right mastoid process appeared to have been sawn off. The skull had never been macerated, but wind and rain long ago had clearly done all that was necessary in that direction.

On April 19th, 1873, Mr Henry Irving, with Miss Bateman, opened at the Lyceum in *Eugene Aram, A Tragedy*, by the Irish playwright, William Gorman Wills. A stage property used in the performance was said to be the authentic lantern which had once hung outside Aram's school in Knaresborough. This was not the case, however. The genuine lantern was in the possession of the poet, Dante Gabriel Rossetti. The play ran for three months, during which Lord Lytton of Knebworth passed peacefully away.

Thomas Wormald, for long demonstrator of anatomy at St Bartholomew's hospital, passed peacefully away the following year. Mrs Wormald then presented the skull and limb bones of John Thurtell to the Royal College of Surgeons. The skull was numbered 338 by the conservator, Flower. In estimating Thurtell's probable height, he found a curious anomaly between what it must be calculated to be from the length of the humerus and what it must be calculated to be from the length of the femur. The latter would give him a height of almost six feet, the former little over five feet four. His legs must therefore have been long in proportion to his arms. The massiveness and almost exaggerated masculinity of the skull suggested rather a big man with disproportionately short arms than a small man with disproportionately long legs.

The new skull appeared particularly massive in comparison with 337. The cranium was six millimetres longer, six broader and thirteen taller, the bones, on the other hand, thick and somewhat contorted, while Aram's was lightly made, of even ovoid outline, internally smooth and regular. The French school had not yet provided a formula whereby cranial capacity could be determined from external measurements. One might turn the skulls upside down and fill them with water, which could then be poured off into some form of laboratory measure. The weakness of water was that it formed a plane surface at the lowest point of a highly irregular rim, against which solid particles might be carefully disposed with the hand. A litre and a half of lead shot would be heavy. To drop 338 full of shot on the toe would be a crippling experience. Poppyseed would be little better than water. Dried peas, on the other hand, were too large and uneven. Enquiry at home elicited the suggestion of peppercorns or coriander, and it seems that the latter was used. It gave

Thurtell two hundred and forty cubic centimetres more of cranial capacity (and therefore of brain size in life and for a while thereafter) than Aram, whose cranial capacity was a mere fourteen hundred cubic centimetres, not much more than the average for women.

Apart from the need for assistance in maintaining a fully articulated skeleton upside down, Wild presented special difficulties in view of the removal of the posterior part of the vault of the skull. In the course of his life, Sir William Flower was nevertheless to come to a conclusion about Jonathan Wild's cranial capacity, which he determined *by seed* to be a mere twenty-five greater than that of Eugene Aram, two hundred and fifteen less than John Thurtell's. From the external measurements still possible, it was clear that Wild had been conspicuously long-headed, while Aram and Thurtell had been no more so than is common among Englishmen.

As only his upper jaw was present, an odontological colleague could say little more than that Aram's back teeth seemed to have been removed from that in his lifetime. Of teeth remaining in their sockets, Wild had only three, two in the upper and one in the lower jaw, but all the teeth in his upper jaw and all but one in the lower would have been present at the time of his death, while the teeth still present were free of caries, and there were no signs of sepsis in the sockets. In Thurtell's case, by contrast, of the four teeth remaining three were carious, while there had been root abscesses in most of the sockets vacated live.

As we know, Newgate prison was finally demolished in 1904. Robert Dow's famous handbell thereafter remained in the vestry of St Sepulchre's church. It is now locked away safely in the rector's office. In Watson's *Eugene Aram, his Life and Trial*, there is a photograph of Aram's cranium as it was in 1913, mounted and so neatly hinged that, unless you had read about it, you would not know that it was in two parts. It does not look like that now.

What happened twenty-seven years later to so many of the

City churches is well known and much lamented. The great tenor and the other bells in the tower of St Sepulchre's must have come crashing down. Whether they were salvaged and recast, the librarian of the Central Council of Church Bell Ringers has failed to discover. In the late evening of May 10th, 1941, the unforgettable double pulse of German bomber engines was increasingly audible over central London. Fearful damage was done in Lincoln's Inn Fields. Rooms IV and V, containing the larger specimens of comparative osteology, were quite destroyed with their contents. In other rooms, something remained among the broken glass and pools of surgical spirit. It was estimated by the recorder, Jessie Dobson, that one third of the Hunterian collection might be saved. In Room I, the skeletons both of the Irish giant and of Mr Jonathan Wild, the Great, were intact. So was the skull of John Thurtell, and the bones of his limbs were identified with fair certainty. The cranium of Eugenius Aram gaped. Pickard's neat hinges had not fully withstood such violent wrenching. The bone itself was not seriously impaired, externally at least.

For more than seven years after the war, London showed little inclination to rebuild, preferring to expose its sores to the pitying attention of foreign visitors. Miss Dobson arranged temporary exhibitions variously about the remaining premises.

There were new acquisitions. In October 1949, for instance, Mr Wood, the assistant librarian, brought to Miss Dobson's attention a newspaper announcement that the Suffolk Infirmary in Bury St Edmunds wished to dispose of the skeleton of William Corder. This was written off for.

Corder had been small in stature, a mere five feet three. The basilar suture at the top of the spine was obliterated, but those of the vault were open both within and without. Though not strictly brachycephalic, the regular oval of the skull was broad. The chin was sufficiently round and prominent, the facial bones slender but undoubtedly masculine, the forehead rather high. In contradistinction to those of Jonathan Wild, the orbits were markedly oblique (the man had not had that same level look). The temporal lines were much higher than in most small-jawed skulls. The palate also was high, as well as narrow. Three first molars had been lost in life. The wisdom teeth had erupted, but had not had time to meet.

Miss Dobson measured the skull. Its height was a hundred and thirty millimetres, its breadth a hundred and forty, its length a hundred and eighty-seven. There was no longer a need for peppercorns or coriander. Employing a formula happily provided by one of Broca's pupils, Manouvrier, Miss Dobson calculated that this skull's cranial capacity was fifteen hundred cubic centimetres. That made it, according to Sir William Fowler's determinations seventy years before, rather larger than Aram's, rather smaller than Wild's, decidedly smaller than Thurtell's.

Sir William's measurement by seed ought to be compared with the capacities determined by Manouvrier's formula. To this end, Miss Dobson took her own external measurements. Comparing these with Sir William's, she was astonished to find that only in the height of Aram's skull did they agree. Her illustrious predecessor had made this two millimetres too short and two too broad. He had clearly been best at measuring height. The heights he gave for Wild and Thurtell were only one millimetre short. Whereas his Aram breadth was two millimetres too much, his Wild and Thurtell breadths were two too little. He had been two millimetres short with Wild's length and three with Thurtell's.

That would not have affected the determination of cranial capacity by seed, but, when Miss Dobson applied Manouvrier's formula to her own external measurements, she discovered that Flower was seventy cubic centimetres under for Aram, ninety-eight for Wild and no fewer than a hundred and sixty-eight for Thurtell. Really, one might think the man had used dried peas after all and poured these with shaking hands recklessly into his measure, so that for days people were treading on peas.

What Miss Dobson would aim at, when the new museum was ready, was a single show-case for all four of her criminals. In the meantime, she would write them up. First, she must read them up. For Corder, her new acquisition, the only thing Mr Wood was able to turn up was Camden Pelham's *Chronicles of*

Crime. It appeared, however, that, to celebrate his removal from Bury St Edmunds or, as Ipswich possibly saw it, his elevation to national status, an Ipswich firm, the East Anglian Magazine, Ltd, had just put out a new book, *The True Story of Maria Marten*, which Mr Wood would get.

Pelham also had something on Thurtell, Aram and Wild. On Thurtell and Aram, there were separate volumes, rather heavy going, by the Mr Watson who, in this latter, had even printed a photograph of their skull as it had been before the First World War, looking better than it did since the Second.

Completed eleven years ago in traditional style, the museum is on two levels, the second a gallery over the first. As you go in, you are first aware of some of the pickled foetuses in jars for which the museum is famous. They look like imps and demons, such as may be seen illustrated in old books of hours or as gargoyles projecting from the gutters of cathedrals (it is clear that the Middle Ages knew more embryology than we may have thought). The Irish giant then catches the eye, his skeleton so towering that you might suppose it a model.

The criminals are in the gallery, at the end farthest from the curator's office. They are all four in a single case, about six feet square, a foot or eighteen inches deep. To your left is Jonathan Wild, to your right William Corder, the two skeletons suspended, Wild's in a position which suggests that he has remained where he was hanged. The skulls of Eugene Aram and John Thurtell are placed between, at the level not of your eyes but of your shins. As the book says, Aram's lower jaw is missing. Thurtell's is there, with some of the teeth in. His spine and pelvic girdle (no longer, it seems, the bones of his limbs) have also been preserved, and there are some of his ribs in a box.

The arrangement is clearly open to criticism. The four heads ought to be presented at the known or computed height at which each was maintained in life. In the cases of Wild and Corder, this would mean removing the plinth so that the soles of their feet descended to ground level. Since other bones of Thurtell's remain, these, I suggest, should be cleverly suspended beneath his skull in the positions they occupied in his body when this was alive and for some time thereafter. As things are, the position of the skulls of Aram and Thurtell is degraded with respect to those which top whole skeletons. This is especially the case with Aram's, which is small and lacks its lower jaw. To my mind, it is hard that you should have to squat like a miner or sit on the floor in order to examine the marks left by the rusted iron of the gibbet and the sharply projecting mastoid processes, the tip of the right one sawn off. To gaze into those orbits, you would need to lie prone in such a position that other visitors (admittedly, the traffic is not heavy) might tread on your spine or trip over your legs. Brittle as the bone must be now, I should also not have thought it beyond the capacity of a skilled repairer of antiques to fit that cranium with new and invisible hinges, so that it did not gape.

While the aqueous humour glistened in those sockets, beneath this vault the neopallium occupied itself with thoughts of exceptional range. It is true that some of the more characteristic of these were mistaken, but they were less so than those concerned with similar percepts which most other thalami passed on then or allow helplessly through now. If we indulged in the whimsical supposition that these heads chatter when Miss Allen has gone home or that they are communicating silently while the visitor stands before them, looking slightly up at the leftmost, levelly to the right or downward, straight down or a bit to left or right, we might be sure that Aram would still be listened to by the others, but that Wild's amusing stories would have palled by now, especially as his skull lacks all that once shaped his seats of self-esteem, love of approbation and believingness, as well as most of what shielded his cautiousness and firmness.

We cannot in fact suppose that bone retains any power of sensation, however attenuated. It had very little in life, perhaps none where it was fully compacted. And yet it grew and changed, the fontenelle ceasing to beat, the sutures closing. Itself subsists as a form of memory, the most nearly immortal we know.

Their souls may be in Hell, but some of the bones of those four at least are still to be seen by prior arrangement in Lincoln's Inn Fields. Literature is less precise, but, together with others I have used, their names also may be found in many books, including this one. It will not be the case with all of us.

Victims also have their memorials. Wherever it may be now, sixty years ago a piece of Daniel Clark's skull belonged to the coroner nowhere in Yorkshire but at King's Lynn. It was borrowed in early 1912 by Eric Watson, of the Inner Temple, then working on his *Eugene Aram* for the Notable British Trials series. He submitted it to a fellow Scot, Arthur Keith, at that time both Hunterian professor and conservator of the Hunterian collection, who, on March 26th, returned it to the Inner Temple, with his comments and a helpful sketch.

The condition and staining, he wrote, of this part of a left parietal bone suggested burial in blackish mould. It was quite of the consistency and preservation of a bone which dated back to the eighteenth century. It had been broken after the skull was already stained by burial, for the whole of one edge and two other fractures were unstained and must therefore have occurred after exhumation. Between these two and traceable across the specimen to the long edge, however, occurred a partial fracture which had been made before burial. It might very well be the prolongation of a severe occipital fracture.

It was clear that the fragment was part of a skull which had been riveted after it was artificially broken, perhaps to examine the interior. The head had been rather small and evidently of the same shape as Eugene's.

The remains of William Weare, formerly of Lyon's Inn, were buried in the churchyard at Elstree, exhumed and reburied. It is supposed that they rest near those of Martha Reay or Ray, the earl of Sandwich's mistress shot by the Rev. James Hackman out of love. No pleasanter company can be imagined. He, on the other hand, can hardly have seemed a desirable companion for her.

At Polstead, in a corner of the churchyard where there are no headstones, only footstones, a handsome board indicates that the remains of Maria Marten lie thereabouts. Polstead is a sufficiently pleasing village on the hilly edge of the Constable country. The church of Stoke-by-Nayland on the skyline dominates the approach from Colchester. Across a handsome pond, the half-timbered front of the Corder farmhouse can be seen over other roofs, on high ground. The Red Barn no longer exists, but to the left of the road rising beyond a dip towards where it stood, end on to the road, well kept, could be seen recently, though it was threatened, the substantial cottage from which Maria Marten set out in man's clothes to meet her end.

Bibliography

ON THE various original Calendars, I fancy I have said all that was needed in the body of my text. Among reprints between the two world wars, the most ambitious was a (so-called) *Complete Newgate Calendar*, edited by J. L. Rayner and G. T. Crook and published by the now defunct Navarre Society in five volumes, which also included some of the Calendars' predecessors, notably Captain Alexander Smith's *Complete History of the Lives and Robberies of the Most Notorious Highwaymen*, etc. (1719) and Captain Charles Johnson's *General History of the . . . most famous Highwaymen, Murderers, Street Robbers, and . . . Pirates* (1734). John Osborn's *Lives of the most remarkable Criminals . . . condemned and executed for Murder, Highway Robberies, Housebreaking, Street Robberies and other Offences* (1735) was reprinted by Routledge in 1927. An American *Newgate Calendar* was distributed in the United Kingdom the following year under the imprint of John Lane, the Bodley Head. The Werner Laurie omnibus mentioned in my preface had earlier been put out in two volumes. Some of these reprints are no doubt kept in the basement at some of the larger public libraries. They turn up with varying frequency in the second-hand trade.

Since the second world war, there have been two Folio Society selections, edited by Norman Birkett (1951 and 1960), and of course, in and out of print, the paperback digest of Wilkinson in three volumes. A little editorial information would have increased the usefulness of these, but they should not be altogether despised. Brown paper may be used to conceal their horrible covers. At the speed with which books and especially paperbacks are in and out of print these days, it is impossible to predict where these will be when the present volume appears, but, if they are then in print, they are likely to be the only

Newgate Calendar which is. It is interesting to note that the publishers claim copyright protection for their arrangement from a work which could never have come into existence as it did if there had been any such thing at the time.

Of the works of the Newgate novelists, only a bookseller can tell one which, at any given moment, are in print, in one or another of the gradually disappearing standard editions. The most relevant are *Eugene Aram*, *Jack Sheppard*, *Barnaby Rudge* and *Catherine*, with *Rookwood* and *Oliver Twist* following close. Of the works of their predecessors, *Moll Flanders*, *Jonathan Wild* and *Caleb Williams* are of special importance. More and more, public libraries are displaying only recent books, but may keep older novels off the shelves with pornography.

Among those Notable British Trials volumes which deal with cases in the Calendars, only one can still, for the moment, be bought new. This is *The Duchess of Kingston*, edited by Lewis Melville. The case is boundlessly fascinating, though I have found little space for it. The others are, with the names of their editors, *Captain Kidd* (Graham Brooks), *Jack Sheppard* (Horace Bleackley and S. M. Ellis), *Captain Porteous* (William Roughead), *Lord Lovat* (David N. Mackay), *Mary Blandy* (William Roughead), *Eugene Aram* (Eric R. Watson), *Katharine Nairn* (William Roughead), *Abraham Thornton* (Sir John Hall, Bt.), *Henry Fauntleroy* (Horace Bleackley), *Thurtell and Hunt* (Eric R. Watson). On slightly later cases mentioned in the present work, there is a Notable British Trials volume on Burke and Hare (Roughead), and the Bles series of Famous Trials included a volume on Professor Webster and a reprint of Curtis's contemporary account of the case arising from the murder in the Red Barn, Polstead.

In the course of half a century, Messrs. Hodge of Edinburgh published eighty-three Notable British Trials volumes dealing with cases from that of Mary Queen of Scots to that of John Reginald Halliday Christie. New copies of some twenty-eight of these were recently in stock. Notable British Trials set, in the first half of the present century, a new and unsurpassed standard for the detailed, scholarly treatment of individual cases. Wherever it existed, they included a complete transcript of the evidence heard in court, with much else of relevant interest. Most of those on old cases contained very adequate bibliographies, Bleackley's *Henry Fauntleroy* not only for that of Fauntleroy himself but for those of nine other forgers, including Dodd and Hadfield. It is by collating the bibliographies in the Notable British Trials volumes listed above that a scholar would start work if he undertook the huge task of compiling a general bibliography for *The Newgate Calendar*. What he would not find is much help in tracking down many of what copies may still exist of the countless pamphlets and broadsheets upon which the original and later Calendars drew in the first place. The editors of the ten volumes listed were not concerned with *The Newgate Calendar*, but with individual cases which happened to be dealt with in it as well as elsewhere.

For the really arduous part of his undertaking, I must leave my imaginary bibliographer to the care of librarians, archivists and the larger secondhand booksellers. The literary historian may be glad of a note of the writings on criminal and related matters of Henry Fielding. Most of these were included in the Saintsbury, Gosse or Harvard editions of Fielding's works. They are *Charge to the Grand Jury of Westminster* and *A True State of the Case of Bosavern Penlez*, both 1749; *An Enquiry into the Causes of the Late Increase of Robbers*, 1751; *A Proposal for Making an Effectual Provision for the Poor* and *A Clear State of the Case of Elizabeth Canning*, both 1753. Less readily accessible, for some reason, appears to be *A Plan for Preventing Robberies within Twenty Miles of London* (also 1753). For the scheme mentioned in the Author's Introduction to his *Journal of a Voyage to Lisbon*, we must turn to John Fielding's *Account of the Origin and Effects of a Police set on foot by His Grace the Duke of Newcastle in the year 1753, upon a Plan presented to His Grace by the late Henry Fielding*, published in 1758. Three years later, Sir John, as he became that year, published his late half-brother's *A Treatise on the Office of Constable* as an appendix to his own *Extracts from such of the Penal Laws as particularly relate to the Peace and Good Order of the Metropolis.*

For Johnson, Horace Walpole, Hazlitt and De Quincey, the scholar may be left to his own devices. The general reader who yet orders new books will find that the Oxford University Press has run out of the volume which formerly contained all the Johnson contributions to the Dodd case, but on the other hand has a splendid scheme in progress for the publication of all Horace Walpole's letters, which I have somewhat ignored. They bear, indeed, on the Cock Lane ghost, on Dodd and on some other cases I have instanced. They are invaluable most conspicuously on that of the improperly so-called duchess of Kingston, which I pass over with most of the criminal activities in high life. The Nonesuch edition of Hazlitt's essays contains 'The Fight'. De Quincey's 'On the Knocking at the Gate in *Macbeth*' is in a World's Classics volume of *Shakespeare Criticism*. Him 'On Murder considered as one of the Fine Arts' I know only from the first of two volumes of *Essays Narrative and Imaginative* published, with Manson's useful notes, as long ago as 1888. These may still be found in the shops of quite small secondhand booksellers.

That, apart from the basements of public libraries, is where alone the general reader is likely to find copies of most of the Suggestions for Further Reading I now list. The place of publication is London except where otherwise shown.

ALDICK, RICHARD D. *Victorian Studies in Scarlet*. 1972. (Thurtell, Corder.)

ANON., ed. *The Trial of Eugene Aram*. Knaresborough, 1878. (Includes the autobiographical letter to Collins, Hood's poem and selections from the *Gleanings* and *Memoirs* of Norrison Scatcherd, of which Watson is perhaps unduly contemptuous.)

BIRKENHEAD, F. E. SMITH, 1st earl of. *Famous Trials of History*. 1926. (Captain Kidd, Jonathan Wild, the wardens of the Fleet, Eugene Aram, Duchess of Kingston, Dr Dodd.)

BLEACKLEY, HORACE. *Some Distinguished Victims of the Scaffold*. 1905.

—— *The Hangmen of England*. 1929.

BURTON, BRIAN J. *The Murder of Maria Marten*. Birmingham. 1964. (An actor's reconstruction of the melodrama. It has the advantage of remaining in print, which Montagu Slater's similar reconstruction of 1928 does not.)

CHILDERS, HUGH. *Romantic Trials of Three Centuries*. 1913. (Elizabeth Canning, Duchess of Kingston, Dr Dodd.)

COLLINS, PHILIP. *Dickens and Crime*. 1965.

CRITCHLEY, T. A., and P. D. JAMES. *The Maul and the Pear Tree*. 1971. (The Ratcliffe Highway murders.)

CROSSLAND, T. H. *Wainewright in Tasmania*. Melbourne, Wellington and Oxford, 1954.

DOBSON, JESSIE. *The College Criminals*. 1951–2. (Essays on Wild, Aram, Thurtell and Corder, which appeared in the published proceedings of the Royal College of Surgeons of England.)

FITZGERALD, PERCY. *A Famous Forgery*. 1865. (Dr Dodd.)

GRANT, DOUGLAS. *The Cock Lane Ghost*. 1965.

GRIFFITHS, MAJOR ARTHUR. *Chronicles of Newgate*. 2 vols, 1884.

—— *Mysteries of Crime and Police*. 2 vols, 1898.

—— *Secrets of the Prison House*. 2 vols, 1894.

HODGE, HARRY, ed. *The Black Maria*. 1935. (The introductory essays to fifteen of the Notable British Trials volumes, including Roughead's *Mary Blandy* and Watson's *Thurtell and Hunt*.)

—— and JAMES H. HODGE, eds. Penguin *Famous Trials*. 1941–64. (Vols. VI and VIII include, respectively, the introductory essays to Watson's *Thurtell and Hunt* and Brooks's *Captain Kidd*.)

HOOPER, W. EDEN. *Newgate and the Old Bailey*. 1935.

HOWSON, G. *Thief-Taker General*. 1970. (Jonathan Wild.)

IRVING, H. B. *Occasional Papers*. 1926. (Goodere, Aram.)

JONES, B. M. *Henry Fielding, Novelist and Magistrate*. 1933.

LAURENCE, JOHN. *A History of Capital Punishment*. Undated, about 1930.

LESLIE-MELVILLE, R. *The Life and Work of Sir John Fielding*. 1934.

LUCAS, E. V. *The Life of Charles Lamb*. Fifth edition, 1910.

MacClure, Victor. *She Stands Accused.* 1935. (A chapter on Sarah Malcolm.)

McCormick, Donald. *The Red Barn Mystery.* 1967. (Fascinating but unreliable, more particularly on all that suggests a connection between Corder and Wainewright.)

Machen, Arthur. *The Canning Wonder.* 1925.

Manwaring, G. E. *My Friend the Admiral, the Life and Letters of James Burney.* 1931.

Martelli, George. *Jemmy Twitcher, a Life of the 4th Earl of Sandwich.* 1962.

Norman, Charles. *The Genteel Murderer.* New York, 1956. (Wainewright.)

Pelham, Camden. *Chronicles of Crime.* 2 vols, 1886.

Phillip, Alban M. *The Prison-Breakers.* 1927. (Nevison, Sheppard.)

Pringle, Patrick, ed. *Memoirs of a Bow Street Runner.* 1950.

Seccombe, Thomas, ed. *Twelve Bad Men.* 1894. (Lord Lovat, Wild, James Maclaine and Wainewright.)

Shepherd, Thomas H. *London in the Nineteenth Century.* 1829, reprinted 1970.

Stubbs, Jean. *My Grand Enemy.* 1967. (A novel which sticks very closely to known facts in the case of Mary Blandy.)

Tobias, J. J. *Against the Peace.* 1970. (An illustrated history of the police.)

Torre, Lillian de la. *Elizabeth Is Missing.* 1947. (Eliz. Canning.)

Turner, Cecil Howard. *The Inhumanists.* 1932. (Resurrection men and the Anatomy Act.)

Vincent, Arthur, ed. *Twelve Bad Women.* 1911. (Jenny Diver, Elizabeth Brownrigg, Eliz. Canning, Duchess of Kingston.)

Wilde, Oscar. *Intentions.* 1891. (Wainewright.)

Willcocks, M. P. *A Trueborn Englishman, being the Life of Henry Fielding.* 1947.

Wilson, Colin. *A Casebook of Murder.* 1969. (A chapter on the period as a whole, more detailed treatment of Catherine Hayes.)

—— and Patricia Pitman. *Encyclopaedia of Murder.* 1961. (Summaries of the cases of Aram, Mary Bateman, Mary Blandy, Eliz. Brownrigg, Arundel Coke, Corder, Lord Ferrers, Gardelle, Hackman, Catherine Hayes, the Mannings, Catharine Nairn, William Sheward, Thurtell, Wainewright and the Ratcliffe Highway murders. The treatment of these last is updated in Mr Wilson's *Order of Assassins*, 1972.)

Woodcock, George. *William Godwin.* 1946.

Wraxall, Sir Lascelles, Bt. *Criminal Celebrities.* 1863. (Earl Ferrers, Duchess of Kingston, Professor Webster.)

Index

INDEX

INDEX